THE VIEW FROM HERE

THE VIEW FROM HERE

On Affirmation, Attachment, and the Limits of Regret

R. Jay Wallace

OXFORD
UNIVERSITY PRESS

OXFORD
UNIVERSITY PRESS

Oxford University Press is a department of the University of Oxford.
It furthers the University's objective of excellence in research,
scholarship, and education by publishing worldwide.

Oxford   New York

Auckland   Cape Town   Dar es Salaam   Hong Kong   Karachi
Kuala Lumpur   Madrid   Melbourne   Mexico City   Nairobi
New Delhi   Shanghai   Taipei   Toronto

With offices in

Argentina   Austria   Brazil   Chile   Czech Republic   France   Greece
Guatemala   Hungary   Italy   Japan   Poland   Portugal   Singapore
South Korea   Switzerland   Thailand   Turkey   Ukraine   Vietnam

Oxford is a registered trade mark of Oxford University Press
in the UK and certain other countries.

Published in the United States of America by
Oxford University Press
198 Madison Avenue, New York, NY 10016

© Oxford University Press 2013

First issued as an Oxford University Press paperback, 2017

Library of Congress Cataloging-in-Publication Data
Wallace, R. Jay.
The view from here: on affirmation, attachment, and the limits
of regret /R. Jay Wallace.
p. cm.
Includes bibliographical references.
ISBN 978-0-19-994135-3 (hardback: alk. paper)—ISBN 978-0-19-994136-0 (updf)
ISBN 978-0-19-066075-8 (paperback: alk. paper)
1. Life. 2. Values. 3. Life change events. 4. Regret. I. Title.
BD431.W2255   2013
128′.4—dc23   2012033338

To the memory of my father

CONTENTS

ACKNOWLEDGMENTS

I have incurred many debts in writing this book. Different parts of the argument were presented to philosophical audiences at several venues, who provided extremely helpful feedback, and whose interest also encouraged me to continue my work on it. These venues include: Ohio University; the University of Leeds; the University of Pennsylvania; the Ludwig-Maximilians-Universität München; the Universität Dortmund; the Universiteit Leiden; the University of Oxford; the Universität Wien; the Kulturwissenschaftliches Institut Essen; Stanford University; the 2012 meetings of the Pacific Division of the American Philosophical Association in Seattle; and the Universität Bielefeld. I am particularly indebted to audiences in Japan, where I discussed material from the book in three research seminars at Keio University in Tokyo and at Kyoto University in August of 2011, and in China, where my thoughts about regret and affirmation were the basis for the two Ethics Lectures I presented at Peking University in May of 2012.

Many colleagues and friends have taken the trouble to offer helpful written comments on one part or another of the manuscript, for which I am very grateful. They include Ulrike Heuer, Gerald

Lang, Erasmus Mayr, Samuel Scheffler, Nicholas Southwood, and Gary Watson. Niko Kolodny provided characteristically incisive and illuminating written comments on the entire manuscript, which were a great help as I revised and reworked it for publication. I also received extremely valuable comments on the entire manuscript from Bernard Reginster and a second (anonymous) reader for Oxford University Press. In addition, I enjoyed stimulating discussions of themes from the book with R. Lanier Anderson, Michael Bratman, Hannah Ginsborg, Logi Gunnarsson, David Hills, Kazunobu Narita, Michael Smith, George Tsai, and Xiangdong Xu. Kirsten Pickering prepared the index and helped with the page proofs. Finally, I am indebted to the staff at OUP for encouragement and assistance at every stage (especially Peter Ohlin, Emily Sacharin, Natalie Johnson, Ryan Sarver, Emily Perry, and my able copyeditor, Ben Sadock).

Work on the manuscript was generously supported by a visiting professorship at the Ludwig-Maximilians-Universität München; by a sabbatical leave and a Humanities Research Fellowship from the University of California, Berkeley; by a fellowship from the John Simon Guggenheim Memorial Foundation; by a Research Award ("Forschungspreis") from the Alexander von Humboldt Foundation; by research funds from the Frank and Lesley Yeary Endowment for Ethics in the Humanities at the University of California, Berkeley; and by a Research Assistantship in the Humanities from the UC Berkeley Committee on Research. I am also indebted to the Humboldt-Universität zu Berlin, which provided research facilities and an institutional affiliation during the sabbatical year when much of the work was carried out.

I would like, finally, to acknowledge a significant debt of a different kind, to Bernard Williams. The line of argument developed in this book has its origin in a paper I wrote for a conference and volume on Williams's ethical philosophy, which explored some questions about regret and justification that are raised by Williams's influential paper "Moral Luck." As I have expanded and developed the ideas from that earlier paper, I have found myself returning repeatedly to arguments from different parts of Williams's work. These include not only his discussion of Gauguin and luck (which are the main subject of chapter 4), but also his broader reflections on agency and regret, his account of the role of "ground projects" in enabling us to affirm our lives, and his later writings on Nietzsche and liberalism, which argue that we need to face up to the unlovely historical conditions of our most important values. The book might be regarded as a sustained reflection on some themes from Williams's philosophy. It is not a defense of Williams's own views, which I criticize more often than I endorse,[1] but it is animated throughout by a sense of the importance of some of the comparatively neglected issues that Williams hoped to provoke philosophy to confront.

Material from the following paper of mine is reprinted in the book with the permission of Oxford University Press: "Justification, Regret, and Moral Complaint. Looking Forward and Looking Backward on (and in) Human Life," in Ulrike Heuer and Gerald Lang, eds., *Luck, Value and Commitment: Themes from the Ethics of Bernard Williams* (Oxford: Oxford University Press, 2012), pp. 163–92.

---

1. Though there are also some substantial points of agreement. To anticipate: I think that Williams was right to emphasize the perspectival character of our retrospective thoughts about the things that we have done and undergone. I also agree with him that our most basic attitudes toward our lives are in the nature of existential commitments that outrun our ability to provide them with a rational justification.

THE VIEW FROM HERE

Chapter 1

Introduction

The perspective of deliberative choice on one's life is constitutively *from here*. Correspondingly the perspective of later assessment with greater knowledge is necessarily *from there*, and not only can I not guarantee how factually it will then be, but I cannot ultimately guarantee from what standpoint of assessment my major and most fundamental regrets will be.

—Bernard Williams, "Moral Luck"

This book is a study of perspectival elements in practical thought. The "view from here" that is my title is the view that agents take on their lives and on the world in which they live. In particular, it is the backward view they adopt when they take a stand on these things, affirming or rejecting them in retrospective thought. A central idea is that this practical outlook is decisively shaped by historical contingencies that constitute the point of view from which we engage in practical reflection. As a result of such contingencies, we can find ourselves unable to regret actions of ours that were unjustifiable at the time, and committed to affirming features of our lives and of the world we inhabit that are objectively lamentable.

To get a feel for the issues that I will eventually be discussing, it might help to start with a very simple example. Here is a brief passage from an article in the *New York Times Magazine* about Billy Beane, the general manager of the Oakland Athletics baseball team, as he looks back on a decision he made a few years earlier about an offer from a different and much wealthier club:

> He has no regrets, he said, about turning down the Red Sox job, even though it's easy to think, in hindsight, that by combining his insights with that team's resources, he might have been the one to make history there. "I have a wife and kids and parents who all live out here," he said. "If it was strictly driven by the desire to just win games, and if that was the end-all for me, then yes. But this is the type of environment I like and enjoy."[1]

The attitude attributed to Beane in this passage is utterly commonplace, something whose expression has become a virtual cliché in contexts in which public figures of various kinds are invited to reflect on a decision they have made or an experience they earlier underwent. It is an attitude of affirmation, in which Beane abjures regret for the earlier events he looks back on, and says (in effect) that he would make exactly the same choice if he had it to do all over again. Two further things are noteworthy in the passage, even if they are also familiar enough from this genre of article that they are easy to overlook. First, Beane emphasizes that his later attitude toward the decision he made about the Red Sox offer is conditioned by his family relationships. He has attachments to his parents and his own children, and these shape the point of view from which he looks back on the earlier events, and provide a basis for his affirmative attitude toward them. Second, Beane does not express his retrospective attitude by claiming that he made the right decision in turning down the offer from the much richer team. He allegedly has no regrets about the decision, but for all he literally says, it might not have really been

---

1. Adam Sternbergh, "Billy Beane of 'Moneyball' Has Given Up on His Own Hollywood Ending," *New York Times Magazine*, September 21, 2011.

justified under the circumstances. There is, after all, the tantalizing suggestion in the article that Beane "might have been the one to make history" if he had taken the Red Sox offer.

The present book is a systematic study of situations that have this general structure. It discusses attitudes of a kind that are utterly familiar to us, but considers applications of them that are both puzzling and disturbing. The argument proceeds through consideration of a series of cases. One of them is the case of the young girl's child, which involves a teenager who makes the questionable decision to conceive a child, but who later comes to love the child to whom she has given birth. This case has provoked a large philosophical literature, which centers around the so-called non-identity problem for moral thought. I focus on a particular aspect of this problem, which concerns the temporal shift that is induced by the birth of the daughter in the young mother's deliberative situation. The basic idea I defend is that the girl had good reason not to become a mother when she faced the decision about whether to conceive, but that she later has good reason to affirm the decision that she made, insofar as she is now attached to the child to whom she gave birth. There is a rift between her earlier decision and her later attitudes toward it, which makes her unable, in virtue of her later attachments, to regret a decision that she continues to recognize as having been wrong or mistaken.

What we see in this case is that our present attachments condition fundamentally the view we take toward our own lives and toward the larger world that we inhabit. There is a kind of "affirmation dynamic," which leads us to affirm unconditionally the things we are attached to—the people we love, the projects we are engaged in, and our own existence—including the necessary historical conditions for those things. Affirmation, to a first approximation, involves a preference about how things should have been in the past. Specifically, to affirm something is to prefer on balance that it should have existed, or that it should have had the features that it actually had. The contrary attitude to this kind of affirmation is regret, which in its most interesting form also includes a backward-looking preference, the preference that things should have been otherwise than they were in the respect that occasions regret. If this much is right, however, then we can immediately see that our ongoing attachments in life will determine corresponding limits on our susceptibility to regret. My leading idea is that this process has momentous effects on the view we form when we look back on our lives, reflecting both on the decisions we have made in the past and on our relation to the larger social world in which we live. It is the source of the perspectival elements in our thinking about these matters to which I referred above, and its effects ramify across a range of significant philosophical debates.

There are cases that involve disability, for example, in which agents find themselves unable to regret their own handicaps if those are conditions for the projects that have come to give meaning to their lives. Writing about these cases, commentators have supposed that agents in this situation are committed to endorsing the objective value of the disabilities to which they are subject. But the framework I offer shows that this conclusion is false; the inability to regret a condition by a situated agent doesn't entail that the agent endorses the condition, or thinks that it would, e.g., be better if other people were subject to it as well. Another prominent example with this structure is Bernard Williams's reimagining of the case of Gauguin in his influential paper "Moral Luck."[2] Williams notes that the successful Gauguin is unable to regret his earlier decision to abandon his family in Paris, since that decision was a condition for the artistic projects that define his later point of view. Williams concludes from this that the earlier decision has come to be justified ex post facto by Gauguin's artistic success. But this conclusion, again, does not follow: from the

---

2. *Proceedings of the Aristotelian Society, Supplementary Volume* 50 (1976), pp. 115–35, reprinted in Bernard Williams, *Moral Luck: Philosophical Papers, 1973–1980* (Cambridge, U.K.: Cambridge University Press, 1981), pp. 20–39; subsequent page references are to the latter.

fact that Gauguin's attachments prevent him from regretting his decision, we should not infer that the decision was the right one to have made after all.

Finally, there are cases that involve our attitudes toward objectionable social conditions that shape our present projects. In a generic situation that I call the "bourgeois predicament," many of us find that we have built our lives around fairly expensive projects and activities, such as the academic pursuits that are carried out in the context of elite research universities, which would not be possible in their present form in a social world that did not involve massive deprivation and inequality in human life prospects. Our affirmation of our projects, under these circumstances, arguably commits us to affirming the social inequalities that are their historical and contemporary conditions, even though we continue to view those inequalities as objectively lamentable. Here, the affirmation dynamic leads to a rift between ourselves and the larger world in which we live, one that frustrates our ambition to live lives that are worthy of unconditional affirmation.

There is no single thesis that the book defends. Its aspiration is instead to explore some important perspectival elements in our attitudes toward ourselves and the world, focusing in particular on the role of ongoing attachments in relation to both affirmation and regret. If the book lacks a single thesis, however, it does pursue a single large theme, which is the divergence between our attitudes of retrospective affirmation and questions of justification and evaluative assessment. This theme provides the general framework for an investigation of a number of more particular situations and phenomena. Some of these involve cases—such as those of the young girl's child and of Gauguin—that have already been extensively discussed in the philosophical literature. Here the hope is to advance the discussion by situating the cases within a more general context that emphasizes the role of attachments in shaping our outlook on our lives. This will help us to see, for example, where Williams's influential argument really goes wrong, and why the attitudes of the mother in the case of the young girl's child do not involve the elements of paradox that are commonly ascribed to them.

Other situations that will be explored, such as the one involved in the bourgeois predicament, involve common attitudes that have been neglected in contemporary philosophical discussions. Here my aim is to bring into focus some aspects of the human condition that are of great existential significance for all of us, but that at the same time are difficult for us to acknowledge. A striking feature of human life, it will emerge, is our commitment, in virtue of our attachments, to affirming historical events and social structures that we cannot ultimately regard as worthy of affirmation. This situation involves an element of absurdity, which I shall characterize as "modest nihilism." But I suggest that the absurdity is endemic to the condition of finite creatures like ourselves, who form emotional attachments that sustain them as they make their way through a world of compromise and imperfection.

Some philosophers hold that practical thought is perspectival all the way down. They maintain, for instance, that deliberative and evaluative reflection always begins from, and is colored by, the contingent desires and emotions of the person who engages in such reflection.[3] This is not a position that I find plausible, nor will I be assuming that it is true in the argument that follows. The perspectival elements in practical thought that interest me can be traced to the distinctive role of attachments in constituting our practical situation. In the sense relevant to my argument, we form attachments in the first instance to many of the people that we interact with in life (including, most strikingly, the

---

3. See, for instance, Bernard Williams, "Internal and External Reasons," as reprinted in his *Moral Luck*, pp. 101–13; this is also a theme in his *Ethics and the Limits of Philosophy* (Cambridge, Mass.: Harvard University Press, 1985).

individuals who raise us as we progress through infancy and child-hood).[4] But attachments, as I shall understand the notion, range more widely. We are attached to our lives, both as we are living them and as we look back on them, and we are also attached to the projects that sustain us and help to constitute our practical identities. Attachments, in the sense that is at issue, involve familiar patterns of emotional vulnerability and identification; we care about the things that we are attached to, in a way that renders us susceptible to distress and sorrow when they are damaged or threatened. More specifically, attachments typically involve a distinctive attitude toward their objects, which I shall eventually refer to as unconditional affirmation.

The framework I adopt for thinking about these issues takes it for granted that both our actions and our attitudes are subject to normative assessment, and that the terms of such assessment are fixed by objective standards of some kind.[5] There are reasons for action and for emotion, and these determine facts of the matter about what we should do and think and feel. Among other things, our attachments give us agent-relative reasons, looking forward, for various actions and attitudes that we wouldn't have reason to adopt in their absence. They also give us agent-relative reasons, looking backward on the lives we have led, to be glad that things happened as they did in various respects. It is the involvement of such agent-relative, attachment-based reasons that

4. Relationships of this kind are the object of what is sometimes called attachment theory. See, e.g., John Bowlby, *Attachment and Loss*, Vol. 1: *Attachment*, 2nd ed. (New York: Basic Books, 1982), and Susan Goldberg, Roy Muir, and John Kerr, eds., *Attachment Theory: Social, Developmental, and Clinical Perspectives* (Hillsdale. N.J.: Analytic Press, 1995). In what follows I shall not take for granted any of the specific claims of attachment theory in this sense (such as the claim that there are distinct styles of attachment, varying along dimensions such as security or insecurity, that involve characteristic syndromes of emotional and behavioral response to threats, and that may persist, once formed, through a person's adult life).

5. This is one reason why I call the position defended at the end of the book "modest" nihilism. A more immoderate form of nihilism would reject the idea that there are any objective reasons or values; the position I defend, by contrast, grants that there are objective reasons and values, but identifies a class of basic attitudes we take toward our lives that cannot ultimately be justified in terms of those reasons and values.

primarily contributes the perspectival element in our backward view on the lives we have led. That view is responsive to reasons that presuppose the attachments that ground them; we have to occupy the position of an agent with those attachments in order to have and to act on the reasons that they provide. Only if we ourselves stand in a relationship of parenthood to someone, for instance, do we have reasons that are grounded in such a relationship to care for our children and to affirm their lives (though we can of course understand that parents in general have such reasons from other points of view). But there are also reasons that are not specifically grounded in attachments, including, importantly, reasons that have their source in morality. These reasons interact in various ways, and their interactions shape the overall standpoint from which we regard ourselves when we deliberate about what to do and when we reflect retrospectively on the lives that we have led.[6]

My discussion will center around two important normative phenomena. One is the fact that an agent's reasons can change over time, depending in part on changes in the agent's situation and attachments. Thus I can have good reason not to do something at one time, and subsequently develop relationships and projects that give me reason to affirm the decision I have made when looking back on it in reflection. Changes of this kind can give rise to some puzzling

---

6. My reference in the title to the "view from here" echoes Williams's characterization of the "perspective of later assessment" in the passage quoted in the epigraph to this chapter; but it is also meant as an implicit contrast with the title of Thomas Nagel's *The View from Nowhere* (New York: Oxford University Press, 1986). Nagel's "view from nowhere" is an objective standpoint that, in its practical applications, is only responsive to agent-neutral reasons. Nagel contrasts this standpoint with a subjective point of view that we occupy when, in the practical domain, we acknowledge and act on agent-relative reasons. The "view from here" that I describe in the present book is in this way subjective or—as I prefer to put it—perspectival, insofar as it is shaped by the agent-relative reasons our attachments provide for affirming things when we look back on our lives. On the general distinction between agent-relative and agent-neutral reasons, see, e.g., Nagel, *The View from Nowhere*, pp. 152–59, chap. 9, and also my "The Publicity of Reasons," *Philosophical Perspectives* 23 (2009), pp. 471–97.

situations, involving the rifts between present and past to which I referred above, and one ambition of my discussion will be to come to a clearer understanding of their structure and implications. A different normative phenomenon that will concern me involves the persistence of attitudes in the face of objections to them that the bearer of the attitudes acknowledges and understands. Our unconditional affirmation of the people and projects to which we are attached can lead us to also affirm their necessary causal and historical conditions, even in cases in which we know those conditions to be intrinsically objectionable. This is the situation of modest nihilism, involving rifts between the self and the world, and I shall eventually defend the claim that such rifts are endemic to the human condition. Our plight is that we are implicated in the objectionable social and historical structures we inherit, in virtue of our attachment to our own lives and to the things that give them meaning, in ways that frustrate the ambition to live in a way that is ultimately worthy of being wholeheartedly affirmed.

One of my challenges in writing this book was to find an analytic vocabulary that is adequate to its topic. The issues I grapple with, about our most fundamental retrospective attitudes toward the lives we have led, are issues that have not attracted a lot of attention in contemporary English-language philosophy. The thinkers who have come closest to addressing them are probably Friedrich Nietzsche and Bernard Williams; I engage selectively with works by both philosophers repeatedly in the pages that follow, and have drawn on some concepts familiar from their work to advance the discussion at various points (such as Williams's notion of a "ground project" or a "categorical desire" and Nietzsche's thought experiment of the eternal recurrence of the same). But I have additionally found it necessary to introduce some distinctions of my own, including those between conditional and unconditional affirmation, between regrets and all-in regret, and between modest and immoderate nihilism. My own conviction is that these analytic categories mark important distinctions in human attitudes, and that they help to bring into focus issues that are of existential significance to all of us. But readers will ultimately have to judge for themselves whether the distinctions I have drawn illuminate attitudes and concerns that they can recognize as their own.

The discussion that follows divides into four main chapters, plus a shorter conclusion. In chapter 2, I discuss in general terms the emotions of retrospective assessment that humans naturally form when they look back on things that have happened in the past. I defend these emotions as a class against a certain kind of skeptical challenge, tracing their connections to the phenomenon of attachment. I then turn to some of the more specific features of regret, focusing on its relations to affirmation and agency. The general upshot is that attachment constitutively involves a susceptibility to regret (in conditions in which the object of attachment has been harmed or damaged). But it also commits us to affirming things—the immediate objects to which we are attached and their conditions—in ways that preclude regret about them.

Chapter 3 addresses cases involving prospective life and disability. Cases of this kind are often thought to involve paradoxical or labile attitudes: the young mother allegedly cannot affirm the life of her daughter, for instance, unless she also thinks that it was after all the right thing to do to become a teenage mother. And those with disabilities seem unable to affirm the valuable lives they have led, unless they are prepared to conclude that it is in general a good thing that people should be subject to their disabling conditions. I argue against these claims, showing how the retrospective attitudes of the agents in the cases do not commit those agents to the paradoxical conclusions. We sometimes find ourselves in situations in which we are unable to regret something that directly affects our lives, without thinking that it is a condition that is therefore justified or desirable.

Chapter 4 turns to Bernard Williams's influential discussion in "Moral Luck." Williams claims that actions can be justified retroactively by their consequences, illustrating the claim with the case of an artist ("Gauguin") whose life projects preclude his feeling regret about a decision that was subject to serious objections when it was made. I show that Williams's argument fails, for the simple reason—familiar to the reader at this point in my argument—that an inability to regret a decision one made in the past does not entail that the decision was justified after all. I also highlight some disanalogies between the Gauguin case and those discussed in chapter 3. Gauguin's attachments might determine that he affirms the decision that he looks back on in reflection; but from the retrospective point of view, the serious objections to the earlier decision also provide continuing grounds for all-in regret about it, in a way they do not seem to do for (e.g.) the teenage mother.

This possibility, that attachments might commit us to affirming things that we also have good reason to regret, is also at the foreground of chapter 5. Here I start from the observation that many of the projects that ground our attachment to our lives have a bourgeois character; they are genuinely valuable, but they also presuppose resources and opportunities that would probably not be available to us in a world in which there was less absolute poverty and deprivation. Under these conditions, our affirmation of our lives will lead us to affirm unconditionally the projects that give them meaning, including the social conditions that make those projects possible in the first place, despite the fact that those social conditions are objectively lamentable. This is the "bourgeois predicament" to which I earlier referred, and I argue that it involves the frustration of our ambition to live lives that are worthy of unconditional affirmation.

Chapter 6 reflects briefly on some of the larger implications of this argument. If the attitude of unconditional affirmation commits us to affirming the historical conditions of the things that give meaning to our lives, then for all we know we might be committed by our attachments to affirming the most obscene atrocities and disasters. Our fate, in other words, might well be that we are committed to affirming things that cannot possibly be regarded as worthy of affirmation, and only our ignorance of the ways in which we are causally implicated in the past would seem to save us from having to face up to this unsettling nihilistic thought.

Chapter 2

Looking Backward (with Feeling)

It is a strange and striking fact about us that we care deeply about the past. We form attitudes, often intensely felt attitudes, about things that it is no longer possible for us to affect one way or another, because they occurred some time ago. In this chapter I shall discuss some forms that this backward-looking concern can take, focusing both on its positive and on its negative expressions. I call these attitudes affirmation and regret, and one aim of the chapter will be to isolate some of their characteristic features. Another aim will be to make sense of these retrospective attitudes as a class, explaining their distinctive function and point. A central theme will be the connection of the retrospective attitudes with evaluative phenomena that are of central importance to human life. A particular crux will be the role of our attachments—to people, our lives, and the projects that give them shape—in underwriting the attitudes we adopt when we look back on the past.

The chapter divides into four parts. In section 2.1, I consider a skeptical challenge that naturally arises in regard to our negative emotions about the past. Those emotions occur at a point in time at which nothing more can be done about the circumstances that are their objects, and this raises a question about their rationale. I suggest in response that they are constitutively connected to the stance of valuing something, which precisely involves a vulnerability to negative emotions of assessment when the object we value is damaged or threatened in some way. Our most profound sorrows about the past are connected with our attachments, and their rationale lies in the value and role of such attachments in our lives.

I turn next to some specific questions about the internal structure of the emotions of negative retrospective assessment, focusing specifically on regret. This emotion can be occasioned by reflection either on impersonal misfortunes or on voluntary past performances by the person who is subject to the emotion. But Bernard Williams has argued that there is a distinctive form of agent-regret whose objects involve the agency of the person subject to them but that are not restricted to the voluntary. I argue in section 2.2 that this distinction does not track any significant difference in the kinds of regret to which people are susceptible. But agency might be said to have a different kind of importance for regret; I develop this suggestion in section 2.3, arguing that the element of preference involved in our most profound regrets can fruitfully be thought of in analogy to the attitude of intention that is involved in human action. The final section of the chapter takes up a positive counterpart of regret, which I call affirmation. Our attachments give us reason not only to feel sorrow when their objects have been harmed but also to be glad when things are going well for them, and to prefer on balance that they should exist and play a role in our lives. In particular, they ground attitudes of unconditional affirmation, which commit us to affirming the necessary conditions for the existence of their objects, and ultimately render inaccessible to us all-in regret about past events and circumstances that are objectively worthy of condemnation.

2.1. "FOR SORROW THERE IS NO REMEDY"

Should we regret things that we have done? Why, more generally, does it even make sense to be subject to feelings of distress about events that have occurred in the past (regardless of whether they result from acts of ours, or instead involve situations that came about independently of our agency)? Retrospective feelings of these kinds are familiar aspects of our emotional biographies, and most of us probably just take them for granted as we experience them. But when we step back from them in reflection, they can easily start to seem pointless, or worse. They occur at a node in time at which it is no longer possible to do anything about the events that occasion them. Moreover, they seem to make a bad situation worse, adding to whatever is unfortunate about the past event that is their object a second and distinct misfortune, which consists in an emotion of present pain.[1]

To come to terms with this line of thought—the skeptical challenge, as we might call it—it may be helpful to begin by considering some familiar situations: the team you have been following since childhood has just lost the World Series in heartbreaking fashion (after leading in extra innings in the sixth and potentially deciding game). Or the political situation in your country goes from bad to worse, as insane demagogues score huge electoral successes during a period of increasing economic stagnation and misery. A close friend or relative is diagnosed with severe cancer, and dies shortly thereafter. Or you yourself lash out cruelly against someone who is sensitive and vulnerable, in a mood of anger and general frustration.

Someone who experiences an event of one of these kinds will typically be prone to a range of familiar emotions in its aftermath. In their most generic forms we might speak of grief or sorrow,

---

1. For a forceful presentation of this skeptical line of thought, see Rüdiger Bittner, "Is It Reasonable to Regret Things One Did?," *Journal of Philosophy* 89 (1992), pp. 262–73. (Bittner's skepticism is focused on regret for one's own past actions; I am considering in this section the generalized variant of this skeptical worry, which applies to all emotions of regret or grief that are occasioned by things that happened in the past.) Compare Samuel Johnson, "The Proper Means of Regulating Sorrow," *Rambler* 47 (1750), from which this section takes its title: "The other passions are diseases indeed, but they necessarily direct us to their proper cure. . . . But for sorrow there is no remedy provided by nature."

experiences that involve acute feelings of pain or distress on account of an event or situation that is contemplated by their bearer.
I want to make two observations about the feelings that are involved
in these situations. First, they seem utterly familiar and even natural. A person who would not be subject to some version of retrospective sadness or sorrow in situations of the kind we have
sketched would be a very odd bird, indeed pathologically so in
some cases. Thus the "Unfähigkeit zu trauern" (incapacity to
mourn) of the Germans in the years immediately following the Second World War was famously taken by Alexander and Margarete
Mitscherlich to be a remarkable phenomenon, involving collective
neuroses that required a psychoanalytic explanation.[2] If you aren't
able to be pained by contemplation of a serious misfortune in the
recent past that you yourself were directly involved in, then it seems
there is probably something wrong with you. Second, considered
as a natural emotional tendency, sadness about one's own bad actions seems to be continuous with the negative emotions about the
past that we are prone to in cases that do not involve our own
agency. Our remorse or regret about the things we have done (to
ourselves or to others) are no more or less remarkable than our sadness or sorrow at the loss of a beloved friend or at political developments that we view as dangerous and incomprehensible.[3]

The basic structure of these retrospective attitudes involves an
emotion of present pain or distress, occasioned by an event or situation that lies somewhere in the past. But the "occasioning" relation
that is at issue is not merely a matter of brute causality. It is not just
that a present pain or distress emerges in a person as a result of

2. Alexander Mitscherlich and Margarete Mitscherlich, *Die Unfähigkeit zu trauern: Grundlagen
kollektiven Verhaltens*, rev. ed. (Munich: Piper, 2007).

3. It is of course compatible with this point that regret that takes one's own past agency as its
object has features that set it apart in important respects from other forms of grief and sorrow
about the past; this is a possibility to which I return in secs. 2.2 and 2.3 below.

something that happened some time ago. Rather, the relation between past occurrence and present pain is mediated by the person's own thoughts. In particular, those who are subject to emotions of this kind think of the past event or situation that is their object, conceptualizing it in negative terms, as something that is unfortunate or lamentable along some dimension or other. Their consciousness of the past occurrence thus involves an element of negative assessment, one that is crucial to our understanding of the painful emotions that are at issue. Those who are in the grip of an emotion of these kinds apply standards of evaluation in reflecting on things that lie (at least partly) in the past, and their doing so renders the feelings to which they are subject fitting or appropriate, from their own point of view. It makes sense to be pained about an event or a situation that you evaluate in negative terms.

Of course there are variations in our experience that are covered only imperfectly by these generalizations. Among other things, the element of negative assessment does not always involve a form of conscious awareness that would admit of easy articulation by the agent. I can be subject to feelings of guilt, or to emotions of mourning or inchoate grief, without being entirely clear myself what it is that has given rise to these forms of emotional experience. But cases of this kind are not genuine counterexamples to my generalizations; the emotions in question, I submit, only count as cases of grief or mourning or guilt insofar as they have proper objects, and these objects are fixed by the evaluative cognitions of those who are subject to them. What the cases bring to light is that the evaluative cognitions in question are not always easily accessible to the subject's own conscious reflection. In some cases it might take quite a lot of introspection or conversation or even therapy to get clear about what exactly the unfortunate event might be that has occasioned in one feelings of grief or of guilt. (The fact that "it is Margaret you mourn for" is not, for instance, something that is yet clear to Margaret herself in the well-known poem by Gerard Manley Hopkins.)[4]

The emotions under discussion thus involve a negative evaluation of their object, which is an occurrence or situation that lies at least partly in the past: the outcome of an important game, the death of a loved one, political developments in one's community, or something that one has oneself done or left undone. We may therefore think of these emotions as feelings of retrospective assessment. If some assessment of this kind is partly constitutive of the emotions at issue, however, then we might suppose that it could help us respond to the skeptical challenge. The challenge concerns the significance and point of feelings of present pain when they are occasioned by situations that lie in the past, and that we are therefore no longer able to affect one way or another. But the pains in question are, as we have seen, connected constitutively to a negative assessment of the past event that occasions them. Perhaps we can find in this connection an explanation that renders intelligible to us the present pain that these emotions involve. Thus to assess something negatively is, it might be thought, to be subject to a range of behavioral and emotional dispositions with regard to it, including dispositions to effect changes in the negative situation if one can, and to experience sadness or grief if one cannot. *Emotions* of retrospective assessment, on this line of thought, would then derive their point and significance from the assessments that they constitutively involve. Insofar as those assessments are called for or justified, the corresponding feelings of present pain will be as well. The two things stand or fall together, and the emotions of retrospective assessment are simple byproducts of a realistic assessment of things that have happened in the past.

4. Gerard Manley Hopkins, "Spring and Fall: To a Young Child."

This way of responding to the skeptical challenge is not successful, however. The problem is a fairly fundamental one: evaluative assessment does not in general involve the behavioral and affective tendencies that this account ascribes to it. Thus to evaluate something is not the same as to value it. I can judge that something is good or bad, welcome or unfortunate in various ways, without thereby acquiring any particular behavioral or affective tendencies in regard to the target of my evaluative judgment. Values are complex and multifaceted, and we can and often do acknowledge that they have been realized or thwarted in the world, without that in any way moving us to action or engaging our emotions. I can acknowledge that the standard of play in the recent test match between England and Australia was exceptionally high, and yet remain utterly dispassionate about this state of affairs, so long as I don't care all that much about the sport of cricket. Or I might concede that the musical practices of classical performance are in a bad way in the contemporary world, and still fail to be moved to do anything about it, or even to feel any particular emotion in response. This might simply represent one of the countlessly many evaluative questions that I happen not to take a lot of interest in myself.

If this is right, however, then we cannot make sense of retrospective pain simply by citing the retrospective assessments that fix the content of the backward-looking emotions. There is lots of scope for endorsing negative verdicts about events or situations in the past, while lacking the element of pain or distress that is characteristic of the emotions of retrospective assessment. But if this emotional affect is ancillary in relation to the element of retrospective assessment, then the question remains as to its significance and point, even after we have acknowledged the role of the evaluative assessments that these emotions constitutively involve. We could in principle arrive at well-grounded assessments of events and situations in the past, without that inducing in us feelings of present pain or distress.[5] So what is the rationale for our tendency to experience such feelings?

A plausible answer to this question, it seems to me, will not take the form of a justification of our susceptibility to present pain about past events, considered in isolation from other psychic phenomena. The key, rather, is to situate this form of retrospective pain precisely in relation to other aspects of our lives; only then will its significance come into clear focus. But what other aspects are of interest in this connection? We have just seen that feelings of present distress cannot be made sense of by connecting them to the evaluative element that the retrospective emotions include. A different possibility, which I shall attempt to defend and develop in what follows, is to connect the feelings of present pain and distress with the phenomena of valuing and attachment.

It is a familiar idea that there is a difference between judging something valuable and valuing it. As we have seen, it is entirely possible to acknowledge the value of something, without caring much about it one way or another oneself, or being invested in it personally. I know perfectly well that bluegrass music and organic chemistry are valuable fields of human activity, but I don't myself happen to value them. That is to say, I am not concerned personally about how things fare with activities in these domains, in the way I am concerned about how things are with (say) my friends or with research in philosophy. To acknowledge the value of activities in these various domains is— according to a line of thought that I find attractive—in part to make a claim about reasons for action and attitude. It is to hold, among other things, that the activities in question are ones that people have reason

---

5. Thus Bittner asks us to imagine a Spinozistic agent who "sees that what he did was wrong and . . . [is] perfectly aware of the suffering he inflicted on others. He just does not grieve," in "Is It Reasonable to Regret Things One Did?," p. 265.

to engage in (if, e.g., they are drawn to them and have the requisite talents), and also activities that the rest of us have some reason to support or at least not to interfere with. It is to say, furthermore, that there are reasons for at least some people to learn about the activities in question, and that they are appropriate objects of consideration and concern. But one can endorse normative judgments of these kinds without oneself valuing the activities whose value one thereby acknowledges.

Valuing goes beyond judging valuable in, among other things, involving an element of emotional engagement.[6] To value something is not just to believe that it is a locus of reasons for positive responses of various kinds. It is also, and crucially, to take an active interest in the thing, caring about it in a way that renders one emotionally vulnerable to how it fares. If I care about philosophy, then I will find that my attention is drawn toward its problems and results, which engage my interest and generate in me (under appropriate circumstances) affective responses of attraction and excitement and satisfaction. I will also be subject to a range of characteristic emotional reactions, depending on how things are going with the object of my concern. I will tend to be pleased or delighted, or at the very least relieved, when I learn something that indicates that philosophical research is in an interesting and fruitful phase. I will also become discouraged or despondent upon hearing of serious setbacks to the contemporary activity that I care about and value, or if I have been prevented from

---

6. I draw heavily, here and in what follows, on Samuel Scheffler's important work on the topic of valuing; see, e.g., his "Valuing," in R. Jay Wallace, Rahul Kumar, and Samuel Freeman, eds., *Reasons and Recognition: Essays on the Philosophy of T. M. Scanlon* (New York: Oxford University Press, 2011), pp. 23–42. See also his "Relationships and Responsibilities," as reprinted in Samuel Scheffler, *Boundaries and Allegiances: Problems of Justice and Responsibility in Liberal Thought* (Oxford: Oxford University Press, 2001), pp. 97–110, and "Projects, Relationships, and Reasons," in R. Jay Wallace, Philip Pettit, Samuel Scheffler, and Michael Smith, eds., *Reason and Value: Themes from the Moral Philosophy of Joseph Raz* (Oxford: Clarendon, 2004), pp. 247–69. Also important for my treatment of this topic are Elizabeth Anderson, *Value in Ethics and Economics* (Cambridge, Mass.: Harvard University Press, 1993), chap. 1, and Niko Kolodny, "Love as Valuing a Relationship," *Philosophical Review* 112 (2003), pp. 135–89.

engaging in the activity myself (on account, e.g., of tedious administrative assignments that have made it impossible for me to pursue my own research). This is the phenomenon of emotional vulnerability to which I referred, and we can already see that it exhibits the basic pattern that is characteristic of the emotions of retrospective assessment that are our larger topic.[7] In particular, there is a susceptibility to a feeling of present pain (or pleasure), which is occasioned by an event or situation that lies at least partly in the past, and in a way that is mediated by evaluative thoughts on the part of the subject. What secures the crucial link between these different elements is the phenomenon of valuing, which *consists* in part precisely in a susceptibility to retrospective emotions of these kinds. To value something just is, inter alia, to be subject to feelings of distress when one recognizes that things are not well with the object of one's interest and concern.[8]

But if this is on the right lines, then we can begin to see the outlines of a response to the skeptical challenge. To understand the emotions

---

7. The precise degree and nature of emotional vulnerability involved in one's valuing a given object will depend on the nature of the object. As Scheffler observes, some of the things we value—e.g., the life lessons imparted to us by our grandparents—are not things that can be said either to flourish or to be in a bad way, and to the extent this is the case there will be less scope than there is in other cases for feeling sad or distressed on account of our valuing them; see Scheffler, "Valuing," pp. 28–29.

8. It might be suggested that mere judgments of value also implicitly involve a susceptibility to negative emotions, so that the distinction between valuing and judging valuable cannot be maintained. Thus to judge something valuable is, among other things, to think that one ordinarily has some grounds for resentment in the event that the valuable thing is wantonly attacked or destroyed. But (a) one can affirm reasons for reactive sentiments of these kinds without actually being subject to them in practice, and (b) insofar as one is subject to indignation under the postulated circumstances, one's emotional condition shows that one values not the thing that has been attacked but the moral values that generally enjoin respect and consideration for worthwhile objects and activities. For a defense of the suggestion that the reactive emotions show that one cares about the values at the heart of morality, see my paper "Dispassionate Opprobrium: On Blame and the Reactive Sentiments," in Wallace et al., *Reasons and Recognition*, pp. 348–72, sec. 5. On the general moral requirement to respect what is valuable (even if one does not engage with it personally and emotionally), see Joseph Raz, *Value, Respect, and Attachment* (Cambridge, U.K.: Cambridge University Press, 2001).

of retrospective assessment, it seems, we should see them in relation to the phenomenon of valuing. These emotions, in particular, appear to be symptoms of valuing, which involves a susceptibility to retrospective feelings of just this variety. It follows that the point of the retrospective emotions will be closely connected to the point of valuing things in the first place. That is, if we want to understand why people should be subject to feelings of pain about events and circumstances that lie in the past, we need to look at the phenomenon of valuing with which those feelings are constitutively connected. The retrospective emotions will have a point so long as valuing itself does, and their rationale (such as it is) will be the rationale for having this form of response in our repertoire and for sustaining rather than suppressing its instances when we are subject to them.

Friends of the skeptical argument might object, at this point, that it is question begging to assume that valuing constitutively involves a susceptibility to retrospective sorrow. They are not against the broader stance of valuing things, but merely want us to detach it from the disposition to experience negative feelings of retrospective assessment. But this does not seem to me to be a realistic proposal. The positive aspects of the stance of valuing include dispositions and experiences that would not even be possible for us unless we were also susceptible to feelings of retrospective pain and sadness under certain circumstances. That one takes pleasure in an opportunity to engage in a valuable activity or experiences satisfaction when one is able to achieve some measure of success in the activity reflects the very same underlying stance that also makes one vulnerable to retrospective sadness when (for instance) the activity one values has been impeded. It is the investment of things with personal interest and importance that renders one susceptible to both of these forms of affect; the positive and negative tendencies are thus two sides of the same coin, constitutively connected to each other as different aspects of a single underlying syndrome or stance. So it isn't a real option for us to attempt to retain the positive dispositions that the syndrome involves while jettisoning the vulnerability to retrospective sadness.[9]

Once we appreciate this constitutive connection of the retrospective emotions with valuing, however, the skeptical challenge seems to lose much of its force. Note, for one thing, that there is hardly any genuine question as to whether human beings will cease valuing things. We are, for better or worse, valuing creatures, and it is simply part of our nature to respond to values by coming to care about and engage with them. Of course, there are individuals who lose the capacity for this kind of response, over a shorter or a longer period of time, ceasing to take an interest in anything that happens to them or to others in their world. But this is a pathological condition, a form of depression or anomie that requires treatment or therapeutic intervention of some kind. Thus the naturalness of the retrospective emotions, which I noted above, seems connected to our nature as valuing beings. There is something amiss about people who are never subject to feelings of retrospective assessment, and this can be traced to the generalized indifference that such people display, their utter lack of the emotional engagement characteristic of valuing.

A psychological tendency might be part of our nature, however, without it being on that account desirable or worthy of celebration. Thus, even if we are by nature valuing creatures, it is at least conceivable that we might be better off without this familiar tendency, and that we should therefore seek to wean ourselves from it. But this possibility, though minimally coherent, hardly seems worthy of serious attention. The investment of things with emotional significance that

---

9. It might be suggested that this is ultimately an empirical question, one that is not finally subject either to confirmation or to refutation by the armchair speculation of philosophers. I do not disagree with this suggestion, but think that reflection on our own emotional experience, and on the nature of the positive and negative dispositions involved in valuing, gives us reason to think that the skeptic's empirical hypothesis about the severability of those dispositions is implausible. That is the spirit in which these remarks are to be taken.

is characteristic of valuing is among the most important sources of value in our lives. Emotional engagement involves forms of experience that are themselves desirable, animating the spirits and intensifying our sense of being alive. Furthermore, engagement of this kind is bound up with other things that are intrinsically valuable in human existence.

Consider our *attachments* to the individuals and projects that give structure to our lives, and that imbue them with meaning and subjective significance. Examples include important interpersonal relationships of various kinds, such as those between friends or romantic partners or family members. There are also our personal commitments to ends and projects, as in the case in which I not only care about philosophy but make it my life's work to engage in this activity and to teach other people about it. To be attached to a person or a project in these ways is, among other things, to value the object of one's attachments, adopting toward them a stance whose structures of evaluative judgment and emotional vulnerability we have already identified. We take ourselves to have good reasons to engage in suitable activities together with our friends, for instance, and to care about them, to help them when we can, and to share aspects of our lives with them. We also value both them and our relationship to them, and this element of emotional engagement involves in part a tendency to grief and distress when things are not well with our friend (or with our relationship to them).[10] Similarly with projects: to be committed to something like philosophy is not just to value philosophy in the abstract but to take oneself to have special reasons to engage with it and to care about how things are with one's own philosophical activities in particular—whether or not, e.g., one is teaching

10. For a sophisticated statement and development of these ideas, to which I am much indebted, see Kolodny, "Love as Valuing a Relationship." See also Scheffler, "Relationships and Responsibilities."

it effectively, or making some kind of progress with one's own reflections and research. This kind of emotional engagement, as we have seen, consists in part in a disposition to emotions of retrospective assessment when one's projects are or have been in a bad way.

Two observations about attachments of these kinds are in order. First, their emotional and affective aspects involve experiences that are themselves of great value to us. It can be exhilarating to be invested in something in these ways, to be drawn to a project or a person, to take an active interest in them, to find that it matters to one how they are faring. This is in part because the affect that is involved in these value-laden experiences is itself often pleasurable. Consider in this connection, for example, the delight or familiar comfort one takes in the company of a good friend, or the satisfaction that is involved when one has met with interim success in one's philosophical activities. These experiences are deeply pleasurable; indeed, they are among the most profound pleasures that human beings are capable of. The pleasures at issue are, moreover, intrinsically valuable, so long at least as they are not premised on a fundamental misapprehension of their objects (for instance, the investment of value in an activity or relationship that is itself not worthy of that kind of response). But the experiential value of attachment is not merely a matter of the satisfactions that it undoubtedly involves. There is a quickening of the senses, an intensification of experience, that is present in many of the emotional ingredients of attachment, including those that could not justly be described as forms of pleasure. The anguish or anxiety that is occasioned by loss or defeat may be regrettable on balance, but there is something positive to be said on their behalf. Our experiences are more textured and complex in virtue of containing these forms of emotional reaction; they help in these ways to enrich our lives, at least when they reflect a truthful understanding of the events that occasion them and a proper valuation of their objects.

But there is a second and more important point to make in this connection as well. Not only are the experiences to which attachment makes us prone valuable, our attachments are themselves valuable. That is, it is a good thing that our lives include projects and loving relationships, where these in turn are understood to constitutively involve patterns of affective engagement and emotional vulnerability. Attachments are among the most important measures of the success of someone's life. They are the main sources of meaning for us, and their presence adds depth and value to our existence. This is the case, at any rate, so long as the condition mentioned above is also satisfied—that the relationships and projects to which we are attached are themselves of genuine value.[11] Thus, to be emotionally invested in activities that are base and jejune, or in relationships that are one-sided and demeaning, is not something that really makes for a meaningful or worthwhile individual life. Attachments are of undeniable value, however, when they involve emotional engagement with things that are worthy of that kind of response. Our basic human capacities for emotional engagement, for taking an interest in things and caring about how they fare, are in good order when they light on objects of concern that are independently valuable. Moreover, the realization of attachments of this kind, to worthwhile projects and relationships, is the most significant dimension in which our lives can go well. We live better to the extent we achieve attachments that meet this condition, and attachments are to that extent important sources of value in their own right.

I would maintain that these points about the value of attachments form the proper context for thinking about the skeptical challenge to the emotions of retrospective assessment. Those emotions involve, as we have seen, feelings of present pain that are occasioned by an event or

---

11. For a defense of this general approach to issues of meaning in life, see Susan Wolf, *Meaning in Life and Why It Matters* (Princeton, N.J.: Princeton University Press, 2010). I return to the question of meaning and its conditions in sec. 5.1 below.

situation in the past, and that are mediated by evaluative thoughts about that event or situation. The challenge was to elucidate the point or rationale of feelings of this kind, given their unpleasant phenomenology and the fact that at the time they are experienced, it is no longer possible to do anything about the events that gave rise to them. But we are now in a position to articulate a convincing response to this line of thought. The fundamental idea is that the emotions of retrospective assessment need to be seen as part of a larger syndrome of attitudes and emotional tendencies, which together count as cases of valuing or (more specifically) of attachment. Once we view them in this light, they start to look much less puzzling than they do when looked at in isolation.

Consider the suggestion that it is pointless to feel pained about an event or situation that it is no longer in our power to affect one way or the other. This suggestion seems troubling when we think about the episode of retrospective emotional distress simply on its own. But it is not in fact a self-sufficient emotional phenomenon, but belongs to a broader pattern of emotional and affective tendencies that hang together to constitute a single, complex phenomenon. These tendencies include, among other things, motivations to action with regard to the object that one values or is attached to. Thus if some misfortune befalls the cause or person that one values, it may no longer be possible to do anything about that event, insofar as it lies in the past. But the underlying stance that renders one susceptible to grief or sorrow about the past misfortune also renders one disposed to take constructive steps going forward: to help the victim of misfortune cope with its effects, for instance, or to assist in other ways with that person's undertakings.[12] The larger syndrome to which the emotion of

---

12. These tendencies should not be thought of as brute behavioral dispositions. They are rather dispositions to be subject to motivations that have characteristic phenomenal and affective aspects; compare T. M. Scanlon's discussion of desires in the "directed attention sense," in his *What We Owe to Each Other* (Cambridge, Mass.: Belknap Press of Harvard University Press, 1998), chap. 1.

retrospective assessment belongs, in other words, might well have a constructive point, even if the individual emotional episode, considered in isolation from that syndrome, does not appear to be a constructive response to the event that occasions it.

But this is only a partial response to the skeptical challenge. It leaves us without anything to say, for instance, about those cases in which we are grieved by the death or demise of the object of our concern, so that there is no longer anything that can be done to assist that object in the future. The more significant point to make here is that the value of the larger syndrome we have identified does not lie solely in its production of beneficial effects. As we have seen, attachment is valuable in itself, at least when it latches onto appropriate objects of evaluative concern. It is the main source of meaning in human existence, and a constitutive part of human flourishing or well-being. This, it seems to me, is the deeper rationale for the emotions of retrospective assessment. They are elements in a complex emotional syndrome that has great intrinsic value, and our lives would be immeasurably impoverished if we were no longer susceptible to them. This is the fundamental point that we lose sight of when we focus on instances of retrospective emotion in isolation from the broader psychological structures that give rise to them.

This last point applies, strictly speaking, only to cases of what I have called attachment, involving our emotional bonds to individuals or activities that constitute valuable interpersonal relationships and life projects. But valuing is a more general phenomenon, and it is possible to value something without being connected to it through a relationship of love or a pattern of meaningful individual activity. To return to an example mentioned above, one might care about one's political community in a way that renders one vulnerable to feelings of sorrow or distress during a period of rampant injustice and political dysfunction, without being an activist or someone who has made it a personal project to fight for social change. (Perhaps one just doesn't have time for that sort of thing, because one has decided to devote oneself to other worthy causes instead.) Insofar as one's evaluative stance in this example does not amount to a case of attachment, it would seem to lack the intrinsic value that inheres in significant personal projects and relationships.

Even here, however, the connection of the retrospective emotions with valuing helps us to understand their role in our lives. Valuing things, in the way that characteristically involves emotional vulnerability with respect to them, is among the factors that most significantly shape our identity and constitute our perspective on the world. Our values are in large measure a matter of what we care about in this distinctive way, and they help to define who we are. This connection of the retrospective emotions with identity may not exactly serve to justify them. But it does help us to make sense of the emotions in this class, adding thereby an additional and complementary line of response to the skeptical challenge. To suggest that we might be better off without these emotions is to suggest, in effect, that it might be better for us if we lacked one of the things that most importantly define our distinctive point of view as individuals. Couched in these terms, however, the suggestion seems absurd on its face. We are the individuals we are partly virtue of caring about some things rather than others. To the extent this is the case, there can be no real question for us of ceasing altogether to care about things, and the emotions to which we are susceptible in virtue of this valuing stance are in that way beyond justification.

2.2. REGRET AND AGENCY

To this point I have addressed in general terms the broad category of emotions of retrospective assessment. I now want to focus on a special case of this more general phenomenon, that of regret.

Regret is of course a retrospective attitude. It emerges when we look back on something that we did or experienced in the past from a standpoint that in the nature of the case is shaped by events that have taken place in the interim. In its basic structure, regret exhibits the generic features that we have seen to be characteristic of the emotions of retrospective assessment. It involves a kind of present distress that is caused by some event or situation in the past and that is mediated by one's evaluative understanding of that past event or situation. Thus the *Oxford English Dictionary* defines regret as a kind of "sorrow" or "distress" or "disappointment" that is occasioned by "reflection on something that one has done or omitted to do," or in response to "some external circumstance or event." This definition does not explicitly mention the element of evaluative thought, but it might naturally be taken to be understood. It seems intuitively plausible that events or actions will give rise to regret only if they are seen by the subject as in some way unfortunate or "regrettable." (Though again, this is not to say that the subject will always be able to articulate consciously what it is about the object of regret that makes it worthy of this kind of attitude.)

Bernard Williams famously distinguished between impersonal and agential forms of this distinctively retrospective sorrow or pain.[13] Impersonal regret is an emotion that it is open to anyone to feel about an unfortunate occurrence in the past, regardless of their own agential relation to the circumstance in question. Thus it is possible for me to regret the destruction of a distant village through the eruption of a volcano, or the natural extinction of an insect species in the Amazon forest, without my in any way having had a hand in these unfortunate events. Insofar as impersonal regret exhibits this kind of independence from agential involvement in the regretted circumstance, it is

---

13. Bernard Williams, "Moral Luck," as reprinted in his *Moral Luck: Philosophical Papers, 1973–1980* (Cambridge, U.K.: Cambridge University Press, 1982), pp. 20–39.

an emotion that anyone might feel (assuming, that is, that they are alive after the regretted event has occurred, and that they have some knowledge of its occurrence). Agent-regret, by contrast, presupposes agential involvement, in a way that renders it more exclusive. As Williams understands the concept, it applies both to cases in which the object of regret is a voluntary performance on the part of the person subject to regret and to cases in which the regrettable event resulted directly from that person's agency (without however being something that the agent voluntarily brought about). Agent-regret is thus by definition something that can be felt only by those who stand in an agential relation to the thing that occasions regret; I cannot in this way regret *your* voluntary performances (or their unintended consequences), though I might impersonally regret the fact that they occurred.

Williams's larger aim in introducing this notion was to isolate a form of retrospective feeling that is appropriate to a realistic understanding of the nature of agency itself. Remorse is of course familiar to us as a peculiarly agential form of regret, appropriate especially to cases in which our actions attract moral objections of one kind or another.[14] But as Williams observed, its proper target is the class of performances that are voluntary in some suitable sense (including both the things we have intentionally done, and the things that could have been foreseen to result from the things we intentionally did). His basic point is that intentional agency is embedded in the larger world of causal processes, which connect us, in ways that couldn't have been anticipated in advance, to events that are not under our

14. There are also cases of voluntary agential regret that don't involve specifically moral lapses on our part, and that therefore aren't clear cases of remorse. Consider, e.g., your regretful attitude about the stupid or embarrassing comment you made at the party last night. There are other familiar cases, however, in which we speak of remorse without the implication that the agential failing involved a moral offense in particular: cf. the phenomenon of buyer's remorse in the context of consumer behavior. I return to cases of nonmoral regret about the voluntary later in the present section.

direct control, including things that we could not properly be said to feel remorse about. Thus the lorry driver of Williams's famous example acted in ways that brought about the death of a child, even though this wasn't something that he intended to cause, and even though he took all reasonable precautions in driving the vehicle to prevent an occurrence of this kind. (We may suppose that the child dashed out into the road from behind a hedge in pursuit of an errant ball, emerging into the lorry driver's field of vision after it was too late for him to react.) It is a matter of luck, relative to the lorry driver's epistemic situation at the time when he deliberately turned into the road, that this unfortunate event came about. But come about it did, and in a way that directly implicated the lorry driver's agency. Agent-regret is meant to be the category of retrospective feeling that is peculiarly suited to one's involvement in unfortunate situations in cases of this kind.

There are a number of questions that might be asked about Williams's suggestion, however. One set of issues has to do with the nature of this emotional reaction. Agent-regret is an attitude that it is allegedly open to people to feel only if they are relevantly involved in the regrettable occurrence. But what is it about the emotion that blocks its availability to uninvolved third parties? As we have seen, it is perfectly possible for observers or bystanders to feel a kind of regret about agency-involving events, even if they were not themselves the agents in those events. I can regret the fact that the child was run over by the vehicle, even if I only read about this event in the newspaper or heard about it through the grapevine. What exactly is supposed to distinguish this feeling from the agent-regret that is available only to the lorry driver himself? Is it that there is a quality or intensity of feeling that only those whose agency gives rise to an unfortunate situation are subject to? This seems to be a questionable suggestion. There is nothing in the nature of impersonal regret that would preclude its being as intense as you like—indeed, someone who is emotionally attached to the young victim of the accident (a parent or a close uncle, say) will probably be subject to a quality of regret about its occurrence that is at least as intense as anything that the lorry driver might reasonably be expected to feel.

Perhaps, then, the exclusive character of agent-regret should be traced to something in the thoughts that it characteristically involves. But how exactly is this suggestion supposed to get fleshed out? The uninvolved observer or third party, after all, can perfectly well appreciate that the unfortunate event occurred, and also that it is unfortunate; the evaluative thoughts involved in these forms of awareness of the past event are precisely what make it possible for such third parties to experience impersonal regret about it. So what proprietary form of conscious awareness might be taken to be available only to the agent? Is it just the indexical thought that it was *my* agency that gave rise to the unfortunate event? It is true that an emotional reaction that constitutively involved an indexical thought of this kind would not even be available to those who were not themselves caught up as agents in the regrettable events (not at any rate in the absence of massive delusion or fantasy). But it isn't obvious that emotions of retrospective assessment that involve such indexical thoughts really constitute an interesting natural kind of psychological phenomenon. Nor is it clear why it should be important to insist that agents such as the lorry driver rightly feel emotions of this kind, if their defining feature is the involvement in them of indexical thoughts about one's own relation to the regretted circumstance. What exactly would be deficient in the attitudes of a lorry driver who felt profound and persistent regret about the fact that the child died, but only of an impersonal kind that was not tied constitutively to the thought that the death resulted from his agency in particular?

I suspect that agent-regret, as Williams understands it, is meant to unite the two aspects that I have so far treated in isolation. That is, we should probably understand it as regret that is more intense in affect than impersonal regret ordinarily tends to be, where this inten-sity is connected to our conceiving the regrettable occurrence as something that came about specifically through *our* intentional ac-tivities.[15] If this is the general idea, however, then another and to my mind more important question arises. Williams's larger concern is to identify an emotional formation that fits with the facts about the re-lation between our agency and the world that contains it—in partic-ular, with the fact that "[o]ne's history as an agent is a web in which anything that is the product of the will is surrounded and held up and partly formed by things that are not."[16] Note, however, that this web of agency includes threads of causality that run in both direc-tions. Not only are there causal consequences of our volitional acts that outrun our intentions and beliefs about them; there are also causal effects that we are subject to, both as persons and as agents, in which we are "held up" and "partly formed" by things that are not themselves the products of our own agency. We affect the world, often in ways that elude our capacities to control what happens; but we are also affected by the world, through the operation of causal forces that similarly exceed our capacities to control them. This is, among other things, the dimension of our situation that gives rise to the phenomena of constitutive and circumstantial luck: luck, that is, in the conditions that help to constitute who we are, and in the cir-cumstances of agency that we happen to find ourselves in as we go through life.

Our web-like history as persons thus extends in two directions, involving nonvoluntary causal influences on us as well as nonvolun-tary causal effects that are brought about through our agency. If this

---

15. I don't mean for this to be a complete account of the phenomenon that interests Williams. He himself emphasizes a third element that I have not yet touched on, suggesting that agent-regret is distinguished in part by its characteristic mode of expression ("Moral Luck," pp. 27–30). I take up this interesting suggestion below.

16. Williams, "Moral Luck," p. 29.

is the salient feature of our predicament, however, then there ought to be a form of regret that is adequate to both of the ways in which we are linked causally to the larger network of events within which we operate. That is, not only should we expect people to feel a special kind of regret when untoward effects are inadvertently brought about as a result of their intentional actions. We should equally expect people to feel a special kind of regret when they in particular have been acted upon by the world in ways that are unfortunate. And we do in fact seem to expect this of people. Consider again the situation of the child's close relatives in the lorry driver case: they were not involved as agents in the tragic incident of the child's death, and yet it seems natural to suppose that they should feel a kind and quality of regret about it that would not equally be open to uninvolved third parties to experience. Indeed, that we expect this of people seems to be connected to facts about the nature of attachments that were canvassed in the preceding section of this chapter. To be attached to something, in the way of a relationship of love or a ground project, is among other things to be peculiarly susceptible to emotional distress in situations in which the object of one's attachment has been grievously harmed. Uninvolved third parties, who are not in the same way personally connected to the victim in this case, will not exhibit the same pattern of emotional vulnerability. They may regret that the child was run over, but not in the distinctive way that those who loved and cared about the child will regret the event.

But what is the special way of regretting the event that is at issue? Partly it is a matter of intensity of feeling. But intensity of feeling is not all that is involved; there is, in addition, the sense on the part of the subject of the intense emotions that they are warranted under the circumstances. If one is the victim of an unfortunate event, or if the event implicates one's relationships and projects directly in some way, then it makes sense that one should be subject to specially intense feelings of distress in looking back on it. What renders these feelings fitting, under the circumstances, is presumably just the fact that one is personally affected by the regrettable circumstances, either directly (insofar as one is the agent or victim of them) or through individuals to whom one is personally attached. To comprehend this aspect of *personal regret* (as we might call it), we must suppose that it constitutively involves an appreciation of the special reasons that one's experiences and attachments provide for feelings of pain and distress about something that has happened. Uninvolved third parties do not have the same special reasons for regretting the unfortunate circumstances, and they will therefore be unable to regret it in this distinctive way; they can only feel a more generic pain or distress that it is in principle open to anybody to experience.[17]

If the argument of section 2.1 is correct, however, then even this more generic form of pain or distress can be traced to an attitude of valuing on the part of the person subject to it. Impersonal regret is not completely disinterested; it reflects the emotional vulnerability that is characteristic of the phenomenon of valuing, showing that one is invested in some way in a value that has been affected by the situation that occasions regret. The remote third parties who regret that the child has been run over by the vehicle, for instance, may not be personally attached to the child, but their susceptibility to retrospective distress of this kind reveals the value they place on human life, and their empathetic concern for the strangers who have been more directly affected by the tragedy. The difference between personal and

---

17. Note that "involvement" in the unfortunate event can take many different forms. The lorry driver is involved in the accident, insofar as it is caused by his own agency. But a group of immediate bystanders with no attachments to the victim might also be said to be involved, insofar as their biographies bring them into direct causal contact with the unfortunate event (a form of traumatic experience to which those are not subject who merely read about the accident in the newspaper the next day). Experiential involvement of this kind is potentially different from involvement through one's agency—the lorry driver, after all, might not experience directly the death of the child that he runs over, but find out about it in the same way the uninvolved third parties do (i.e., by reading about it in the paper a day later).

impersonal regret is not a difference between attitudes that do and that do not presuppose valuing, but a difference in the way one's values are affected by the situation that occasions regret. This difference, furthermore, is one of degree. In cases of personal regret, our attitude involves the acknowledgment of agent-relative reasons for distress that presuppose direct or indirect involvement in the circumstance that occasions regret.[18] Impersonal regret is also in a sense agent-relative, insofar as it is available only to those who satisfy the contingent condition that they value something that has been adversely affected by the lamentable state of affairs. But this condition is less exclusive than the conditions associated with personal regret; it is capable of being satisfied even by those who were neither involved in the regrettable circumstance as agents, victims, or immediate bystanders nor connected to individuals who were so involved via relationships of personal attachment.

Agent-regret, as Williams understands it, appears to be a special case of personal regret. It is called for in cases in which one's personal involvement in the regrettable circumstance takes the form of being causally implicated in something unfortunate through one's agency. The question arises, however, as to why we should suppose that this form of personal involvement gives one special agent-relative reasons for retrospective distress. In saying this, I do not at all mean to deny that agency has special significance for our retrospective attitudes. Our voluntary performances, in particular, form a special category within the broader class of things that are possible occasions for personal regret. What is particularly unfortunate in these cases is a lapse of agency on our part, a failure to do something that we ought at the time to have done, and lapses of this kind have features that set them

---

18. These reasons might stem from the fact that one cares about the character and quality of one's own experiences, or from one's special concern for the trajectory of one's own individual biography.

apart from other misfortunes that befall us. Among other things, they affect our ongoing efforts to live up to values or ideals that are important to us as grounds of deliberation and choice. Furthermore, they are occurrences that we can be held accountable for, and when they harm or wrong other people, they affect our interpersonal relations in important and familiar ways (attracting reactions of blame in those who are wronged, for instance, and corresponding expectations from us of apology and repair). But this, of course, is the familiar domain of remorse, which attaches, as Williams himself acknowledges, to our voluntary performances (what we might think of as the core expressions of our agency). Agent-regret, by contrast, is meant to be appropriate to a much wider class of cases, including a variety of situations in which our actions inadvertently play a causal role in the etiology of a lamentable state of affairs. What allegedly makes agent-regret appropriate in these cases is its realism, its fidelity to the facts about our embeddedness in a web of events in which agency is thoroughly interwoven with impersonal causality.

If this is the crux, however, then personal regret, as I have introduced it, would seem to be the more fundamental category of attitudes. Personal regret acknowledges our implication in a larger network of causal interactions, being in place precisely in cases in which we ourselves are affected in some way by that larger network (through our actions, our experiences, or our attachments). What it doesn't do is ascribe special importance to the subset of these cases in which the causal links between ourselves and the larger network operate via our own agency. But why *should* we attach special significance to these cases, once it is clear that agency of the voluntary kind that potentially grounds accountability relations is not at issue? It is perhaps a personal misfortune for the lorry driver that the child died as a result of his own actions; insofar as this is something that happened to him, he has special agent-relative reasons for regret about the outcome that don't equally extend to uninvolved third parties.

But the death of the child is at least as great a misfortune for the child's parents and close relatives; they, too, have special reasons for regret, and their retrospective emotions will therefore be of a kind that it is not open to other observers to feel. The fact that their agency was not involved in the outcome does not in any way seem to diminish the urgency and significance of the emotions of retrospective assessment they are subject to on account of it. If anything, their attitudes would seem to have greater weight than those of the lorry driver, since their own attachments seem more extensively affected by the unfortunate outcome than is the case with him. They, after all, have lost someone they love, while the lorry driver's biography has merely taken a macabre turn.

Williams himself emphasizes a different aspect of agent-regret that I have not yet had occasion to discuss. In particular, he suggests that agent-regret is distinguished in part by its characteristic mode of expression.[19] The idea is that one "test" for agent-regret is whether those subject to it feel some need to perform an act of reparation for the harm that has come to another person through their agency, or whether they would instead feel content to allow compensation to be paid through an impersonal insurance scheme. This in turn might seem to distinguish agent-regret from the more passive cases of personal regret that I have attempted to assimilate it to, since personal regret does not necessarily go together with a felt need to make amends. But this suggestion cannot work for all cases. There are situations in which we feel regret about voluntary expressions of our own agency, but without having done anything that clearly wrongs another party or provides an occasion for reparations. My regret about the embarrassing thing I said at the party last night, or about my stupid decision to see the latest Hollywood thriller (despite the lousy reviews it attracted), clearly implicates my own agency, but there is

19. Williams, "Moral Luck," pp. 27–30.

no possibility of expressing these attitudes through the performance of reparations.

Even when reparations are possible, however, doubts can be raised about Williams's suggestion. In particular, there is a real question about whether he is right to insist on this mode of expression for regret in cases such as that of the lorry driver. The need for reparations is part of the complex of normative expectations that are clearly in place when we act in ways that wrong other people, violating moral requirements through exertions of voluntary agency of some kind. It is of a piece with such responses as apology, acknowledgment of wrongdoing, and the attempt to make amends, which are all responses that are expected of people when they disrupt their relations to others through a failure to comply with basic moral demands. But it is just not clear that this syndrome of normative expectations applies to the situation of the lorry driver. By hypothesis he did nothing to wrong other people, violating none of the moral demands we make of each other as we go about our business on the public roads and highways. Under these conditions, it strikes me as simply implausible to maintain that the agent's retrospective attitudes toward what happened rightly include a felt need to make amends.

Things might be otherwise in the different situation in which the lorry driver was at fault in some way, driving a little over the speed limit, for instance, or with tires and brakes that he had neglected to maintain. In cases of this kind, there was a clear lapse of agency on the driver's part, one that violates our basic moral expectations of each other. It might be a matter of bad luck that the child darted in front of the vehicle as it progressed through the curve. Still, the harm that occurred resulted at least in part from an agential failing of the most basic kind on the driver's part, and that is enough to trigger the network of normative expectations that constitute responsibility relations between people (including the demand that the driver places on himself to make reparations, insofar as it may be possible to do so). This, however, is precisely not the situation of Williams's lorry driver, who is explicitly described as having brought about the death of the child "through no fault of his."[20] In a still different variant of the case, the lorry driver might not have been certain after the fact that he was completely without fault, even if we postulate (with Williams) that he acted impeccably under the circumstances. Perhaps he wonders whether he was driving a bit too fast, or suspects that he might have been distracted by the radio program he was listening to as he entered the fateful curve in the roadway. Even if these thoughts are false, his epistemic situation might be such that it is reasonable for him to entertain them, and this provides a different opening for the felt need to make reparations that Williams associates with agent-regret. Here too, however, the basis for this special mode of expression is a thought on the agent's part about a voluntary lapse in the exercise of his powers of agency. It is not the mere involvement of one of his actions in the outcome that makes this special form of regret appropriate, but the suspicion that he might in fact have done something wrong.[21]

To summarize, I have suggested that the interesting contrast with impersonal regret is not Williams's notion of agent-regret but what I have called personal regret. This is distress that you feel only when you have special agent-relative reasons for feeling pained by an unfortunate circumstance in the past, reasons that derive from the fact that the circumstance affects you or your attachments in some significant way. That we are specially affected by things that are first-personally accessible to us is connected with the nature of valuing, which as we

---

20. Williams, "Moral Luck," p. 28.

21. In these cases, in which there is some (real or suspected) fault on the agent's part, it is plausible to suppose that there is a "nameless virtue" that involves a willingness to take responsibility for effects that are thereby set in motion, even when those effects were not under our direct control; for this suggestion, see Susan Wolf, "The Moral of Moral Luck," as reprinted in Cheshire Calhoun, ed., *Setting the Moral Compass: Essays by Women Philosophers* (New York: Oxford University Press, 2004), pp. 113–27.

have seen precisely involves a vulnerability to special feelings of distress when its objects suffer harm or damage. There is, within this broader class of feelings of personal regret, a coherent subclass of cases that are occasioned by voluntary or deliberate exercises of our own agency. But this is just the familiar territory occupied by remorse,[22] not the broader phenomenon of agent-regret that it was Williams's aim to defend.

2.3. PREFERENCES ABOUT THE PAST

Regret, as we saw above, is typically understood to involve an affect of pain or distress about a past event that is judged to be in some way unfortunate or lamentable. Understood in these affective terms, regret is an emotion that can tolerate a wide range of possible inflections and instantiations. It needn't be a stable or considered condition, nor is it necessarily free from ambivalence and tension. One might have a tendency to feelings of sorrow or sadness about some past event that are transient, waxing or waning depending on one's mood, or such as to be undermined by sustained and realistic reflection about their proper object. Even if one's attitude of retrospective sorrow is stable and robust, it might coexist with some element of emotional satisfaction or pleasure about the very occurrence that prompts one's backward-looking pain. In these situations, there will be no overall verdict that one arrives at when one looks back in thought on the earlier action or event. One's view is essentially conflicted, in a way that precludes a simple answer to the question of whether the earlier occurrence is welcomed or deplored.

---

22. Remorse is the paradigm here, but there are similar forms of regret about voluntary lapses that do not involve specifically moral failings; consider, again, one's regret about an embarrassing comment one made or about a stupid consumer decision.

Under these conditions of emotional ambivalence, we might be reluctant to say without qualification that agents simply regret the occurrences that they are looking back on. To speak in this way suggests the presence of a single on-balance emotional tendency, of a kind that is lacking when one is emotionally conflicted; we might describe ambivalent persons as "having regrets" about the event they are reflecting on, but it would potentially be misleading to describe them simply as regretting those events.

Regret typically involves not just emotional affect but also thoughts that are appropriate to the affect in question. As I argued earlier, it is connected to the phenomenon of valuing, a manifestation of the emotional vulnerability we are subject to when we are attached to a person or a project, or when we care about a cause of some kind or other. To value something is, as we have seen, not merely to judge that it is valuable along some dimension. One can think that an object or a situation is good or admirable or worthy of pursuit, without being emotionally invested in it in the way that is characteristic of valuing. But valuing something typically does presuppose the thought that the valued object is valuable, i.e., that it is the sort of thing that people with the relevant talents and inclinations have good reason to take an interest in, to learn about, to become proficient at, and in general to care about.

This normative context helps us to understand the evaluative thoughts that mediate between the past event that occasions regret and the affect involved in the present emotional state. The evaluative beliefs that regret normally involves focus on an object to which one ascribes value, saying of that object that things are in a bad way with it. If the valued object is a person or an individual organism of another kind, then a typical cause of regret will be the judgment that the individual in question has suffered some sort of harm or misfortune. Similar remarks apply to cases in which one values a cause or a project, where we are subject to regret if we feel that the cause or project has been dealt a setback. A different case is that in which one values a normative ideal, such as the ideal form of interpersonal relationship that is made possible by compliance with basic moral requirements. Here, the evaluative belief that occasions generic regret is standardly the belief that some individual or other has failed to live up to the relevant ideal. Thus we feel moral remorse or guilt in situations in which we have fallen short by reference to the moral standards that define what we owe to other people, and what claims they have against us. And we are subject to a different kind of moral regret (e.g., resentment or indignation) when we see that other people have comported themselves in ways that flout important moral demands.[23]

Regret is often thought to be connected to beliefs about the comparative badness of some past state of affairs. In "Moral Luck," for instance, Williams writes: "The constitutive thought of regret in general is something like 'how much better if it had been otherwise', and the feeling can in principle apply to anything of which one can form some conception of how it might have been otherwise, together with consciousness of how things would then have been better."[24] Formulations of this kind suggest a link between regret and judgments about the overall value of the regretted situation, as compared with an alternative that is accessible to retrospective reflection. But the suggestion seems potentially misleading. To experience regret, one need not believe that it would have been better overall if things had been otherwise. Beliefs of this kind would involve apparently impersonal ascriptions of comparative value to states of affairs or situations. But those subject to regret need not entertain thoughts of this form (indeed, they might not even be convinced that they know what such predications of impersonal goodness mean).[25] The evaluative

---

23. On the connection between valuing moral ideals and the reactive emotions, see (again) my "Dispassionate Opprobrium."
24. Williams, "Moral Luck," p. 27.
25. Compare Judith Jarvis Thomson, *Normativity* (Chicago: Open Court, 2008).

thoughts at the center of personal regret, for instance, seem to be of a more focused and perspectival kind. They specifically concern the object that one is attached to, and they say of that object that it has been damaged or harmed or is not flourishing.

The person subject to such thoughts will agree that there is some respect or other in which it would have been better if things had been otherwise. The mother of the young victim of Williams's lorry driver, for example, would surely accept that it would have been much better for her child if the accident hadn't occurred. And remorseful agents typically think that their own behavior would have been better, in respects that matter to them, if they had acted otherwise than they in fact did. But thoughts of these kinds do not entail, and need not be believed to entail, that (for instance) the world would have been an impersonally better place if the regretted actions or events had not occurred. They entail, at most, that it would have been pro tanto better, in a respect that matters to the subject, if those actions or events had not occurred.

What exactly is it to think that it would have been better, in this way, if things had been otherwise in the past? On an approach that I find attractive, predicative uses of the language of value are understood to ascribe a second-order property to things, the property of having first-order features that give people reasons for responding positively or negatively toward them.[26] So to judge that it would have been better if a past circumstance had not obtained is to judge that there is some feature of the circumstance that gives us, for example, a reason to be pained that it has occurred, if we stand in the right relation to an individual or project or ideal that has been affected by that circumstance. The particular kind of effect that most often gives rise

---

26. See, for instance, Scanlon, *What We Owe to Each Other*, chap. 2, and my "Reasons, Values, and Agent-Relativity," *dialectica* 64 (2010), pp. 503–28. In these terms, to say that an occurrence is "impersonally" bad would be to say that it has features that give anyone reason to resist or fight against it when they can, to regret or to deplore it after it has occurred, etc.

to a reason of this kind is, I would suggest, a form of harm or damage to an object of attachment. It would have been better had things been otherwise in the past, because and insofar as the actual state of affairs that obtained involved a misfortune or a setback or a harm for something that one is attached to (an individual or project or ideal). This kind of effect is one that is normatively significant for the person who is so attached, giving that person (but not necessarily other persons) a reason for the complex of responses that are constitutive of regret. This explains the perspectival character of personal regret; it involves the acknowledgment of agent-relative reasons that are not necessarily shared by people whose attachments have not been directly affected by the circumstance that occasions regret.

But evaluative thoughts of these kinds do not just identify reasons for negative affect in cases of regret. A distinct element that can be isolated is an orectic attitude on the part of the agent toward the situation or circumstance that occasions regret. Thus if I regret some past event, I not only believe that it was in some way unfortunate with regard to things that I value (be they individuals, institutions, causes, or ideals); I also wish that things had been otherwise in the regrettable respect.[27] This backward-looking preference, it should

27. Compare Williams, "Moral Luck," p. 31. Insofar as regret involves such a preference, its object can be described in counterfactual terms; we can say that we regret having done X, or equally that we regret not having refrained from X-ing. David Velleman has argued that it doesn't make sense to regret "what might have been" in this way, because we are not "on first-personal terms" with the subject of events and experiences in the possible worlds in which things were otherwise. See J. David Velleman, "Persons in Prospect," *Philosophy & Public Affairs* 36 (2008), pp. 221–88, at pp. 239–42 (this passage is from Part 1, "The Identity Problem," of Velleman's three-part article). But Velleman's skeptical argument fails to convince, for two reasons. First, as we have seen, not all regret is personal in nature, and so it doesn't seem essential to regret that it should be based in our special self-concern. Second, even in the personal cases that are grounded in self-concern, it is not clear why our ability to regret what might have been presupposes that we are actually concerned in this way about the subjects of the counterfactual scenarios we entertain in thought. We are concerned first-personally about the self who actually did or suffered something in the past, and this leads us to regret what might have been, insofar as what might have been involves possible actions or experiences of that very subject (something that Velleman does not deny).

be emphasized, is not unrelated to the negative evaluation of the regretted circumstance, as something that harms or damages an object
that one is attached to or an ideal or cause one cares about. Regret
would not make sense to the person subject to it if it simply involved
a brute unmotivated preference to the effect that things in the past
should have been otherwise in some dimension or other. The preferences that are involved in regret should instead be understood to be
connected to and derived from two other elements in the person's
outlook that have already been touched on: the stance of valuing an
individual or object or cause or ideal and the belief that the thing one
values has been harmed or has suffered a misfortune or setback of
some kind. It is because one has these background attitudes that one
forms the wish that things had been otherwise in the unfortunate
respect, and the backward-looking preference can therefore be said
to be normatively grounded in one's evaluative assessment of the situation one wishes had not obtained.

Returning to the case of ambivalence, it is noteworthy that there
is lots of room for conflicts in both the evaluative and the desiderative aspects of regret. The very situation that harms or damages
something that one values might also be positively valenced in relation to a different set of concerns. It might for instance frustrate the
interests of a person one is attached to, even as it advances significantly an important professional project that one is involved in. The
agent who reflects on the past situation might be subject to a correspondingly conflicted set of backward-looking preferences: both
wanting and not wanting that things should have been otherwise in
the relevant respects.[28] Conflicting attitudes with this content are
often appropriate to a situation that is evaluatively complex, constituting an ambivalence of stance that involves simultaneous sadness

---

28. In the terms I propose below, the person in this situation hasn't yet taken a stand on the question of whether the circumstance in question should or should not have occurred.

and satisfaction about the contemplated past event. A different situation with this general structure might be that in which one looks back on actions that were performed under circumstances of deep ethical conflict, in which there were powerful moral objections to each of the options that it was open to one to perform. In a situation with this structure, there will be retrospective dissatisfaction whatever one ends up doing, insofar as each of the alternatives that are available involves damage or failure by reference to something that one values (an individual affected by one's action, for example, or a moral ideal that one cares about living up to). One was condemned to acting in a way that would eventually leave one with some wish that one had done otherwise, where that desire in turn is grounded in one's awareness of how things that one values have been affected by what one has done.[29]

But there are of course other cases as well, in which one's retrospective attitudes are less conflicted or indeterminate. In situations of what I shall call "all-in regret," a person experiences a stable reaction of sorrow or pain about a past action or circumstance, taking into account the totality of subsequent events that they are aware of having been set in motion by it. But the person is subject, in addition, to an on-balance preference that things should have been otherwise in respect of the action or circumstance that now occasions retrospective

29. Williams discusses cases with this structure in "Ethical Consistency," as reprinted in his *Problems of the Self: Philosophical Papers, 1956–1972* (Cambridge, U.K.: Cambridge University Press, 1976), pp. 166–86. He argues, specifically, that in cases involving deep ethical conflict, agents will appropriately continue to experience regret about the options that they did not choose, and that this emotion can be thought of as the expression of a desire that wasn't satisfied through the agents' earlier actions; see "Ethical Consistency," pp. 170–79, also "Moral Luck," p. 31. Williams adds, however, that agents in such tragic situations needn't think that their earlier decision was a mistake, or feel that they would have decided differently if they had it to do over again ("Ethical Consistency," pp. 184–86). To the extent this is the case, the conflicts he is envisaging do not involve the kind of all-in regret I go on to discuss but something that falls short of that—"regrets," in the terminology I have suggested, rather than simply regret.

sorrow. There are not conflicting desires about what should have happened in the past, but a single, determinate preference that the regretted events should not have happened, one that is itself based in the agent's retrospective understanding of the past situation that is the object of reflection and assessment. It is when this condition is satisfied that it is most clearly appropriate to say not just that a person has some regrets about the past event or occurrence but that the person regrets that event or occurrence, full stop.

But how are we to understand the attitude of retrospective preference that all-in regret, on this way of interpreting it, seems to involve? What exactly is it to have a preference of this kind that things should have been otherwise in the past in the respect that is regretted? Preferences are ordinarily taken to be action tendencies of some sort. But in cases of the kind under consideration, there is nothing the agent could possibly do to bring about the state that is preferred, since the preference precisely concerns a situation that is settled and in the past. Under these conditions, a natural suggestion would be that the preference can only manifest itself as a disposition to affective distress or sorrow that its proper object cannot be realized. One wishes that things should have been otherwise, but because there is nothing that can now be done to bring about this state of affairs, one is subject to a feeling of present pain. According to this interpretation, to say that the agent has an on-balance preference that the past situation should not have occurred is basically to say that the agent's present affective reaction to the past event is exclusively negative in valence, in the range of pain or distress or anguish. There is no room for mixed feelings of the kind that are both natural and appropriate in cases in which one's desires about the past are conflicted (in a way that specifically reflects one's appreciation of the evaluative complexity of the past situation that one contemplates).

But this won't do as an account of the element of preference that is involved in all-in regret. The reason is that the presence or absence of mixed feelings isn't a reliable indicator of the presence or absence of fundamental ambivalence about the situation that agents look back on in reflection. We sometimes experience mixed feelings in cases in which our retrospective attitudes are basically affirmative; likewise, we can be conflicted at the level of fundamental assessment, without that manifesting itself in a present susceptibility to simultaneous emotions of both distress and satisfaction. To begin with the latter point, consider (again) situations of tragic conflict, which leave agents unable to adopt an attitude either of stable endorsement or rejection in retrospective reflection. People in this situation are often fundamentally conflicted about what they have done, but the conflict need not express itself in an ambivalence of present affect when they think back on their past decision. They will feel pained or sorrowful about what has happened, but will typically not be subject to any positive affect of satisfaction. Their conflicting attitudes will not involve ambivalence of present affect so much as present regret that is accompanied by an awareness that they would be feeling just as regretful if they had acted otherwise under the tragic circumstances that earlier obtained.

Conversely, people who take a basically affirmative stance toward an earlier state of affairs may nevertheless be subject to mixed feelings when they look back on it from their present point of view. To see this, consider cases in which one made a decision that one continues to stand behind, but that also involved serious costs of some kind (either to oneself or to others who were affected by what one did). People in this situation will not be subject to what I have called all-in regret; they will not wish on balance that they had made a different decision when they reflect retrospectively on what they have done. Despite this, however, it would be perfectly natural in these situations to feel some anguish and distress—some regrets, in the idiom earlier introduced—on account of the costs associated with the decision that one continues to affirm.

For these reasons, we cannot understand the element of on-balance preference exclusively as a disposition to experience present affect (of satisfaction or distress, depending on whether the preference is or isn't satisfied). It seems to involve an attitude that is directed in some different and more focused way at the past circumstance that is the proper object of regret. To make sense of this attitude, it may be helpful to consider our future-directed action tendencies. It is common, in thinking about the future-directed case, to distinguish between desires on the one hand, construed as states of present attraction or repulsion, and intentions on the other.[30] One can feel drawn toward a course of action without actually intending to pursue it; conversely, one can intend to do something without its being something that one particularly feels attracted to doing. There are different ways of accounting for this difference between intentions and desires, depending in part on whether one takes intentions to be sui generis attitudes or, rather, states that can be reduced to attitudes of other sorts (such as special reflexive beliefs about one's own behavior).[31] But some distinction of this kind seems unavoidable when we think about our future-oriented tendencies to action. Intentions are settled resolutions to act, determinations of the will that have the function of defeasibly resolving some practical question that the agent faces, and they are primary manifestations of our capacities for activity. Desires, by contrast, are states that we are subject to that we may or may not stand behind or endorse, and their presence does not

---

30. The distinction is more or less explicit, e.g., in Scanlon, *What We Owe to Each Other*, chap. 1, and in G. F. Schueler, *Desire: Its Role in Practical Reason and the Explanation of Action* (Cambridge, Mass.: MIT Press, 1995).

31. For an impressive account of intentions as sui generis states, see Michael Bratman, *Intention, Plans, and Practical Reason* (Cambridge, Mass.: Harvard University Press, 1987). Reductionistic accounts that treat intentions as a kind of belief about one's own future behavior are developed, e.g., by J. David Velleman, in *Practical Reflection* (Princeton, N.J.: Princeton University Press, 1989), and by Kieran Setiya, in *Reasons without Rationalism* (Princeton, N.J.: Princeton University Press, 2007).

entail that the practical questions that the agent confronts have been resolved one way or another. Intentions represent commitments of the kind that bring practical deliberation to a provisional conclusion, whereas desires are states that precede deliberation and provide a potential basis for choice.[32]

Now if we consider some prospective candidate for action, and ask whether I prefer on balance that I perform it, we will potentially get different answers depending on whether preference is understood as a matter of intention or of mere desire. I might desire, on balance, that I perform the action, insofar as I feel myself strongly drawn toward it and experience no countervailing aversions. But this might be true of me without it yet being the case that I have resolved for myself the question of what to do in the matter, or committed myself to performing the action toward which I am in this way attracted. To form the intention of performing the action is, by contrast, precisely to have resolved that practical question, at least in a provisional way, and to have a corresponding commitment to doing the thing that one in this way "prefers." It is to take a stand on the question of whether to perform the action, in a way one does not necessarily yet take a stand if one merely finds that one is very strongly taken with the idea that one might perform it.

My suggestion is that we should understand the element of preference that is involved in all-in regret in analogy with intentions to action of this kind. To prefer on balance that things should have been otherwise in some respect is to have an intention-like attitude toward that prospect; one takes a definite stand on the question as to whether things should have been otherwise, and is committed to the answer that one thus affirms, in a way that resolves for oneself the question of

---

32. The distinction between desire and intention, as I have drawn it here, is denied by some; see, e.g., Michael Smith, "Instrumental Desires, Instrumental Rationality," *Proceedings of the Aristotelian Society, Supplementary Volume* 78 (2004), pp. 93–109. Those who take this approach understand all desires as primitive dispositions to action, which are in this respect similar to intentions as I understand them. See also Michael Ridge, "Humean Intentions," *American Philosophical Quarterly* 35 (1998), pp. 157–78.

whether things should or shouldn't have been otherwise in the relevant respect. Of course, for the agent looking backward in reflection, that question is in an important respect theoretical rather practical. There is no way of bringing it about, from the present point in time, that things should have been otherwise in some particular aspect or other in the past, and so it isn't really an option for me, now, to bring it about that things should have been otherwise. But intentions typically take as their objects prospective actions that represent real options for the agent at the time when they are formed. In this respect at least, the backward-looking attitudes that are involved in all-in regret are different from genuine intentions for the future. This is why I suggested that we understand the backward-looking attitudes in analogy with intentions, rather than as special cases of intention.

In support of the analogy, it is noteworthy that we sometimes form literal intentions for the future without believing that the actions we intend to perform are real options. Consider, for instance, conditional intentions, such as the intention to walk home rather than hitchhike if one should ever again find oneself stranded on that stretch of road out by the quarry, or the intention to work on one's paper for the conference tonight if one can't get tickets to the play. One could resolve for oneself the question of what one is going to do under such conditions, without yet believing that the conditions will in fact be satisfied. On-balance preferences regarding past states of affairs could be thought of as a special kind of conditional commitment, where the relevant condition is contrary to fact. One has resolved for oneself the question of what one would do as regards a past state of affairs, under the counterfactual supposition that it was open to one to make a difference in the matter one way or another.[33]

---

33. Compare the treatment of plans in Allan Gibbard, *Thinking How to Live* (Cambridge, Mass.: Harvard University Press, 2003). I disagree with Gibbard's suggestion that normative judgment is in general to be understood in terms of the formation of plans of this kind, but believe they may have a limited role in the genesis of our attitudes toward past misfortune.

Indeed, the backward-looking attitudes that we form in these cases often seem continuous with the conditional intentions for the future that one also naturally forms—different expressions of the same underlying attitude. The person who regrets, on balance, that they hitched a ride back from the quarry will also, and for the same reasons, typically have the conditional intention never to do so again if they should find themselves in a similar situation. They have resolved for themselves a question about what to do under certain conditions, where the conditions in question have both counterfactual (past) and still possible (future) instantiations.

A different consideration that supports the analogy with intentions is that our backward-looking attitudes admit of strong forms of akrasia (or resistance to "better judgment").[34] Looking back on our history with a romantic partner, we might judge that it was a disaster all around for everyone concerned, and that it was definitely for the best that it finally came to an end, and yet still find that we are unable to regret either entering into the relationship or sticking with it as long as we did. In cases of this kind, it strikes us that evaluative features of the past situation we were involved with give us overwhelming reasons for regretting it, and yet we fail to form the attitude that we ourselves believe is called for. The failing that is exhibited here seems to go beyond the milder forms of akrasia that sometimes afflict our emotional lives, such as the persistence of fear in the presence of an arachnid that we know to be perfectly harmless. It seems more robustly irrational, and this lends support to the suggestion that the attitudes involved in all-in regret might fruitfully be conceptualized in analogy to intentions for the future.

The fundamental advantage of this way of thinking about all-in regret is that it captures very nicely the wholehearted character of the subject's attitudes regarding the past. In cases of this kind, one wishes

---

34. I am indebted to Gary Watson for this suggestion.

fervently that things should have been otherwise than they were, where this attitude toward the past seems to involve a kind of agential commitment. One doesn't just find oneself abstractly attracted to the idea that things should have been otherwise in the past, or subject to present affects of various kinds in regard to the past state of affairs one regrets; rather one has taken a definite stand on the question of whether the regretted state of affairs should have obtained. Granted, it might seem infelicitous to describe one's attitude in a case of this kind as an intention, strictly speaking, precisely insofar as one will never have a real opportunity to bring about the state that one in this way prefers. To the extent this is the case, one has not through one's attitude resolved a genuine practical question that one does or might face. But one has, all the same, settled for oneself a counterfactual question, one that is structurally very similar to the questions that are resolved through the formation of conditional intentions for the future.[35]

Even if it is possible for us to settle in this way issues about what we would do if certain counterfactual conditions were to obtain, the next question that arises is why we should go to the trouble of doing so. What is the point of expending mental energy on an issue of this nature, given one's awareness that the condition one is planning for is impossible? It makes sense to form conditional commitments to action when it is at least a live question whether the condition about which one is deliberating is a condition that might conceivably obtain as one makes one's way through life. But this is not the situation in regard to preferences about the past, which precisely involve conditions that cannot in the nature of the case arise. We know for a fact, looking back on the past circumstance that we regret, that it will never be a real option, either for

---

35. One can be committed, in this way, on the counterfactual question at issue even if one hasn't explicitly formulated a plan or policy for the question. It would be enough if it is true, in virtue of one's present attitudes, that one would effect a change in the regretted past circumstance if one were given an opportunity to do so. A preference of this kind would be more like an intention than a desire in the above sense, which is a phenomenologically salient state of present attraction.

us or for anyone else, to prevent that circumstance from obtaining. So why should we bother to resolve the question of what we would do if (contrary to fact) this were to become a real option for us? The intention-like account I have proposed of the preferences involved in all-in regret provides a new opening for the skeptical line of inquiry about such attitudes that was raised in section 2.1 above.

Part of the answer to this new skeptical question lies in the aforementioned connections between our future-directed and our retrospective attitudes. Having made a significant mistake or been through a traumatic experience of some kind, we often form conditional intentions for the future as a result, resolving (for example) never to hitchhike in remote areas late at night, or to avoid films by the director of the ridiculous and offensive movie we went to last week. There is no question that it can make perfect sense to form conditional intentions of these kinds for the future, insofar as it remains a real possibility that the conditions in question might eventually be realized. But as I noted above, the attitudes at issue are often continuous with the retrospective attitude of all-in regret, on the interpretation of it that I have proposed. The single resolution to do X under conditions C can be understood to have both future and past applications, depending on whether C is an ongoing real possibility for the agent (a situation in which one has it in one's power to do X, given that C actually obtains), or merely a matter of counterfactual speculation (responding to reflection about what one would do in a past situation in which C obtained, if one had it to do over again).[36]

---

36. Two qualifications are in order about this. First, the point applies only to cases in which the immediate object of regret is an exercise of one's own agency, since it is only in these cases that the retrospective attitude can be understood to be continuous in the way described with a conditional intention for the future. Second, even in cases that involve one's own agency, it is always possible to draw a line between the future and the past instantiations of C, precisely insofar as the past ones occurred under circumstances in which the agent did not yet have experience of the failure to do X. Thus one might consistently think, "I don't regret going to the movie by that director last week, since I had no idea how stupid and offensive his movies were, but I'll never see another one by that director, that's for sure."

But there is a different and more fundamental point to make about this issue. In responding to the earlier skeptical challenge, I emphasized the connection between regret and the phenomena of valuing and attachment. The same connection can help us to understand why we should trouble to settle for ourselves merely counterfactual questions about the past. The deeper significance of the attitudes through which we settle such questions, I believe, is underwritten by our attachments. When a situation in the past has harmed or damaged an individual, institution, or ideal that we are attached to, this is typically a matter of great concern to us. We naturally entertain counterfactual reflections about how things might have been otherwise in circumstances of this kind, reflections that (as we have seen) do not leave us completely indifferent. On the contrary, a resolution that the harm or damage should have been avoided, if it had been at all possible for us to bring this outcome about, can be considered a spontaneous expression of our concern about the object to which we are attached. It is our capacity to entertain counterfactual thoughts that makes it possible for us to form on-balance preferences of this kind regarding past states of affairs. And it is our attachment to the things that have suffered damage or harm that leads us to exploit this possibility. We take a stand on the question of whether things should have been otherwise as soon as we form a clear picture in our minds of the alternatives, and this reflects the basic fact that we care about the individual or cause that has been visited with misfortune in the actual course of events.

Of course, from the fact that we can entertain counterfactual thoughts about the past, it does not follow that we have to entertain such thoughts. The backward view we adopt when we contemplate historical events and circumstances of various kinds is in this way different from the view we take up as we move forward through our lives. As agents, we are often confronted with situations that force us to choose between actions that it is open to us to perform, situations in which we can hardly avoid taking a stand on the practical question that we face. Nothing forces us in the same way to confront the counterfactual question of how things should have been in the past, and it is therefore possible in practice for us to avoid thinking about that question. We might be so caught up in the ongoing challenges that life presents us with that we have no real leisure to expend on merely counterfactual questions about the past, devoting ourselves instead to just getting on with our affairs. And even if this is not our situation we might deliberately refuse to pose for ourselves the counterfactual question, pursuing a "method of avoidance" in regard to it. These are important possibilities, which I shall come back to in section 5.4 below. Still, it remains the case that *when* we reflect on how things went in the past, we naturally entertain counterfactual questions, especially when the past circumstances we reflect on involve misfortunes or setbacks for things to which we are attached. And once these questions are raised, we are led, equally naturally, to take a stand on them in virtue of the same attachments, forming intention-like attitudes to the effect that things should have been otherwise in the respects that affect the objects of our attachment. Indeed, our concern for those objects might well be such that we cannot help taking a stand on the counterfactual question once it has been raised for us in thought.[37]

The on-balance preferences that we form in these circumstances are perspectival in several different senses. They are formed from a point of view that is conditioned by the subject's attachments, which give the subject special agent-relative reasons for concern about the ways in which the objects of attachment might have suffered damage or harm. But they are also formed from a point of view that involves superior knowledge, as compared to the standpoint contemporaneous with

---

37. The backward-looking commitments involved in all-in regret thus need not be under our direct control. Their agential character (to which I return below) stems from their similarity to intentions rather than from our having it in our power to determine whether or not we are subject to them.

the events that are the object of regret. We look back on those events from a point of view that is essentially conditioned by our awareness of what has happened in the interim. The question on which we take a stand, then, is this: would we, knowing what we now know about how things have since played out, bring it about that things were otherwise in the respect that we are focusing on, if it were in our power to do so?

The thought experiment that underlies this question has a curious double aspect. On the one hand, we hold fixed the way things have actually gone, insofar as we pose the question of whether things should have been otherwise from a standpoint that is conditioned by what has actually happened in the past. On the other hand, we entertain the counterfactual possibility that things might precisely have been different in the past, taking a definite stand on whether that possibility should have been realized. But of course, if things had been otherwise in the past, then the point of view from which we look back on them would also have been different. The all-in preference that things should have been otherwise is thus formed from a point of view that would not even have existed if the preference had been satisfied. This initially sounds paradoxical, but the appearance of paradox is superficial. There is no real inconsistency or incoherence involved in committing oneself to a counterfactual possibility whose realization would undermine the standpoint from which one formed the commitment in the first place. One might believe, or at least hope, that the alternative standpoint of retrospective assessment that the counterfactual possibility would have brought into existence would have preserved the values and attachments that characterize one's actual standpoint, eliminating merely the grounds that those values and attachments currently provide for all-in regret about what happened in the past.[38]

---

38. I shall return in later chapters to a range of cases in which these assumptions are not in place, cases in which all-in regret is ruled out because of the ways in which counterfactual possibilities would threaten the values and attachments that shape one's actual current outlook.

In entertaining the counterfactual possibilities that are involved in regret, we unspool the film of time in thought back to the point at which the events or circumstances we are focusing on occurred. If the event in question is an action of ours, then the preference we form about it is fairly straightforward. It is the wish that we had not performed the action, which in cases of all-in regret may be thought of as a kind of resolution not to perform the action under the counterfactual circumstance that one had it to do over again (a resolution that, as we have seen, is formed in the light of our knowledge of what has actually happened in the interim). In cases in which the object of regret is not an action of ours, however, the counterfactual thoughts involved are correspondingly more complex, incorporating elements of fantasy. If I regret the loss of life and property that were caused by the Tōhoku tsunami, then I form a preference regarding that past state of affairs, which might be thought of as a resolution to prevent the loss of life and property under the counterfactual circumstance that I had it in my power to do so. But the conditional supposition at issue in this case involves two distinct scenarios that are contrary to fact. I suppose, first, that the film of time might be unspooled, taking me back to March 11, 2011, when the tsunami occurred. But I suppose, second, that there is something I might then have done to bring it about that the tsunami did not lead to loss of life and property. As there is, in fact, nothing that I could then have done that would have brought about this result, my resolution in this case makes implicit reference to a set of further counterfactual hypotheses: e.g., that there was some mechanism in place that could have been deployed to prevent the loss of life and property (such as fantastic machines or godlike beings with the power to hold the wall of water at bay), and that it was in my power to activate the mechanism.[39]

39. If this seems too artificial, an alternative would be to suppose that the preferences involved in regret might differ in nature, depending on whether regret takes an action of ours as its object or an impersonal circumstance that does not involve our own agency. In the former cases, we can understand the element of all-in preference in close analogy to a conditional intention for

This reinforces the earlier suggestion that all-in regret has a distinctive character when it takes a voluntary action of the subject as its immediate object. It is in cases of this kind that the analogy between backward-looking preferences and intentions is most straightforward. The wholeheartedness of our attitude toward the thing that we regret can be understood as involving something that is very like a conditional intention for the future, and that is often continuous with such an intention: a resolution or a commitment to act otherwise under the counterfactual scenario that we had it to do over again. This is the territory of remorse, which focuses on voluntary performances by the agent who is the subject of the attitude, and which is typically characterized by an unambivalent, on-balance preference to have acted otherwise than one in fact did.[40] We might say that our capacities for agency are doubly implicated in our attitudes about the past in cases of this kind. They take voluntary expressions of agency as their immediate object; and in addition they can themselves be understood to involve an intention-like attitude that directly expresses our capacities for agential self-determination.

---

the future, since the immediate object of our attitude is something that is under our volitional control (i.e., an action that it might be or might have been open to us to perform). In the latter cases, by contrast, the preference could be understood to take impersonal states of affairs as its direct object. A preference of this kind would be a potential basis for the counterfactual commitment we might form concerning the steps we would take if presented with an opportunity to change the past in the relevant respect. A challenge for this account, however, would be to explicate the notion of preference that it presupposes, which would be a wholehearted attitude of the agent's that represents a ground of choice, rather than a resolution or volitional commitment of some kind; I am skeptical that this challenge could be met, which leads me to favor the analogy with intentions that is explored in the text.

40. As noted in sec. 2.2 above, remorse is also morally inflected, in a way that generally renders it appropriate to cases in which the objection to the voluntary action that is its target is grounded in the claims or entitlements of other beings. Cases of voluntary performances that do not involve wrongs to other parties would ordinarily be said to occasion merely (all-in) regret, though the element of preference that is characteristic of this attitude will closely resemble that which is involved in remorse. I return to the topic of remorse in the next chapter.

In cases in which the object of regret is a state of affairs that does not in the same way involve the agency of the subject, by contrast, the analogy with intention is somewhat more strained. We can understand all-in regret about such circumstances to involve a counterfactual intention, and this is indeed the best way to make sense of the wholeheartedness of the retrospective attitudes that we form in situations of this kind. But the remoteness of the counterfactual conditions that are thus implicated in such attitudes makes them less like ordinary future-directed plans than are the preferences involved in remorse.

2.4. REGRET AND AFFIRMATION

All-in regret, as I have interpreted it, contrasts with a different and positively valenced attitude, which we might call affirmation. To affirm something, in the relevant sense, is to judge that it is valuable along some dimension or other, and also to prefer on balance—taking everything into account—that it should not be otherwise than it is.

Affirmation, like regret, can range widely over a variety of different kinds of objects. One can affirm an action that one has performed in the past, just as one can regret or feel remorse about something one has done. But one can also affirm an individual, being glad, for example, that a person that one loves exists. One can also affirm a variety of different states of affairs, including the states and events that together make up the life that one has lived, or other states of affairs that affect one only indirectly (if at all). I can be happy that I met you, or (as a Red Sox fan) that the Yankees suffered an excruciating late-season collapse, or that the recent uprising in Egypt was resolved without a significant loss of life.

Affirmation differs from regret in that it isn't really an emotional state. In particular, it lacks the element of affect that is characteristic of emotions. To affirm your life or the existence of someone that you love is not necessarily to be subject to positive feelings that take these things as their objects. You can have an affirmative attitude toward them without, for example, experiencing anything on the order of elation or joy or even satisfaction, and without having your attention directed toward opportunities to interact with the object of affirmation (in the way that is characteristic of many emotional states). Affirmation is better understood to be a matter of one's preferences as regards the things it takes as objects, which typically go together with normative beliefs about the ways in which those objects provide reasons for the preferences one has about them. As with the case of regret, these preferences in turn can be thought of in analogy with conditional intentions for the future. So affirming an action one has performed involves something like the persistence of the intention that originally led one to perform it: one would do just the same thing if one had it to do over again. But cases involving the affirmation of other objects or states of affairs can also be thought of as involving intention-like attitudes. To take an affirmative attitude toward a person or a situation is to "will" that the person should exist or the situation should have obtained. "One wouldn't have it any other way"—which is to say that one is committed to its being the case that the object of affirmation exists or has the features that it actually has (even though there may not in fact be anything that one can do about the matter one way or another).

The intention-like character of affirmation shows itself in the fact that affirmation is often a kind of achievement. We can sometimes bring it about that we affirm our life or a situation that has affected us in some way, choosing to adopt toward these objects a positive attitude. Thus, the attitude expressed in Edith Piaf's "Non, je ne regrette rien" contains a distinct note of defiance and a strategic commitment to affirm the past, as a condition for a new beginning in life. There is in cases of this kind a voluntary aspect to affirmation that distinguishes it from regret, and that is perhaps connected to the fact that affirmation is not in the same way an emotional state.[41] It isn't open to us simply to make it the case that we experience some positive or negative affect in regard to a situation or state of affairs, and for this reason we cannot regret a past situation or state of affairs at will. With affirmation, by contrast, we can at least sometimes adopt the attitude deliberately, choosing to affirm some aspect of our life or our experience that we contemplate in reflection.[42] Doing this is very much like resolving on a course of action for the future, committing ourselves to that course of action through the adoption of a plan. This provides further support for the suggestion that the preference involved in this attitude might helpfully be conceptualized in analogy to future-directed intentions to act.

Intentions are generally produced in deliberative situations that present an agent with a menu of options to choose between. Reflecting on those options, the agent forms an intention by selecting one of the options from the menu, adopting the plan of pursuing it in preference to the others that are available under the circumstances. It is similar with the backward-looking preferences involved in affirmation. One commits oneself to the thing that one affirms, willing it (as it were) in preference to a set of alternatives that are present to reflection. What the relevant alternatives are is in turn something that will vary from case to case, being determined by contextual factors that depend in part on the nature of the object to be affirmed and the perspective

41. All-in regret, on my account of it, typically includes a volition-like element, insofar as it involves a commitment or resolution that one should have done otherwise. In virtue of this volition-like element, one can refrain from regretting something in this way, even if one is subject to some emotional misgivings about it. But all-in regret is not fully volitional, insofar as this emotional element (of retrospective pain or sorrow) isn't under our volitional control.

42. I discuss in chapters 5 and 6 below a number of situations in which one is unable to help affirming conditions that one recognizes to be unworthy of that attitude. In these cases, at the least, affirmation has the quality of a basic orientation that is not subject to our volitional control.

from which one engages in reflection on it. For instance, to affirm an action that one has performed is to continue to endorse or accept the intention to perform it, as against the alternatives that it was open to one to choose in the deliberative situation one originally confronted as an agent. To affirm the action of another (individual or collective) agent is, similarly, to prefer on balance that that action was performed, as against the alternatives that confronted the agent at the time. In other cases, by contrast, the implicit contrast is fixed by reference to the perspective of the person who is reflecting on the object to be affirmed. Thus, to affirm an individual whom one loves is, among other things, to be glad that they exist, strongly preferring this state of affairs to the hypothetical alternative that they should not have lived at all. And to affirm one's own life, I shall eventually argue (in section 4.2), is not to prefer the actual life one has led to any alternative life that might have resulted from the choices it was open to one to make. It is, rather, to prefer one's actual life to the alternative of not having lived at all, taking into account everything that was involved in one's actually living the life that one led.

Affirmation, insofar as it is not an emotional state, doesn't presuppose attachment in the way that we have seen to be characteristic of regret. There is for this reason a wider range of potential bases for affirmation than for regret, which as I have argued reflects the kind of emotional vulnerability that is in play when we value something or are attached to an individual or a project. Thus, one can have good reasons for choosing one course of action over another that don't have anything in particular to do with one's attachments, and those reasons might continue to give one a basis for affirming the decision when one looks back on it in reflection. You elected the coastal route to the conference, for instance, on account of the bucolic scenery, and this continues to strike you as a good thing to have done even though scenic driving conditions are hardly something that you are invested in emotionally. But attachments are still important potential grounds for affirmation when we look back on what has happened in the past, and they will play the primary role in cases in which the object of affirmation is another individual or one's own life. We have special reasons for affirming the life of other persons, for instance, insofar as we love them. And our primary reasons for affirming our own lives, when we reflect on them, are provided by the projects and relationships that we are emotionally bound up with, which provide the evaluative substance of our lives.

I shall return in later chapters to the role of attachment as a potential basis of affirmation. In the remainder of the present chapter I want to address the different question of the relation between affirmation and regret, a question that will eventually play an important role in the larger argument of this book. The first thing to note here is that there is no space for affirmation and all-in regret that are directed toward one and the same proper object. These attitudes, as I have introduced them, are defined at least in part by the on-balance preferences that they involve. To experience all-in regret is to have an on-balance preference that the thing one regrets should have been otherwise, whereas to affirm something is to prefer on balance that it should have been just as it was. But these are contrary attitudes that cannot be combined. If I form the on-balance preference toward something that is involved in affirmation, then eo ipso I lack the all-in preference that is partly constitutive of all-in regret about that same object.

All-in regret can, however, coexist with affirmation targeted at distinct aspects of the total history that is being contemplated. I might feel happy that we went on the punting expedition yesterday, which was a lot of fun, though I'm sorry that we got caught in a rain shower. Here I am distinguishing in thought between the object of regret (the fact that we were exposed to the storm) and the object that I affirm (the fact that we went punting). I affirm the fact that we went punting, though I also regret on balance the distinct fact that it rained. By contrast, it would be odd to say that I was happy we went punting, insofar as it was fun, though on balance I regret doing so, insofar as we got wet. This would imply an ambivalence of all-in regret and affirmation toward one and the same object of contemplation, and our emotional capacities don't allow for this combination. To combine these attitudes coherently, we need to give them different proper objects.

The parsing maneuver that makes this possible, whereby we distinguish in thought between different targets of retrospective assessment that are part of the same larger flow of events, often comes naturally to us. It makes sense in cases in which the objects that are distinguished are conceptually and causally independent from each other, to a degree sufficient to enable us to form counterfactual thoughts about one object without the other. In the punting example, though I take an affirmative stance toward the outing that we actually went on, even taking into account the fact that it rained, I might also believe that it would have been still better if we hadn't got caught in the rain. In saying that I'm sorry it rained, I'm singling out a feature of the course of events that I wish had been otherwise, an attitude that is compatible with affirmation toward the punting expedition as it actually played out. A different example of the same phenomenon is the classic bureaucrat's non-apology in response to the outraged protestations of some mobilized constituency or interest group: "We regret that our actions in this matter have caused offense." What the official is saying with these words is something that is literally true, even at the level of all-in assessment. An element of the actual course of events—namely, the fact that offense was taken—is being singled out in thought, and the official is saying of that element that they are sorry that it occurred and wish that things had been otherwise in this particular respect. But this is not to say that they are sorry for the action of theirs that caused the offense, which is the attitude that the protests originally sought to elicit.

Are attitudes of these kinds really defensible, however? An objection to them would be that the parsing maneuver that they rest on is always artificial, and that the discrete attitudes that result from applying it are therefore unrealistic. If it in fact rained during the punting expedition, then it isn't really open to us to affirm that we went punting while regretting that it rained. Similarly, if we affirm the action of ours that has in fact caused offense, then we can't truthfully refrain from affirming that consequence of it. The things that we attempt to distinguish in thought in these cases are connected to each other in fact, as part of the larger historical flow of events, and our retrospective attitudes are problematic if they fail to acknowledge that this is the case. The logical conclusion of this line of thought would be the apparently Nietzschean suggestion that affirmation of an object or a state precludes regret about any of the other processes that were involved in the larger world history of which it was a part. On this conception, one can affirm an aspect of one's current life (for instance) only if one is prepared to affirm the entire course of world events of which it is a tiny part, willing, as it were, the eternal recurrence of those events as they have in fact played out.[43]

---

43. See, for example, the remarks about eternal recurrence in Friedrich Nietzsche, *The Gay Science*, sec. 341. It is noteworthy that Nietzsche was concerned primarily with the conditions for the affirmation of one's life (the life one has actually led), and it might be that this particular object of affirmation has features that do not generalize to other potential objects of affirmation. See, for example, Alexander Nehamas, *Nietzsche: Life as Literature* (Cambridge, Mass.: Harvard University Press, 1985), chap. 5. Nehamas traces Nietzsche's doctrine to a view of the metaphysics of the self, according to which the self just is the totality of its connections to everything else, where all such connections are of equal significance; on this interpretation, any given aspect of one's own life can be affirmed only if one is willing to affirm every other aspect. For a different interpretation of Nietzsche's views on this issue, see Bernard Reginster, *The Affirmation of Life: Nietzsche on Overcoming Nihilism* (Cambridge, Mass.: Harvard University Press, 2006), chap. 5. I discuss the topic of the affirmation of one's own life in chapters 4 and 5 below, and offer some brief comments about Nietzsche's eternal recurrence in chapter 6.

The objection misfires, however. Affirmation and regret, it is true, have to take into account the larger processes in which their immediate objects were actually embedded. They are retrospective attitudes, adopted from a perspective that involves cognizance of the flow of events that they have so far set in motion. The on-balance preferences that are central to these attitudes would be unrealistic if they were formed in abstraction from information that is available to their subject about some aspect or other of the history in which the objects of the attitudes are implicated. Thus if I affirm the punting expedition, I prefer on balance that it occurred, even taking into account the fact that it rained while we were on the river. Similarly, I might affirm the action that I earlier performed, despite the fact (which I acknowledge) that it turned out to cause offense to the members of the interest group. Our retrospective attitudes would be objectionable if they were based on willful ignorance about their larger effects and implications; we might call this the realism condition on affirmation and regret. But there is nothing in this condition that prevents us from applying the parsing maneuver to single out discrete parts of the larger flow of events, and to form specific preferences regarding them. I can prefer on balance the fact that we went punting, even taking into account the effects of the rain on our experience, while I also wish on balance that it hadn't in fact rained.

There are other cases, however, in which the realism condition prevents application of the parsing maneuver. These are cases in which the putatively discrete targets of affirmation and regret are *necessarily* connected to each other, so that there couldn't have been one without the other. Thus, there is no way for me to affirm on balance the punting expedition while regretting on balance that we were out on the water in a flat-bottomed craft. The thing that I affirm in this case (the punting expedition) constitutively involved being out on the water in a flat-bottomed boat; for this reason there is no conceptual space for affirming the former while wishing on balance that the latter state of affairs had not obtained. (A person might, perhaps, be extremely confused about what is involved in punting, not realizing that it is in part a matter of being out on the water in a flat-bottomed craft. But then the attitudes of such a person would not include affirmation of the punting expedition, only of the state or object that the person mistook for a punting expedition, e.g., the picnic in the meadow that preceded the episode on the water.)

A different case of this general kind involves the necessary causal conditions of the object or state that one directly affirms. If I prefer on balance that the punting expedition should have taken place as it did, then I am committed also to affirming the sine qua non conditions of its so occurring. I might in this situation regret on balance the fact that it rained, since its having rained wasn't necessary either as a constitutive or as a causal condition of our being out on the river in the punt. But I cannot in the same way regret on balance, for instance, the fact that we organized a punt for the afternoon, since there wouldn't have been a punting expedition at all if we hadn't done that. At any rate, I cannot regret on balance this latter fact unless I am (again) ignorant or confused about the necessary conditions for our going on the expedition that I affirm. This is the sense in which on-balance affirmation commits one to affirming as well the necessary causal conditions of the thing that one affirms. There is no psychological space for affirming the object while regretting on balance its necessary conditions, so long as one is clear that the conditions really are necessary for the thing that one affirms.

This conclusion requires qualification, however, for it applies only to one species of affirmation. There is a range of familiar cases in which one wholeheartedly affirms something, while consistently feeling all-in regret about causal conditions that one acknowledges to be necessary for the thing that one directly affirms. Thus I might celebrate without reservation the heroism of the firefighter who rescued my kids from the flames, while regretting deeply the negligence on my own part that caused the fire, and which was therefore a necessary causal condition for the thing that I affirm.[44] Here, it seems that I affirm on balance the heroic acts of the firefighters, while regretting on balance a necessary presupposition of the thing that I affirm; I do this, moreover, without any internal contradiction. A different example of the same kind is a case in which one is glad that one has lived up to one's obligations, though one wishes that one hadn't entered into them. I might affirm on balance that I should have kept my promise, given the fact that I freely undertook it, but at the same time be subject to all-in regret about the latter fact.

These examples involve a phenomenon that I shall call conditional affirmation. In cases of this kind, one takes it as fixed that a past circumstance obtained, and focuses on events that happened in its train. The past circumstances are "screened off" in reflection, and one forms preferences regarding parts of the subsequent flow of events, taking it as given that the events leading up to it occurred as they did. This is often a perfectly reasonable way to proceed, particularly in cases, such as those just described, in which the object of affirmation is the action of one or several individuals. What I celebrate in the firefighter example is the heroic comportment of the public servants who responded to my emergency call. I wholeheartedly applaud the behavior of the firefighters under the circumstances that they confronted, but I can do this without affirming that those circumstances obtained. Similarly, given that one made the earlier promise, one will affirm in reflection one's decision to fulfill it, even if one looks back with regret on the fact that one made the promise in the first place.

This form of conditional assessment makes sense in application to individual actions, because actions are themselves responses to a set of circumstances that confront the agent as a

44. Thanks to Samuel Scheffler for the example.

matter of facticity.[45] At the moment of action, certain things have to be taken as given, insofar as they are no longer under the agent's power to affect one way or another: the fact that the house is on fire or that a promise has been made. The deliberative task is to select among the options that it is now open to the agent to perform, given the fixed circumstances that constitute the deliberative context. We therefore screen off those fixed circumstances in retrospective assessment of the action, focusing on the question of whether the action was or was not worthy of affirmation, *given* the circumstances that define its immediate context.[46]

There are other cases, however, in which affirmation assumes a different and unconditional form. Consider our attitudes toward the individuals whom we love, or toward our own lives. Our attachments in these cases give us powerful reasons for affirming the immediate objects that are up for assessment in a distinctive way. One does not merely affirm those objects, given that the necessary causal conditions for them obtained; rather, one is glad on balance that those objects are in fact part of the history of the world, taking into account the totality of things that they involved. In a case with this structure, one's affirmative attitude spreads backward from its immediate object, as it were, encompassing as well the historical conditions that were necessary for the existence of the thing that one affirms. One

---

45. One can, however, also conditionally affirm things that are not actions—approving of the fact that it rained, for instance, insofar as it extinguished the fire, without approving of the fact that the fire was started in the first place. My point in the text is just that there are constitutive features of actions, considered on their own, that make them natural candidates for this kind of affirmation.

46. A different factor that is at work in the firefighter example (but not the promising case) is the fact that the value at issue in the agent's activity is ameliorative in character. What we admire in the firefighter's action is the prevention of greater harm or damage, and when something is valuable in this way we generally do not have reason to affirm the threats or dangers that are admitted conditions of its being valuable. (Things might conceivably be different for the firefighters themselves, if the ameliorative values of their professional activities become normative bases for their ability to affirm unconditionally their own lives. I return to this possibility in sec. 5.4 below.)

embraces unconditionally the life of the person one loves, and of one's own life, in a way that commits one to embracing as well the necessary conditions for the existence or realization of the immediate objects of these attitudes. It is in the nature of attachment that the attitudes of affirmation it grounds should in this way often be unconditional.

Of course, attachments can play a role in the justification of attitudes of merely conditional affirmation as well. Part of the reason why one celebrates the heroism of the firefighters, after all, is because one is attached to the children whom they rescued, and an attachment to the values around which morality is organized helps to explain why one affirms the fact that one kept the promise that one made. But nothing in the nature of the relevant attachments requires us to affirm the historical conditions of the things that we affirm in these cases. One's attachment to one's children gives one powerful reason to be glad for the heroism of the crew that rescued them from the flames, but it doesn't in the same way give one reason to be glad that the fire occurred. Similarly, a deep concern for moral ideals determines one to be happy that one was able to keep the promise that one made, but from the perspective of that concern it is typically a matter of indifference that one entered into the promise in the first place. By contrast, if I love my children, then it cannot be a matter of indifference to me that they should have existed; my affirmative attitude toward them is precisely a commitment to affirm the conditions of their being around in the first place, whatever those conditions might have been.

I say "commitment" here, because it is undoubtedly possible to affirm something unconditionally without affirming all the conditions that are in fact necessary for the existence of the thing that one is attached to. I might for instance be ignorant about some of the necessary conditions for the existence of my children, and under those circumstances I will form no attitude, either positive or negative, about those conditions in virtue of my attachment to them. I am committed to affirming those necessary conditions, however, in the sense that my attitude toward my children will lead me to affirm them once I become aware of their relation to the objects I am attached to. Furthermore, the affirmative attitude to which I am thus committed by my attachments is itself unconditional. If a given act or event was in fact necessary for the existence of the child whom I love, then I have to prefer on balance that it should have occurred, taking everything into account about it; it is not enough to prefer that it should have occurred, given the further conditions that provided its own distinctive context. Unconditional affirmation is thus an implicitly extensive phenomenon. It may not necessarily involve the affirmation of everything that actually occurs in the world that the object of our attachments happens to inhabit (as Nietzsche, according to many interpretations, suggests with his idea of the eternal recurrence of world history[47]). But it does commit us to affirming those parts of the actual world history that stand in a necessary constitutive or causal relation to the direct objects of our attachments.

Unconditional affirmation is an extremely important phenomenon, which reflects the significance of attachments in shaping the perspective from which we look back on the past. If we are attached to an individual or to a project, then we will typically affirm the direct objects of our affirmation in a distinctively unconditional way; this in turn commits us to affirming their necessary constitutive and historical and normative conditions in a way that is similarly unconditional, and precludes our regretting that those conditions obtained. We might refer to this as the dynamic of unconditional affirmation (or the "affirmation dynamic" in short). In the chapters to follow I will explore this dynamic in application to a number of particular cases, tracing its systematic implications for our understanding of the retrospective point of view.

---

47. In chapter 6, however, I shall sketch a different interpretation of Nietzsche's idea of the eternal recurrence, connecting it to the unconditional character of our affirmation of our lives, together with our ignorance of the historical conditions that in fact enabled us to adopt this affirmative attitude.

Chapter 3

Affirming the Unacceptable

In the previous chapter we explored the attitudes of retrospective assessment. At the extremes, there are cases of all-in regret and unconditional affirmation, which cannot coexist toward one and the same object of reflection. All-in regret involves a pained recognition that an individual or institution that one values has been harmed or damaged in some way, accompanied by an active wish that things had been otherwise in the relevant respect. This attitude leaves no space for affirmation of the thing that is in this way regretted, since affirmation entails the absence of the desire that things should have been otherwise that is partly constitutive of all-in regret in the first place.

Regret is an attitude of retrospective assessment, insofar as it is mediated by evaluative judgments on the subject's part. At its center is typically the recognition that something that one cares about has been damaged or thwarted in some way, either through one's own actions or through impersonal circumstances of some kind. But situations can arise in which this form of evaluative consciousness does not give rise to the unambivalent regret that would ordinarily accompany it. This happens, in particular, when a person's retrospective point of view is defined by powerful reasons for affirming something that was set in motion by the earlier, regrettable occurrence. Affirmation is incompatible with all-in regret, so there is no psychological space for regretting something in this way when one's retrospective outlook toward it is essentially affirmative. Under these conditions, all-in regret becomes inaccessible to the agent who looks back on the earlier occurrence, despite the fact that the occurrence remains intrinsically objectionable.

In this chapter I explore some situations that have this puzzling structure. A natural assumption to make is that the retrospective point of view of the agents in such situations involves a kind of endorsement or retrospective justification of the earlier situation that they now affirm. I question this assumption, showing that the inability to fundamentally regret an earlier occurrence does not entail that one now either endorses it or views it as justified retroactively. In particular, the attachments that define the retrospective point of view can give people powerful reasons to affirm earlier actions that they acknowledge to be wrong, or situations that they still see to be unfortunate or regrettable. I develop these ideas in sections 3.1–3.2, applying them to an example that has been found interesting and puzzling in the literature on the so-called nonidentity problem. Section 3.3 adds some nuance to the picture, identifying several forms of ambivalence that agents might be subject to when they look back on unjustifiable actions that they are unable fundamentally to regret. The general schema is then applied in section 3.4 to a different class of cases, involving personal disabilities and social injustices that have come to shape an adult agent's defining projects and activities. Agents in this position will understandably affirm the things that have thus conditioned the meanings they have realized in their lives. It does not follow from this retrospective attitude, however, that those conditions are not lamentable, or that we have reason to subject others to the same disabilities and injustices when there are ways of overcoming them going forward.

3.1. THE YOUNG GIRL'S CHILD

There is a well-known example of Derek Parfit's that illustrates what he calls the "non-identity problem."[1] The case involves the decision of a fourteen-year-old girl to conceive a child, and its basic contours are as follows. It seems that we want to say about the girl's decision that there is a strong objection to it; it is wrong to bring a child into the world when you are not yet mature enough to attend responsibly to its interests, and it would therefore be better on balance for the girl to wait a few years before becoming a mother. The non-identity problem in this case arises from the fact that the moral objection to the mother's decision does not appear to be one that can be articulated from the child's point of view. Assuming that the teenage girl gives birth to a child whose life is well worth living on the whole, that child will not object on her own behalf to her mother's decision to conceive as a teenager. After all, she (the child) is not made worse off than she otherwise would have been by her mother's decision; on the contrary, the choice to postpone conception by several years on the part of her mother would have had the consequence that she, the mother's actual child, would never have existed, and this is something that the child will hardly prefer if indeed her life is one that is worth living.

Parfit and others have concluded from such examples that morality has an important impersonal dimension. The objection to the mother's decision cannot be that she has harmed or wronged some individual, but rather that she has failed to produce a state of affairs that is impersonally optimal with regard to human interests. It would have been better for the girl to postpone conception, because she would then have given birth to a child that is better off, or has a

---

1. Derek Parfit, *Reasons and Persons* (Oxford: Clarendon, 1984), pp. 357–61.

higher quality of life, than the child she actually conceived as a teenager.[2]

This analysis of the case of the young girl's child raises a number of issues; one immediately striking aspect of it has to do with temporal perspective. On Parfit's account, we want to say, at the point of the girl's decision, that it would be better for her to postpone pregnancy and motherhood. But if it would then be better not to conceive, it is presumably also the case that it would have been better in retrospect if she had done so; the time at which a judgment is made about the impersonal values that are at issue should not affect the content of the value judgment that is arrived at. But if it would have been better in retrospect had the mother not become pregnant, then we can say of the mother's actual child that it would have been better had that very child not existed. The facts being what they are, we know that that child would not have existed if her mother had decided to postpone motherhood by several years. So if we agree in retrospect that it would have been better had the mother delayed conception, we must also accept that it would have been better had her child never been born.

Parfit himself finds this conclusion plausible, asserting that if he were the teenager's child, he would agree that it would have been better had he not existed[3] (a conclusion that his mother would also presumably have to endorse). He defends the plausibility of these conclusions by distinguishing between evaluative judgments on the one hand and rational regret on the other. Even if it would have been better had Parfit not existed, it might still be the case that neither he nor his mother should regret his existence. More precisely, there might be grounds in this case for "moral regret" on the mother's part about her earlier decision, but this is compatible with her inability to

2. See the "Same Number Quality Claim" in Parfit, *Reasons and Persons*, p. 360.
3. Parfit, *Reasons and Persons*, p. 360.

regret her decision "all things considered."[4] The discussion of regret in the preceding chapter suggests that there is indeed room for a divergence between different kinds of regret in a case of this kind, and this is a possibility that I shall come back to later. Still, there is something puzzling about Parfit's way of conceptualizing the case. If it really would have been better all things considered had Parfit not existed, and if both Parfit and his mother accept that this is the case, then it seems that they rationally ought to regret, now, that Parfit exists. Their failure to do so suggests that they find something in the situation of Parfit's existence that is valuable on balance and therefore such as to merit affirmation rather than regret on their part. But by hypothesis it is not the case that Parfit's existence is on balance for the best, nor are we to suppose that either he or his mother believe this to be the case. Under these conditions, it seems that their inability to experience more than merely moral regret about Parfit's existence doesn't really make sense; there is nothing in their evaluative outlook that would render it rational for them not to experience all-in regret about the fact that Parfit was born.[5]

How else might we conceptualize the apparent temporal shifts in the attitudes of the people involved in a case of this kind? One possibility is to suppose that the evaluative judgments at issue change over time. Thus, Jeff McMahan argues that potential parents might judge,

4. Parfit, *Reasons and Persons*, pp. 360–61.

5. As we saw in the preceding chapter, it is commonly thought that regret is structured around evaluative thoughts of precisely the kind that figure in Parfit's discussion; cf. Williams's suggestion that "the constitutive thought of regret in general is something like 'how much better if it had been otherwise'," in Bernard Williams, "Moral Luck," as reprinted in his *Moral Luck: Philosophical Papers, 1973–1980* (Cambridge, U.K.: Cambridge University Press, 1982), pp. 20–39, at p. 27. If this is right, and if our imagined Parfit agrees that it would have been better had he not existed, then it is hard to see why it would not be rational for him (or his mother) to regret that he exists. Having said this, I should add that, though I reject Parfit's impersonal treatment of the non-identity problem, I shall eventually defend a position that has some affinities with his suggestive but undeveloped remarks about regret in this passage.

prospectively, that life without a child would be better for them, while judging, after they become parents, that life with a child is better.[6] There is a shift, in other words, in the evaluative judgments that such people endorse that is effected by the change in their parental circumstances. McMahan goes on to suggest that the shift should not be understood to involve judgments that are literally inconsistent with each other. There is a plurality of evaluative frameworks for thinking about what makes for a good life, and the framework that is adopted prospectively is different from, but not better or worse than, the framework that is taken up after the child arrives on the scene. The prospective judgment is indexed to one set of values, while the retrospective judgment is indexed to a different evaluative set, with neither evaluative framework being more authoritative than the other.[7]

McMahan is especially concerned to address issues regarding the expressive significance of decisions about conception. If people decide not to have children after preconception screening brings to light a strong likelihood that their offspring would be born with a disability, this might suggest a negative attitude toward actual people who have the disability in question.[8] In particular, it suggests that the burdens of caring for such an individual would not be compensated for by the contributions that the disabled person would make to the quality of the parent's own life. McMahan concedes that this message is sent by the decision of prospective parents not to conceive children who are likely to be disabled. But he argues that disabled persons might take comfort in the fact that the parents of people like themselves typically

---

6. Jeff McMahan, "Preventing the Existence of People with Disabilities," in David Wasserman, Jerome Bickenbach, and Robert Wachbroit, eds., *Quality of Life and Human Difference: Genetic Testing, Health Care, and Disability* (New York: Cambridge University Press, 2005), pp. 142–71.

7. McMahan, "Preventing the Existence of People with Disabilities," pp. 155–57, 161–66.

8. McMahan, "Preventing the Existence of People with Disabilities," pp. 148–52. He also considers the potentially different expressive significance of decisions to have a normal child rather than one who would suffer some serious disability.

come to endorse a different evaluative judgment.[9] They affirm the contribution of their children to the quality of their lives, from the perspective of a set of values that are different from those of the prospective parents who decide not to have disabled children. This is supposed to mitigate the expressive meaning of the decisions that will be made by prospective parents if methods of preconception screening become widespread.

There are several difficulties with this approach, however. For one thing, the rational arbitrariness of the postulated transition from one evaluative framework to another undermines the expressive work that the transition is supposed to perform. On McMahan's pluralist account, there is no rational basis for choosing between the values that inform the judgments of the prospective and the actual parents of disabled children.[10] If that is the case, however, then the fact that people who have disabled children happen to affirm the contributions of those children to their lives should do little to console people who are actually born with disabilities of the relevant kind. It is a mere contingency that parents of such children gravitate toward this evaluative framework, and they might just as well have retained the earlier values that lead prospective parents to decide not to conceive.

Consider the counterpart of this evaluative shift in the case of the young girl's child. We might similarly say about this case that a change in evaluative frameworks informs our attitudes toward the teenager's child. Before the girl conceives, we judge that the burdens of caring for a child at that stage of life will outweigh the satisfactions of parenthood, and this is among the reasons for thinking that the girl should not become pregnant in the first place. But the girl herself

9. McMahan, "Preventing the Existence of People with Disabilities," p. 165.
10. He suggests, specifically, that they are "on a par" rather than being strictly incommensurable (though he thinks his argument would go through if one interpreted value pluralism instead in terms of incommensurability); see McMahan, "Preventing the Existence of People with Disabilities," p. 162.

might come to see things differently after giving birth, adopting a set of values that enable her to affirm the contribution of her child to the quality of her life. This in turn would perhaps explain why the mother finds herself unable to regret her fateful decision when she looks back on it from a later point of view. But the pluralism and contingency that are built into McMahan's approach make it unsatisfactory in application to this case as well. The affirmative judgment that the mother reaches about her child does not seem to be rationally arbitrary, but something that is called for in her situation, as a correct response to the fact of her child's involvement in her life. It is not just that she happens not to regret her child's existence, but also that she has good reason not to regret her child's existence, and any consolation that her child might take from her mother's affirmative attitude toward her is connected to its being in this way justified rather than arbitrary.

How else might we think about the temporal aspect of the attitudes involved in this interesting case? A still different proposal, due to David Velleman, emphasizes the distinction between descriptive and demonstrative modes of access to human life.[11] Prospectively, we judge that it would be best if the young girl did not conceive a child at her current stage of life. This is an "all things considered" value judgment that is couched in descriptive terms and grounded at least partly in moral considerations, having to do with the rights of children to be born in circumstances that are adequate to the predicament they face.[12] But Velleman suggests that the birth of the child makes possible a different, demonstrative way of representing it, and our retrospective evaluations of the child can be understood partly in these demonstrative terms. Looking backward, the young mother

---

11. J. David Velleman, "Persons in Prospect," *Philosophy & Public Affairs* 36 (2008), pp. 221–88. The discussion of the young girl's child is found primarily in Part 3 of this paper, "Love and Nonexistence."

12. Velleman, "Persons in Prospect," pp. 268, 275–77.

will affirm that it is for the best, all things considered, that *this* child exists and plays a role in her life, an attitude that will presumably be shared by the child herself, insofar as she does not regret that *she* was born. These demonstrative evaluations are not available to be made or assessed prior to the child's birth, and this explains the temporal shift that is induced by that event.[13]

But how exactly should this shift be understood? One possibility is the following. The mother (say) continues to endorse the descriptive judgment that it is best, all things considered, that children not be born to fourteen-year-olds. But she does not accept this conclusion in application to individuals who satisfy the relevant description, once those individuals are available to be known to her demonstratively or by acquaintance. Of those individuals (or most of them, at any rate), she might think that it is for the best, all things considered, that they exist.

This approach would account for the shift in evaluation between the prospective and the retrospective points of view. But it raises puzzles of its own. Most significantly, there is the oddity of supposing that we would endorse a value judgment whose subject is picked out using definite descriptions while withholding the evaluative predicate from all actual individuals who satisfy the pertinent description. If our prospective attitudes are to the effect that it is best that individuals born to young teenagers should not exist, how can we rationally fail to think this of every person who in fact was born to a young teenage mother? Velleman, at any rate, does not understand the temporal shift in these terms. His view is not that we make different evaluative judgments about people who can be represented by us demonstratively and who can be represented only by description. The prospective judgment that is couched in terms of definite descriptions is one that we continue to endorse, looking backward on

13. Velleman, "Persons in Prospect," pp. 269–73.

the individuals who satisfy the descriptions in question; it is just that we *also* endorse a demonstrative value judgment about those individuals that is differently valenced. On this account, both the mother and the daughter regret the birth of the child that the mother conceived as a young teenager, thinking that that event was not for the best. At the same time, however, they are thankful for the existence of *this* child, thinking it a good thing on balance that the child with whom they are thus acquainted was born.[14]

But this position has oddities of its own. Most obviously, there is an apparent inconsistency in judging that it is best, all things considered, that children not be born to fourteen-year-old mothers, while also judging that it would not be best, all things considered, that *this* child of a fourteen-year-old mother should not have been born. Velleman, for his part, takes this not to be an objection to his account so much as a consideration that motivates an antirealist account of value. On the metaethical approach he favors, value judgments are not answerable to some real distribution of value among options or outcomes.[15] They are expressions of valuing attitudes that it is intelligible for a given agent to hold, and Velleman believes that it is perfectly intelligible for parents and children alike to have different emotional responses to the existence of the children, depending on whether they are thought of descriptively or demonstratively.[16]

The approach is unconvincing, however. For one thing, it requires us to take on board an expressivist theory of value that is controversial, to say the least. More to the immediate point, it is not at all clear that the retrospective attitudes that Velleman ascribes to parents and children in cases of this kind really are intelligible. The difficulty

---

14. Velleman, "Persons in Prospect," pp. 271–73.
15. Velleman, "Persons in Prospect," p. 273. He notes, in addition, that conflicting judgments would be intolerable if they yielded conflicting advice for agents about what to do, but that the judgments at issue are essentially retrospective rather than action guiding; see p. 272.
16. Velleman, "Persons in Prospect," p. 287.

comes into focus when we note that the demonstrative and descriptive modes of thinking about the young girl's child are not hygienically separate from each other. The mother, for instance, can think of her child descriptively as "the daughter of a fourteen-year-old girl" or demonstratively as "this child." But she can also think of her offspring through hybrid modes of presentation, such as "this child, who is the daughter of a fourteen-year-old girl." What evaluative attitude is this way of thinking of the child supposed to elicit? Insofar as it is demonstrative, one would expect it to give rise to the kind of all-things-considered affirmation that is characteristic of love. Yet insofar as it applies to the child the offending description, it should also express the attitude of all-things-considered rejection that is characteristic of regret. But there is no way of combining complete affirmation and rejection in this way, which is to say that there is no stable set of differently valenced attitudes toward the child that is channeled through demonstrative and descriptive modes of presentation.

Velleman's approach is an attempt to do justice to two important desiderata. On the one hand, the birth of the child does not merely present us with the option of adopting toward her an affirmative attitude; it calls for such an attitude. On the other hand, the weightiest considerations that prospectively speak against the young girl's decision to become pregnant seem to remain cogent even after the child is born; it isn't that the birth of the child leads us to change our minds about that question. This leads Velleman to propose that we entertain two different value judgments after the birth of the child, depending on whether we think of the child descriptively or demonstratively, a view that we have seen to be unsatisfactory.

A better way to do justice to the relevant desiderata, I believe, is to abandon an assumption that is common to the various treatments of the case that we have been considering. That is the assumption that our prospective and retrospective attitudes should be understood in evaluative terms, as involving (for instance) all-things-considered assessments of

the child's existence. Instead, I propose that we think of the case normatively, attending to the changes in the deliberative situations of agents
that are induced by the birth of the young girl's child.[17]

Thus, prior to the child's conception, the young girl is in a situation in which there are compelling reasons for her to put off pregnancy and motherhood. Some of these reasons are of a self-regarding
nature: her own life will presumably be likely to go better in various
respects if she postpones these phases of it until she is more emotionally and intellectually mature. But there are important moral reasons
at stake as well. It is morally objectionable, in ways that are of course
challenging to articulate, to give birth to a child who you know will
face unusual obstacles in virtue of your own immaturity.[18] The totality of reasons thus speaks strongly against conceiving a child at this
stage in the girl's life, a conclusion we might express by saying that she
ought, all things considered, not to follow that path.

Consider now the changes that are effected in the young girl's
deliberative situation by the emergence onto the scene of her child.
At this point in her life, it is no longer an open question whether to
have a child or not; that question has been resolved, for better or
worse, and in a way that alters the normative landscape that she inhabits. In particular, there is now an individual human being, her
daughter, who both exists and stands in a significant relationship of
attachment to her. Actual human beings of this kind make claims on
us, however, of a kind that merely possible people do not. We have

17. Normative considerations, I shall assume, are reasons or (perhaps) rational requirements
of various kinds, and deliberation is here understood as reflection about such reasons and
rational requirements, insofar as they bear on questions about what to do, think, or feel. I
don't wish to deny that reasons are often connected to values in various ways; the point
is rather that the normative significance of values for a given agent often depends on that
agent's deliberative situation, in ways that help us to understand the temporal dimension of
cases such as the young girl's child.

18. Part of the challenge, of course, is to figure out whether the moral objection is essentially
impersonal (as Parfit and consequentialists think) or rather an objection that can be articulated on behalf of the young girl's child; I return briefly to this issue below.

reason to attend to their needs and interests, to nourish, care for, and support them, particularly if we stand in a parental relationship to them. Moreover, we have reason to cherish and to love them, caring not only for but also *about* them, in ways we do not have reason to care about people who are mere strangers to us.[19] Responding appropriately to the reasons of this kind that her new situation brings in its train, the young girl will naturally affirm and celebrate the existence of her child, cherishing her daughter and her daughter's role in her own life. This is part of what is involved in being attached to the child, in the way that is characteristic of relationships of love.

This change in the mother's deliberative situation, I submit, makes it possible for us to understand the evolution in her attitudes, without supposing either that she changes her mind about the relevant normative questions or that she acquires responses that are inconsistent toward one and the same state of affairs. It is true that a person in the young girl's preconception situation has compelling reason to postpone motherhood, and this is a normative judgment that the girl can continue to endorse even after the birth of her child. Looking backward, she still believes that someone in the situation she earlier faced ought to put off motherhood until becoming more mature. But it is also true that parents have special reasons of attachment to love and care for and affirm the lives of their offspring, and this is similarly a judgment that the girl could in principle acknowledge even before she makes the fateful decision to become pregnant. Looking forward, she should grant that parents have special reasons of this kind to care about their children. Indeed, the fact that this is the case is among the considerations that tell against the decision to conceive a child as a teenager; doing so can be anticipated to change her deliberative situation in the way I have described, introducing

---

19. Compare Niko Kolodny, "Love as Valuing a Relationship," *Philosophical Review* 112 (2003), pp. 135–89.

new and compelling normative requirements that she is not yet capable of fully living up to.[20]

Against this, it might be suggested that the deliberative considerations that bear on the young girl's situation do not in fact permit the easy resolution of the apparent puzzles that I have proposed. Consider Parfit's account of the moral reasons against conceiving a child when one is a teenager. Doing so, he argues, would produce an outcome that is impersonally worse than an alternative that is available, insofar as the child she would have as a teenager can be expected to enjoy a lower quality of life than would be enjoyed by the different child she would have if she postponed motherhood for several years. To understand the moral objection to the young girl's decision, in other words, we need to trace that objection to an overall evaluation of the outcome that would be brought about by the decision. But if it was true at the time of the girl's decision that it would be better not to have a child as a fourteen-year-old, it will remain true in retrospect, after she has given birth, that it would have been better not to do so. As we saw above, the mother's acceptance of this retrospective evaluation would seem difficult to reconcile with her attitude toward her child, which is affirmative rather than regretful.

But these considerations do not undermine the approach to the problem that I have begun to sketch, for several reasons. First, it is far from obvious that the moral objection to the young girl's decision is properly conceived in terms of an impersonal comparative value judgment of the kind that Parfit appeals to. One problem is that it is not at all clear that we even understand what is being said when Parfit speaks about one outcome or scenario as being better than another. Such predicative uses of "better than" are notoriously problematic,

---

20. As I noted in the introduction, agent-relative reasons of love are perspectival, in the sense that one only has them if one actually stands in a relationship of love to someone; but they can be understood and ascribed to agents from other points of view, including, for instance, the prospective point of view of the young girl before she has a child.

THE VIEW FROM HERE

and it should not be taken for granted that that any clear meaning can be attached to them.[21] Furthermore, even if we allow that they sometimes make sense, it isn't obvious that the moral objection to the young girl's decision can perspicuously be captured in terms of judgments of this kind. Consider the well-known "buck-passing" theory of value.[22] On this plausible approach, predications of goodness to individuals or states of affairs should not be understood to involve a first-order property of goodness or intrinsic value. Goodness is rather a second-order property, which is rightly predicated of things when they have first-order features that give us reasons for appropriately favorable responses to them.[23] To say that it would have been better had the teenager's child not been born, according to this account, is not to articulate a first-order reason against bringing her into existence in the first place. It is rather to say that the state of affairs of her existing has other features that give us reasons for reacting negatively toward it (as compared to the alternatives that the young girl might have caused through her agency). But then the comparative badness of the state of affairs cannot be the ground of the moral objection to bringing it about. Rather, to say that the state of affairs is bad is to presuppose that there are other and independent bases for objecting to it.

As it happens, there are promising alternative frameworks for thinking about the non-identity problem that enable us to articulate the moral objection to decisions such as the young girl's without recourse to impersonal evaluative assessments of the outcomes of the available actions. We might say, for instance, that individuals have

---

21. For a forceful defense of this skeptical conclusion about predicative uses of "good" or "better than," see Judith Jarvis Thomson, *Normativity* (Chicago: Open Court, 2008).
22. T. M. Scanlon, *What We Owe to Each Other* (Cambridge, Mass.: Belknap Press of Harvard University Press, 1998), chap. 3.
23. For a defense of this approach, see my "Reasons, Values, and Agent-Relativity," *dialectica* 64 (2010), pp. 503–28.

generic claims to a certain level of provision or care as children, and that it is wrong to bring people into existence when you know in advance that these claims will not be met. The wrong that is done to the child, on this way of understanding the case, is not that the young mother has made her worse off than she otherwise would have been (since the decision to postpone motherhood would have had the consequence that her child was not born in the first place). It is rather that she has knowingly brought it about that a person exists whose claim to an adequate standard of maternal care and attention cannot be satisfied. This is a moral objection that can be brought on behalf of the child herself, and it can therefore be articulated without recourse to impersonal value judgments of the kind that figure in Parfit's account.[24] Of course, if there is an objection of this personal nature to the young girl's decision, then we can say on the buck-passing approach that the state of affairs that is brought about through the decision is in at least one respect bad. It is bad insofar as the state of affairs involves a decision that we have moral reason to object to. But on this way of thinking about things, the badness of the state of affairs that is brought about isn't the basis of the moral objection to the mother's decision. On the contrary, it is only because we take there to be an independent basis for mounting an objection to it that we are prepared to ascribe to the resulting state of affairs the second-order property of being (pro tanto) bad.

These remarks raise large and controversial issues, however, which I have hardly done enough to defend. Suppose I am wrong

---

24. See, for example, the approach implicit in Seana Valentine Shiffrin, "Wrongful Life, Procreative Responsibility, and the Significance of Harm," *Legal Theory* 5 (1999), pp. 117–48. Shiffrin contends that procreation can violate the rights or claims of individuals, even if it is also a condition for their existence. (Indeed, she argues that procreation necessarily infringes against the moral claims of offspring, a stronger claim that I do not wish to endorse.) Broadly similar positions are defended, e.g., by Elizabeth Harman, "Can We Harm and Benefit in Creating?," *Philosophical Perspectives* 18 (2004), pp. 89–113; James Woodward, "The Non-Identity Problem," *Ethics* 96 (1986), pp. 804–31; and Rahul Kumar, "Who Can Be Wronged?," *Philosophy & Public Affairs* 31 (2003), pp. 99–117.

about them, and that the moral objection to the young girl's decision is based in the impersonal badness of the state of affairs that it brings into existence. Even then, I want to argue, it would not follow that the prospective and retrospective views of the child's life involve a conflict in judgments about reasons. For impersonal values might be differently normative for our attitudes before and after the child's birth. Looking forward, the fact that postponing motherhood would produce a better outcome than conceiving in the immediate future might be a compelling moral reason for the young girl to favor that outcome. Looking backward after the child has arrived, however, the fact that there was an alternative outcome that would have been better might not give the mother reason to regret that her child exists.[25] On the approach that I am defending, the considerations that most basically structure our thinking about cases of this kind are normative considerations, having to do with our reasons for action and response, and we cannot simply take it for granted that the impersonal values that allegedly ground the moral objection to the young girl's decision are equally normative for her retrospective attitudes. This carves out conceptual space for the interpretation of the temporal shift in the young girl's outlook for which I have been arguing. Even if she has compelling reason to postpone motherhood at the time when she makes the decision to conceive (in virtue of the impersonal disvalue of the outcome to which that decision would lead), she might later have compelling reason to affirm the very same decision (in virtue of her attachment to the child that she has brought into the world).

Still, as I have hinted above, there is something odd about supposing that evaluative considerations might be differently valenced in

---

25. Parfit himself appears to concede as much when he suggests that it might not be rational for either the young girl or her child to regret the fact that she conceived and gave birth when she did, even though both should agree that it would have been better had she not done so; see Parfit, *Reasons and Persons*, pp. 360–61. It remains to develop an account of regret that would accommodate the rational objections to the attitude under these conditions.

this way, depending on whether they figure in prospective or retrospective thoughts about an action or outcome. This is true independently of whether we understand the moral objection to the young girl's decision in impersonal or personal terms. Thus, suppose that what makes it wrong to conceive a child when you are still a young teenager is the fact that your child will have claims to parental attention and support that cannot in the nature of the case be fulfilled. This moral objection on the potential child's behalf renders it true that the young girl ought not to become pregnant and have a child, in the deliberative situation in which she finds herself. But if it was true, at the time, that she ought not to have a child, it remains true, when she looks back on her decision from the perspective of motherhood, that she ought not to have followed that path. Furthermore, this is a normative truth that remains accessible to her from her later point of view, and that she should continue to endorse when she thinks about her earlier circumstances. After all, the fact that she now finds herself in a different situation does nothing to undermine the moral and other objections to conceiving a child when you are still a young teenager yourself.

At the same time, the birth of her child changes the young girl's deliberative circumstances in the ways canvassed above. Specifically, it gives her compelling reason to love and cherish her daughter, to care for and about her, and to affirm and celebrate her existence. These are the considerations of attachment that make it natural to say that the mother, looking back on her life, does not have reason to regret the existence of her daughter and of her life together with her daughter. But if this is right, it seems that her retrospective view of her trajectory will include a mistaken decision that is inaccessible to all-in regret. She will grant that she ought not to have had a child when she did. But she will not be able to regret having taken this course, since her doing so is the condition for the existence of the child that she now loves and has reason to affirm and to celebrate.

It is tempting to suppose that there must be something incoherent in this retrospective conception. To the extent the mother agrees that she ought not to have had a child when she did, shouldn't she regret her decision to become a mother? And to the extent she finds herself unable to regret that decision, aren't we forced to conclude that she doesn't really believe any longer that it is a decision she ought not to have made? Considerations of this kind make it difficult to see how the mother's normative judgment about her earlier decision can possibly go together with her persisting immunity to regret. We seem to be pushed back to the view that the young girl's change in circumstances must induce either a change in her judgments or an incoherence in her overall outlook.

3.2. AFFIRMATION AND JUSTIFICATION

I do not believe that the retrospective viewpoint I have ascribed to the young mother is incoherent. Some decisions and choices that are wrong are also inaccessible to a certain kind of personal regret, and the fact that this is the case does nothing to establish that those decisions either are or are believed to be justified after all.

To see why this is the case, it will be helpful to recall some of the conclusions from the preceding chapter about the nature of regret and its objects. Regret, as we have seen, is a pained apprehension of some past event or state of affairs. It is connected to the phenomenon of valuing and reflects the peculiar emotional vulnerability we experience when we are attached to an individual or a project or an institution. There is room for deep ambivalence of emotional reaction in cases that involve retrospective regret; one might have some regrets about things one did in one's youth, even if one is at the same time also glad that one did them. But there are also cases in which one's retrospective attitudes are less fundamentally conflicted. In particular, when one experiences all-in regret about an earlier event or situation, one has a pained consciousness of the event or situation when one looks back on it in thought, together with an on-balance preference that things should have been otherwise.

As we saw in the preceding chapter, regret of this all-in variety cannot coexist with a certain kind of unconditional affirmation about one and the same object of thought. To affirm something, in the relevant sense, is to judge that it is valuable along some dimension or other, and also to prefer on balance—taking everything into account—that it should not be otherwise.[26] But if one affirms something in this way, then there is no conceptual space left for one also to experience all-in regret about it, since a defining feature of such regret is an on-balance preference that the object of regret should have been otherwise. Nor can one be subject to all-in regret about the necessary causal and historical conditions of the object that one wholeheartedly and unconditionally affirms. To wish on balance that those conditions had been otherwise, in the knowledge that the object that one affirms would not have existed in their absence, would ultimately undermine one's affirmative attitude toward that object. This is the affirmation dynamic that was described at the end of the preceding chapter.

These general points have direct relevance for the case of the young girl's child. Thus the young girl cannot experience all-in regret about her decision to conceive a child at fourteen while affirming unconditionally the existence of her daughter. If she had postponed motherhood, the child she actually loves and cherishes wouldn't have existed. So she cannot realistically reconcile her unconditional affirmation of

---

26. Otherwise, that is, from among a range of possibilities that is fixed by the context and the object of affirmation. As I noted in sec. 2.4 above, the alternatives relevant when we affirm an action are typically different from those that are relevant when we affirm, say, an individual. In the same section, I contrast this kind of unconditional affirmation with the conditional variety, where we affirm (e.g.) an action or event on the assumption that its necessary conditions obtained, but without affirming or being committed to affirming those conditions themselves.

her child with all-in regret for her decision by insisting that these attitudes are directed toward different objects. The thing that she affirms, the existence of her daughter, presupposes the decision that she would attempt to regret, which means that she has to fish or cut bait, as it were. If, looking backward, the totality of events that were set in motion by her decision include compelling reasons to love her daughter and to affirm and celebrate her existence, then she will not be able to prefer, on balance, that she should have decided otherwise.[27] By a particular application of the affirmation dynamic, her unconditional love of her daughter will commit her to affirming the decision to conceive that was a necessary condition for the daughter's being around in the first place. The result is that all-in regret for the decision has become rationally inaccessible to her. She cannot now regret the decision in this way, despite the fact that the balance of moral and nonmoral reasons spoke strongly against it at the time.

This fact about the inaccessibility to her of all-in regret, however, does not entail that the decision has somehow acquired a justification ex post facto that it didn't have when it was made, or that the mother's view about the justification of her choice has changed over time. The totalizing character of all-in regret, emphasized above, renders it ill-suited to tracking justification and its absence. To see this, it will help to consider a different and simpler example that involves moral objections to prospective actions of the kind that might be brought by the people whom those actions wrong. I shall then come back to the prospective-life case that has been my main concern in the present chapter.

Consider a situation in which I have promised to drive you to the airport to catch a flight to the conference in Europe that you are

---

27. What she can still regret, in the all-in way, is the fact that circumstances force her to choose between a better decision and her daughter. Thus she might well say, "I only wish I could have had you when I was older and more mature."

planning to attend. The fact that I have made this promise creates a moral reason for picking you up that is ordinarily dispositive. If I fail to do what I have promised, in circumstances in which there was no personal or other emergency that couldn't have been anticipated at the time when the promise was made, then I have wronged you, and this feature of my relation to you as promisee creates a presumptively decisive objection to my failure to meet my promissory duty.

Suppose now that I break my promise, causing you to miss your flight, but that the flight you were supposed to be on crashes, resulting in the death of all passengers on board.[28] Looking back on what happened, you will certainly not be subject to all-in regret that I failed to pick you up as promised. On the contrary, you will be immensely relieved that this is how things played out and feel fortunate in the extreme to have been caused to miss the fatal flight. You will therefore also be unable to regret in the all-in way that I broke my promise; the parsing strategy breaks down in this case, insofar as the putative target of all-in regret—the fact of the broken promise—is a necessary condition of the circumstance that is the proper target of such affirmative attitudes as relief and gratitude. At the same time, however, the fact that my action ended up benefiting you in this dramatic way that calls for affirmation does not constitute a justification for my decision to undertake it. It was wrong for me to break my promise under the circumstances, and you continue to have a legitimate complaint against me even if things turned out so well in the end that you are unable to regret my acting as I did.

Though they do not affect the *justification* of my earlier action, however, the subsequent events in this case might have some bearing on the truth of judgments about what I ought to have done. Thus, from the perspective of retrospective assessment, the fact that breaking the promise ended up saving your life puts pressure on us to

---

28. Compare Woodward, "The Non-Identity Problem," pp. 810–11.

modify our views about what I really ought to have done under the original circumstances. Some philosophers hold, for instance, that the "ought" judgment about the earlier situation of action has truth conditions that depend on the objective facts about the outcomes of the action. On this view, it was true all along that I ought not to have kept the promise, although this was a truth that I admittedly wasn't in a position to grasp at the time of action.[29] Alternatively, one might maintain that the truth of "ought" claims is relative to the context at which they are assessed. The claim that I ought to have kept the promise is false when assessed from the retrospective standpoint that includes knowledge of what would actually have happened if the promise had been kept, but it is true when assessed at the earlier time of action, since there was then no reason to believe that keeping the promise would have endangered your life.[30]

What generates the pressure we feel in this case to think that the truth of the "ought" judgment might be determined by the actual outcomes that do or would result from the actions available to the agent? A salient feature of the example, as it seems to me, is that the considerations that preclude regret are considerations of a kind that would have undermined your moral objection to the broken promise if they had been accessible to me epistemically at the time. The fact that keeping the promise will lead to your death is the sort of unanticipated emergency circumstance that ordinarily releases people from their promissory obligations when such circumstances can be known by the agent to obtain. Our promissory obligations have built into them exception clauses, suspending the requirement to perform when doing so would have disastrous consequences of a kind that

---

29. For a defense of this possibility, see, e.g., Judith Jarvis Thomson, *The Realm of Rights* (Cambridge, Mass.: Harvard University Press, 1990), p. 229 (a view that is modified significantly in Thomson's later book *Normativity*, p. 198.)

30. This position is interestingly defended by Niko Kolodny and John MacFarlane, "Ought: Between Objective and Subjective" (unpublished manuscript).

could not have been anticipated at the time when the promise was originally made. A conception of promises that lacked this feature would be too restrictive, making it unreasonable for people ever to enter into promissory relationships in the first place. (In the case we have been considering, neither you nor I have reason to want the promise to drive you to the airport to be binding even if it emerges that my doing so would lead to your demise!) This is what encourages us to think that the actual facts about what would have happened if I had kept my promise and enabled you to catch your flight might have significance for the question of whether this is something that I really ought to have done.

Whether we should ultimately favor an objective or relativistic conception of "ought" is not an issue that needs to be decided here. For my part, I acknowledge some pressure to think that the truth of "ought" judgments in these cases might be sensitive to facts about the actual consequences of the options that are available to the agent. But a subjective interpretation seems to me more plausible on the whole. According to this kind of view, the truth of "ought" claims is determined by the facts that are epistemically accessible to the agent at the time of action. On this kind of position, it would remain true that I ought to have kept my promise to you, even from the retrospective standpoint that includes knowledge about what would actually have happened if you had caught your flight.[31] This preserves the connection to the deliberative situation of the agent that is in my view the

---

31. This verdict seems most counterintuitive in situations in which we have good prior information about the consequences of the alternative actions that isn't yet available to the agent whose actions are to be assessed. It seems strange to maintain that the agent ought to keep the promise if (e.g.) we happen to know in advance that it will lead to the promisee's death. But this is because our possession of superior information, under circumstances in which there are channels through which it could be communicated to the agent, makes that information available to the agent in the relevant sense. The function of advice, in circumstances of this kind, is not to comment on the deliberative situation of the agent, as it exists independently of the advice giver, but to make claims about what the agent ought to do that take into account the function of advice as a way of correcting false beliefs that the agent might happen to have.

primary context in which "ought" judgments have application. The odd upshot is that situations can arise, as with the promising example, in which we are relieved in retrospect that agents did not do what they ought to have done. But as we shall see presently, situations of this kind can arise even if we accept an objective or relativistic semantics for "ought."

The more important point to make about the promising example, however, concerns the justification of my earlier action of promise breaking rather than the truth conditions of claims about what I ought to have done. Even if it is (now) true that I ought not to have kept my promise, my failure to do so was not *justified* at the time when I performed it, and it does not acquire a justification ex post facto. Justification, in interpersonal contexts of this kind, is connected to the notion of complaint. If I have a justification for my action, then there is a consideration in its favor available for me to adduce that suffices to undermine your strong prima facie complaint against it. But there is no consideration of this kind that I can appeal to in the case at hand. Given what I had reason to believe at the time of action, my failure to pick you up as promised reflected a serious lack of consideration and regard, and this is something that you have good reason to hold against me. The fact that it all worked out in the end does not make it the case that my earlier action did not after all involve a significant failure to acknowledge your interests and claims; but failures of this kind are precisely the sorts of things that ground legitimate moral complaints in interpersonal contexts. My action was not justified, under the circumstances of its performance, and this continues to give you a reason to protest against it.

It might be objected to this that justification can at least potentially come apart from the question of whether there is a ground for complaint on the part of those potentially affected by my actions. Bernard Williams has argued, for instance, that an action might eventually be justified by its results, even if it affected other people in ways that they continue to have grounds for objecting to.[32] I shall return to this argument in the next chapter, examining it closely in the light of the conclusions arrived at here. But the initial point to make is that it is implausible to suppose that justification might come apart from the notion of complaint in the case at hand. The rational consideration that potentially speaks against the action of failing to pick you up, after all, is the fact that I promised you that I would do so. I would therefore wrong you by failing to do what I have promised, and this is connected to the fact that you would have strong grounds for complaining about my behavior if I were to break my promise. A justification, in this context, would be a consideration that undermines or negates the grounds you have for objecting to it. But in the example as we have described it, there is nothing that would seem capable of playing this role. Your objection to my conduct is based in the fact that I deliberately failed to do what I promised to do, under conditions in which I had no reason for believing that there was any emergency at hand that couldn't have been anticipated at the time when the promise was made; my acting in this way reflects a lack of consideration and regard for your interests, and this is your basis for complaint about what I have done. That it all worked out well in the end does not in any way alter these facts about my conduct, and hence that aspect of the cases does not function to justify the way I behaved.

Of course, because things have dramatically turned out well in the end, it is unlikely that you will now press your objection to my conduct. As I have been arguing, you now have reason to affirm that I acted as I did, and under these conditions it would be somewhat unusual for you to make a big deal about the fact that I wronged you. You are passionately attached to your own life, which has inadvertently been saved as a result of my morally questionable comportment, and the relief that you will feel in consequence is likely to

---

32. This is a large theme of his paper "Moral Luck."

swamp any other focused reactions you might have toward the way I treated you. The mistake is to think that these perfectly intelligible aspects of your present point of view might retroactively affect the question of whether the action that I performed was or was not justified under the circumstances. The features of the situation that lead you to affirm my action do not function to undermine your basis for objecting to it. For that reason they do not constitute justifications for my conduct; you continue to have a basis for objecting to it, though you are in the odd (if intelligible) position that you do not prefer on balance that I should have acted otherwise.

Many of the cases that raise the so-called non-identity problem have a similar structure, at least on the approach to them that I would favor. Thus consider the situation of the young girl's child in the example that has been at the center of attention in this chapter. I believe that people have claims to be given an adequate level of parental care and attention from birth, and that these claims ordinarily ground decisive objections to conceiving a child when one is far too young to be able to responsibly meet its needs for parental solicitude and support. This is, I think, the best way to understand the moral objection to what the young girl does, and the objection that it isolates is one that is articulated on the prospective child's behalf.[33] Now suppose, as we have been doing, that the young girl ignores this compelling objection, proceeding to act on her impulse to conceive and give birth to a child while she is still in her early teens. Looking back on this decision, the person on whose behalf we would object to it cannot, for reasons that are now familiar, experience all-in regret about the fact that it was made. On the story we have been telling, the young girl's child has a life that is well worth living, from her own point of view, one that she takes an affirmative attitude toward; she does not prefer, all things considered, that she should never have

---

33. See the texts cited in note 24 above.

existed. But if she in this way embraces her own existence, she can hardly feel all-in regret for the fact that her mother decided to conceive her, since that decision was a necessary condition for the very thing that she embraces.

As we saw in chapter 2, there are some cases in which affirmation is a conditional attitude. We often affirm actions that we or other agents have performed, for instance, without affirming the circumstances that made those actions necessary or attractive in the first place. The kind of affirmation at issue in this chapter is, by contrast, unconditional, and directed not at actions but at individuals and their lives. The young girl and her child do not merely affirm an action that was performed in a context that the agent was then powerless to affect one way or another. They affirm the existence of the child and the life that the child has led. This attitude involves an on-balance preference that the child should have come into being in the first place, including a preference that the necessary conditions of the child's existence also should have obtained. To use the image deployed in section 2.4, their unconditional affirmation of the child is of a kind that spreads backward from its immediate object, embracing as well the necessary historical conditions for the object's existence.

For these reasons, the young girl's child cannot experience all-in regret about the fact that her mother conceived her; her attitude of unconditional affirmation of her own life makes that kind of regret about its necessary conditions inaccessible to her. It does not follow from this instantiation of the affirmation dynamic, however, that the moral objection to the young girl's decision has been undermined by the course of events that followed in its train. If the needs of the prospective child ground a decisive moral objection to the young girl's decision at the time when she is deliberating about it, they retain their moral force and significance after the decision has been made. To suppose otherwise is to think, absurdly, that the mere prospect of a human need grounds a serious moral objection when a need of the very same kind, once it comes to be felt by an actual human individual, is unable to ground a complaint that is similar in its moral force. We do better to assume that the young girl's child has a moral complaint about her mother's decision, an objection to it on her own behalf, even though she does not and cannot regret the fact that the mother made the decision and acted as she did. The action was wrong, but regret about the fact that it is wrong is not available to the child who was its victim.[34]

There is a difference between this case and that of the broken promise that is worth dwelling on at least briefly. In the latter case, as we saw above, there is some pressure to think that the considerations that preclude retrospective regret also affect the truth of claims about what the agent ought to have done. The fact that the broken promise ended up saving your life can tempt us to suppose that it is (now) true that I ought to have acted as I did, even though that did not appear to be the case at the time, and even though the earlier decision lacks (and continues to lack) a justification. The case of the young girl's child seems different in precisely this respect. What makes regret inaccessible to the child is her unconditional attachment to life, which requires her to affirm the necessary historical conditions of her existence. But these considerations were perfectly available to the child's mother at the point when she made the decision to conceive. That is, even before giving birth to her daughter, the young girl had good reason to expect that both she and her child would have powerful grounds for affirming retrospectively a decision she might make to become pregnant. The fact that this outcome could be anticipated in advance, however, hardly suffices to undermine the weighty moral and prudential objections to having a child at that stage of life. It is not the kind of consideration that is capable of playing this role, and

---

34. Compare Harman, "Can We Harm and Benefit in Creating?," p. 99 (though she doesn't put the point in terms of regret).

so we are not even tempted to think that the presence of these factors affects the truth of claims about what the young girl ought to have done. Thus, even on an objective or relativistic semantics for "ought," the plausible thing to say about the young girl's earlier situation, from the standpoint of retrospective assessment, is that she ought not to have become pregnant as a teenager. Doing so was wrong, and hence unjustified, and it was and remains something that she ought not to have chosen to do. And yet the child she gave birth to, whose entitlement to adequate parental attention grounds these conclusions about the mother's earlier action, and who therefore continues to have a valid complaint about that action, is not in a position to regret that her mother acted as she did.

The interpersonal examples I have been discussing are structurally similar to the first-personal situation that has been the primary focus of this chapter. Just as the young girl's child has an objection to her mother's decision that is not undermined by her inability to regret it, so too with her mother herself: she also acknowledges compelling reasons against the course of action that she undertook, despite the fact that she is not susceptible to all-in regret on account of having acted in that way. This is hardly surprising, since one of the considerations that speaks decisively against the mother's decision at the time when it is made is precisely the moral objection to it that can be brought on behalf of the child that she would then bring into the world. The other considerations, of course, are prudential, grounded in the effects of teenage motherhood on the young girl's own life prospects. These considerations, too, seem to remain in force, despite the emergence onto the scene of reasons to affirm the earlier decision. Indeed, the young girl's awareness of the personal costs of her decision might become increasingly acute as she makes her way through life and observes (for instance) the opportunities and advantages that are enjoyed by her more prudent peers. But she will still be unable to regret that decision in the way that involves an on-balance wish that she had acted otherwise.

The reasons why all-in regret is inaccessible are admittedly somewhat different in the case of the mother and the child. In the mother's case, they have to do with considerations of human relationship. The mother is attached to her daughter, in the manner of maternal love, and this kind of relational attachment undergirds her affirmation of her daughter's existence. To be attached to someone in this way is to have a powerful reason to be glad that the person exists, and it is the mother's acknowledgment of this reason that makes her unable to regret on balance the decision that brought her daughter into the world in the first place. To be sure, there is room for debate about the fine structure of the normative considerations that are at issue in the mother's situation. Is the fact that the mother loves her daughter itself a reason to affirm unconditionally the daughter's existence? Or is maternal love something that is grounded in prior and independent reasons, concerning (for instance) the value of the relationship she stands in to her daughter, where those independent reasons are the ultimate warrant for her affirmative attitude toward the daughter?[35] These are not questions that need to be decided here. The fact is that the mother is emotionally attached to her daughter, in a way that essentially implicates reasons of some kind to affirm unconditionally that her daughter exists; this remains the case, regardless of whether we see the maternal love as itself a reason for affirmation or as responsive to independent considerations that supply such reasons.

The affirmative attitudes of the daughter toward her existence have a different character. They are grounded not in an interpersonal relationship with another individual but in her relationship to her own life. She is attached to her life, in a way that involves a strong preference both to continue living in the immediate future

---

35. For these different approaches, see, e.g., Harry G. Frankfurt, *The Reasons of Love* (Princeton, N.J.: Princeton University Press, 2004), and Kolodny, "Love as Valuing a Relationship."

and to have come into existence in the first place. I suggested earlier that this attitude is warranted so long as the daughter's life is worth living on the whole. This is a condition that can be satisfied even if her life is not as good as it perhaps should have been, because of her immature mother's incapacity to live up fully to the responsibilities of parenthood. Ultimately, I believe that it is the presence in a life of valuable attachments to individuals and projects that makes a life worth living from the agent's point of view, and that provides a normative basis for the agent's attachment to life itself. It is the fact that the daughter has meaningful relationships and activities that she cares about that gives her a basis for continuing her life going forward, and for being glad that she was born; this is an issue to which we will return in chapters 4 and 5. But if she has reason to affirm unconditionally that she was born, she also has a reason to affirm the historical conditions that made her birth possible. The upshot is the same as in the case of her mother (albeit for somewhat different reasons): an inability, looking backward, fundamentally to regret a decision that continues to be subject to powerful objections.

3.3. MIXED FEELINGS

A case that has this kind of structure would naturally be thought to involve some element of emotional ambivalence. The young girl and her child may both affirm the decision that the mother made as they look back on it. But to the extent they continue to endorse the powerful objections to the decision, one would expect that to leave some residue in their retrospective attitudes. One would expect this, at any rate, on the assumption that the young girl and her child both care about the values at the center of morality. To care about those values, as we saw in the last chapter, is to internalize a concern for their realization, where this in turn involves a susceptibility to emotional distress when those values are thwarted or damaged somehow. So if the mother and her child both agree that the mother's decision to conceive was wrong, we should expect them to feel some pain or discomfort about the decision when they look back on it; their natural attachment to morality as an ideal precisely involves a susceptibility to this kind of reaction in a situation of the sort we have been discussing. The question is: How can this element of retrospective distress be reconciled with the fundamentally affirmative stance that the young girl and her child adopt toward the young girl's decision? How can we make sense of a feeling of distress that is directed toward something that these agents are unable fundamentally to regret?

The short answer to these questions is that there is nothing in principle that would prevent people from feeling pained about past situations that they do not wish had been otherwise. What is precluded is all-in regret, a pained awareness of the past state of affairs that goes along with an on-balance, intention-like preference that it should not have occurred. In the absence of such a preference, however, the retrospective view of the circumstance one affirms might nevertheless occasion feelings of distress—regrets, in the vocabulary proposed in the preceding chapter, which might persist even in the absence of the element of on-balance preference that distinguishes the attitude of all-in regret.

These pained feelings can assume a variety of forms. Start with a case in which the values that one offended against were not specifically moral in nature, in that they did not primarily implicate one's relations to other people. Suppose you imprudently cashed in your retirement savings for a gambling spree in Las Vegas (under conditions in which there are no other individuals who are dependent on you for financial support); and suppose, furthermore, that you were spectacularly lucky, winning a huge jackpot for your troubles.[36] Here it seems that you have done something that was foolish at best, and yet the result has put you in a position from which it would be difficult to regret on balance that you acted as you did. Your action has been "justified by its success," as we might naturally say about such a case. But this is just a figure of speech, which should not be taken literally; the fact that your reckless behavior paid off does not constitute a justification for it, even if you find that you affirm the behavior when you look back on it in reflection. In a case with this structure, in which the objections to your conduct are not grounded in claims or entitlements that are held by other people, the element of residual distress about what you have done is apt to be fairly attenuated. You are likely to feel relief and simple pleasure at your personal good fortune that will tend to overwhelm any negative feelings you might be prone to. Still, some disposition to emotional ambivalence in a case of this kind would not be surprising, especially if you are on the sensitive or thoughtful side. The natural expression of this tendency would be a susceptibility to shame and embarrassment if it should come to light that you were willing to squander your retirement savings in a gambling spree in Vegas. It typically matters to us that we should be minimally prudent and responsible in our management of our life affairs, and the public acknowledgment that you have fallen short of this personal ideal can and should occasion discomfort.

Turn next to cases in which the action that was not justified is one that involves moral claims that are held by other parties. In some

---

36. The assumption that this case involves strictly "prudential" rather than "moral" values actually seems to me pretty unrealistic. There is something morally problematic about a failure to make adequate provision for one's own future (a dimension of such cases that we might think of as involving a wrong that is done to oneself). In addition, the decision to spend one's resources on a gambling spree arguably affects the claims of other agents as well. Thus it might be argued that, even if you are permitted to make generous provision for your own retirement (rather than donating the funds, e.g., to famine relief), you are not permitted to squander those same funds when there are acute human needs that you could contribute to meeting. I abstract from these aspects of the case in the text.

cases of this kind, as we have seen, the action that is wrong and that therefore lacks justification cannot fundamentally be regretted, even by the parties whose claims have been violated by it. And yet the fact that it has wronged them will typically leave those parties with some mixed feelings. Sometimes these will be directed primarily toward the continuing agent who acted immorally, including such emotions as suspicion and sorrowful withdrawal of trust. In the promising example that I earlier introduced, for instance, you might not be able to feel all-in regret about the fact that I broke my promise to take you to the airport (since my doing so is a condition of your now being alive). But you will probably find me a little confounding as a result of what I have done, and be disinclined to trust me going forward as you were willing to do in the past. There is nothing in the nature of affirmation that would preclude one from feeling this kind of ongoing suspicion about a person, on the basis of an action of the person that one is strictly unable to regret.

A more interesting possibility that is open to the victims of wrong-doing in cases of this kind is resentment. This is the emotional reaction that corresponds to the moral complaint that people have, insofar as they have been wronged by the actions of another. Resentment is a backward-looking attitude with a distinctively moral content; it is *about* the fact that someone has done something that violates moral requirements that we hold them to, and it constitutes the complaint that agents who are wronged are in a privileged position to feel.[37] Insofar as you were wronged by my action, there was and continues to be a moral objection to it on your behalf. Resentment is the negative emotion that corresponds to the acknowledgment that that

---

37. See my *Responsibility and the Moral Sentiments* (Cambridge, Mass.: Harvard University Press, 1994), chap. 2, and also my "Dispassionate Opprobrium. On Blame and the Reactive Sentiments," in R. Jay Wallace, Rahul Kumar, and Samuel Freeman, eds. *Reasons and Recognition: Essays on the Philosophy of T. M. Scanlon* (New York: Oxford University Press, 2011), pp. 348–72, sec. 5.

objection obtains; it reflects the fact that the person subject to it cares about the moral ideals that were damaged by the behavior that wronged them. It matters to us that people should interact with us in ways that comply with moral requirements, and this makes us susceptible to resentment when this ideal is flouted by people in their dealings with us.

In the promising example, my failure to keep my word gives you grounds for resenting what I did, though realistically a feeling with this emotional tone is likely to be swamped by your overwhelming relief that you escaped the disaster. The effects of my wrongdoing on you seem fairly trivial and limited in scope, especially against the background of the overwhelming personal disaster that my action inadvertently served to avert. In situations of this kind, all that remains may be an ongoing tendency to suspicion and withdrawal of trust on your part, mingled perhaps with inchoate feelings of unease (feelings that are nourished by your recognition of my willingness to flout values that you hold dear).

But in other cases, such as that of the young girl's child, things are different. The persisting effects of the wrong that has been done to her make it intelligible that she will resent her mother's decision to give birth to her, even if that decision is one that she is also compelled to affirm.[38] Her entire life is lived under the cloud of the features of her mother's conduct that made it wrong, and it is only natural that the child would experience resentment toward her mother as a result, and have a corresponding tendency to reproach her for what she has done. This tendency might persist well into her adult life, contributing to an ambivalence of emotional experience that goes together

---

38. Contrast Bernard Williams, "Resenting One's Own Existence," in *Making Sense of Humanity and Other Philosophical Papers, 1982–1993* (Cambridge, U.K.: Cambridge University Press, 1995), pp. 224–32, at pp. 228–30. Williams contends that if one resents x, one necessarily prefers to x some realistic alternative in which the basis for one's grievance is removed; this is precisely what I wish to deny.

with an absence of all-in regret about the action of her mother's that is the direct target of her resentment. Alternatively, her resentment might gradually abate over time, especially if her mother expresses contrition and does what she can as she matures to make up for the disadvantages to which she has subjected her daughter. (An increasingly tolerant attitude toward youthful indiscretions might also accompany the child's own adventures as a teenager and a young adult.) A strong undercurrent of resentment in the child's emotional outlook would in either case be both morally and humanly defensible, especially during the phase of the child's life when she first becomes aware of the way her mother neglected her prospective claims in deciding to conceive when she did.[39]

What, however, is the first-personal analogue of this emotional reaction, the pained response that acknowledges on the *mother's* part the continuing objection to her earlier decision? Guilt would seem to be the most natural possibility. This is precisely the agential counterpart to resentment, the reaction one is subject to on one's victim's behalf when one is aware of having done something to wrong them. We hold not only others but also ourselves to moral demands, and this distinctive stance constitutively involves a susceptibility to guilt on occasions when we have violated the demands in question, and a tendency to self-reproach as the expression of this emotional reaction. Guilt and self-reproach are like resentment in being reactions with a moral content, and this content means that the reactions remain available to the mother ex post facto, despite

---

39. A different and more gruesome example of the same kind would be one in which a woman conceives a child whom she goes on to love and care about as a result of being raped. Here, too, unconditional attachment to her child might prevent the mother from feeling all-in regret about the horrific event that led to the child's existence (including an on-balance preference that that event should not have occurred). And yet it would seem odd if the woman did not continue to experience strong feelings of resentment toward the person who raped her, and a corresponding tendency to blame and reproach him for what he did to her.

the fact that she is unable to regret the decision that she undertook. Their moral content is given by the fact that her daughter continues to have a legitimate complaint against her on account of the decision, and it is in this sense that guilt is the first-personal counterpart of the resentment that her child is entitled to feel.[40] Like resentment, it reflects the fact that the person subject to it has internalized a concern for moral requirements.

What about remorse? As we saw in the preceding chapter, this is a sentiment that focuses on voluntary performances on the part of the agent (or on the things, such as omissions to act, that are under the agent's control).[41] Though an amorphous phenomenon, remorse familiarly includes a negative reaction toward one's own failings as an agent, especially in cases in which the failing is morally inflected. In this deliberative guise, the content of remorse is standardly given by the practical judgment that one did something one ought not to have done, insofar as one's action wronged someone else or violated their claims.[42] Remorse of this kind is a feeling of sorrow or sadness or pain

40. In the sense at issue, guilt needs to be distinguished from the mere susceptibility to guilt feelings. One can feel guilty about something without actually believing that it was wrong (as in cases in which one is in the grip of a system of social norms that one no longer endorses). In the relevant sense, guilt involves an acknowledgment that one has fallen short of moral standards that one accepts, and that the victim of one's wrongdoing has a legitimate complaint about it. Cf. my *Responsibility and the Moral Sentiments*, appendix 1. Williams, of course, is suspicious of guilt when it is isolated from other reactions to immorality, and suggests that there is a way of understanding and experiencing shame, implicit in the literature of ancient Greece, whose structure better reflects the social situation of the immoral agent; see Bernard Williams, *Shame and Necessity* (Berkeley: University of California Press, 1993), esp. chap. 4. Those persuaded by this line of thought (as I am not) might suppose that a certain kind of shame, rather than narrow guilt, would be an appropriate emotional response for the mother to feel.

41. Cf. Williams's suggestion that remorse is a kind of agent-regret that "applies only to the voluntary," "Moral Luck," p. 30. The contrast with "voluntary" in this context is roughly "not under the agent's control"; thus the remoter causal consequences of the lorry driver's behavior in Williams's example (in particular the death of the child) are not in the relevant sense voluntary.

42. Though as I mentioned in the last chapter, one should remember the phenomenon of buyer's remorse, which does not seem to have any connection to thoughts of moral wrongdoing.

about one's own action that is occasioned by and responsive to the fact that the action falls short by the standards that deliberation is answerable to. This is why we familiarly demand of criminals that they should feel not only guilt but also remorse about their actions. We want them to acknowledge explicitly that their wrongdoing involved a failure to live up to moral or legal standards that properly regulate their own decision making about what to do. And we want them, too, to show that they care about those deliberative standards, manifesting the emotional vulnerability to their violation that is characteristic of this evaluative stance.

Is there room in the cases we have been considering for an emotion of this kind on the part of the agent? The answer to this question hinges on whether remorse entails all-in regret, or whether it might instead be compatible with an overall stance of affirmation about the decision that is its target. The mother, looking back on her earlier decision, is certainly aware of it as an agential failing of some kind, one that makes reference to standards that she continues (we may suppose) to care about. On the other hand, she is not subject to an all-in preference that she should have acted otherwise, on account of her attitude of unconditional attachment to the child that was brought into existence through her decision. My own sense, already anticipated in section 2.3, is that it would be odd to speak of remorse under these conditions. Remorse is typically said to involve "deep regret" or "gnawing distress" about a past wrong that an agent has committed.[43] Though the issue is a delicate one, these elements seem to me to point toward the presence of an on-balance wish to have acted otherwise in the cases in which we would most confidently apply the term "remorse" to characterize a person's retrospective attitudes toward something they have done.

---

43. These definitions are from the online editions of the *Oxford English Dictionary* and the *Merriam-Webster Dictionary*, respectively.

Even if remorse is not clearly in place with the mother, however, there is still room for her to experience a range of other negative emotions about her decision, including guilt, anguish, grief, and simple "regrets."[44]

These reflections give us a vocabulary for articulating the ambivalence that we would expect to attend the retrospective perspectives of the parties in this case. Neither the mother nor her daughter will regret the young girl's earlier decision in the all-in way that was characterized in chapter 2, insofar as the decision was a necessary condition for things that they now have compelling reason to affirm unconditionally. They prefer on balance that the mother should have acted as she did, and insofar as this is the case there is no room for the kind of deep ambivalence that precisely involves the absence of on-balance preferences of this kind. But mother and daughter both continue to think that there is a decisive moral objection to the decision, an objection that makes it true that the young girl ought not to have had a child when she did. Though we are reluctant to say that they fundamentally regret the decision that they have good reason to affirm on balance, their continuing acknowledgment of the deliberative objections to the decision will still leave some emotional residue in their retrospective view of their situation, in the form of a susceptibility to resentment, guilt, and nonspecific feelings of sorrow and distress (i.e. some "regrets"). These are precisely the reactions that we would expect of someone who believes that there are objections of this kind to a decision that they are no longer capable of feeling all-in regret about.

---

44. If sentiments of this kind become too dominant in the person's retrospective standpoint, they will tend to crowd out the element of affirmation that we are assuming to be appropriate. But some feelings of anguish and grief about the earlier decision can go together with the present preference that it should not have been otherwise; there is something in the decision that continues to cause one mental distress, even though from the present point of view one is glad, on balance, that the decision was made.

3.4. MEANING, DISABILITY, AND POLITICS

My treatment of the case of the young girl's child has exploited the affirmation dynamic that was introduced in the preceding chapter. This is the process whereby unconditional affirmation spreads backward, encompassing as well the necessary causal and constitutive conditions of its immediate object. In this section I wish to explore a further dimension of this dynamic, whereby unconditional affirmation additionally commits the agent to affirming the normative conditions of its objects—the attachments that make it possible for us to affirm unconditionally our own lives, when we look back on them in reflection.

We can approach this topic by returning to the example of the mother in the case of the young girl's child. As we have seen, the mother is attached to her child, as an individual person whom she loves, and this gives her reason to affirm both the existence of the child and the historical conditions of the child's existence. She prefers on balance that the child should have existed, in an unconditional way that commits her to preferring on balance the morally and prudentially questionable decision without which the child would not have been born. But the mother will also likely affirm her own life, preferring on balance the life she has lived when she looks back in reflection, at least compared with many salient alternative scenarios (such as the alternative that she should not have lived at all). Furthermore, her basis for this affirmative attitude will be provided by the attachments that give meaning and texture to her existence, including important personal relationships such as the one she has with her daughter. My suggestion is that this will give her a further and distinct reason for affirming the decision that led to her daughter's existence. Not only was that decision a necessary historical condition of the person whom she directly loves and affirms, it was also necessary for the inclusion in her life of one of the attachments that provide her with a basis for affirming that life. She would not be able to affirm her life in the same way, when she looks back on it in thought, without the relationship to her daughter that (we may suppose) represents one of the most significantly valuable things she was able to participate in while she was alive. This loving relationship can be understood as one of the normative conditions of her ability to affirm her own life, and an affirmative attitude of this kind commits one to affirming as well the conditions that play this normative role.

There are different philosophical idioms available to us for formulating and developing this point. Thus Christine Korsgaard has spoken of our "practical identities," which she understands as self-descriptions under which we find our lives to be worth living and our activities to be worth undertaking.[45] A practical identity in this sense is a feature of our outlook that has special significance for our ability to affirm our own life. It helps to constitute the standpoint, for instance, from which we endorse many of the actions that we end up performing. Thus a mother will find meaning in her own life in her relationship to her children, and she will endorse the activities that together make up the life she is living from the point of view, in part, of her identity as a mother. If she is also, say, a scholar of classical Augustan poetry, then that identity, too, will contribute to her sense of the value of her life and to her ability to affirm many of the things that she does with it. Korsgaard makes the further point that when a feature of our identity has this kind of significance for our attitude toward our lives and our actions, we will in effect be committed to endorsing the identity itself. That is, if and when we step back and reflect on those features of our identities that shape our ability to find meaning in our lives, we will find ourselves endorsing those features

45. Christine M. Korsgaard, *The Sources of Normativity* (Cambridge, U.K.: Cambridge University Press, 1996), p. 101. The line of argument sketched in the remainder of this paragraph is developed in lecture 3, "The Authority of Reflection," in Korsgaard's book.

too. This is an example of the affirmation dynamic leading us to endorse the normative conditions for the affirmative attitude we take toward our own lives—the conditions, that is, that enable us to adopt that attitude in the first place, by providing a normative basis for it (something in our lives that is worthy of affirmation from our own point of view).

In a different vocabulary, we might follow Bernard Williams in speaking of agents' "ground projects" or "categorical desires," understood as extended patterns of interest and activity that constitute basic features of their identity and character, and that give them their most important reasons to continue living their lives.[46] Ground projects in this sense involve what I have been calling attachments: emotionally inflected commitments to individuals, institutions, or activities that leave one vulnerable to sadness and distress when the object of one's attachments is in a bad way. Projects of this kind provide us with a basis for affirming the life we have led, when we look back on it from the retrospective point of view. And the normative role they play in enabling this affirmative attitude makes them natural objects of affirmation themselves. Unconditional affirmation in this way commits us to affirming not only the necessary historical conditions of the things we affirm but the normative conditions of our affirmative attitude as well. We cannot adopt this stance toward our own life without being prepared to affirm the things in it that ground this very stance. This is a conclusion that Williams, like Korsgaard, takes to be virtually self-evident.[47]

But is this application of the affirmation dynamic really so self-evident as these philosophers suppose it to be? Skepticism about it

---

46. See, e.g., Bernard Williams, "Persons, Character, and Morality," as reprinted in his *Moral Luck*, pp. 1–19. Williams also deploys the idiom of "categorical desires" in his paper "The Makropulos Case: Reflections on the Tedium of Immortality," in his *Problems of the Self: Philosophical Papers, 1956–1972* (Cambridge, U.K.: Cambridge University Press, 1972), pp. 82–100.

47. The assumption plays a central role in the main argument of Williams's "Moral Luck," as I shall explain in chapter 4.

might begin with the observation that there is no literal inconsistency between unconditionally affirming one's life because of one's projects or practical identities and regretting on balance the same projects or identities. The intentional objects of these attitudes seem at any rate to be distinct, enough so that there is no simple contradiction or narrow incoherence involved in being glad that one has lived because (say) of one's identity as a mother or a scholar while wishing that one had not had the experiences or made the decisions that led to one's becoming these things. The pressure toward affirmation is supposed to stem from one's acknowledgment that the object of regret is itself a condition for the presence in the agents' lives of the very thing that grounds their affirmative attitude toward it. But why exactly is this pressure supposed to be irresistible? Can't one affirm on balance the fact that one has lived on account of the projects that one has pursued or the practical identities one has attained even while one wishes on balance that one didn't have those same projects or identities?

There is nothing, I suppose, that renders it psychologically impossible for us to entertain this combination of attitudes. But the combination is inherently unstable, and this generates powerful pragmatic pressure to surrender one (or both) of the unconditional attitudes in question. If you affirm your life unconditionally because of the role in it of a given project, then you are committed to affirming that project itself in the same way, if and when it becomes an object of explicit reflection in its own right. A failure to do this will leave you chronically vulnerable to skeptical worries, of a kind that undermine the unconditional character of your affirmative attitude toward your life. The most likely consequence of such a failure is that you will regret the presence in your life of one of the projects around which it has been lived. In that case you will find yourself wishing that your life did not contain the very things that make it possible for you to endorse it in the first place, and this will lead you to conclude that your life, as you have actually lived it, isn't really worthy of affirmation after all. Alternatively, you might remain ambivalent and conflicted when you reflect on whether you should have pursued the projects that help to define your present identity. But that, too, will erode your confidence in your affirmative attitude toward your life, by raising significant doubts about the only things might have grounded your adoption of that attitude.[48]

This might still seem too quick, however. To regret on balance that your life includes a given project or practical identity, you don't need to think that the project or identity is without genuine value. You need only prefer on balance that the life you actually led should have included different values from the ones that you actually organized your activities around. It seems, then, that you could adopt this regretful attitude toward your project or identity while still acknowledging that it was in fact a repository of value, in a way that might render the life you have actually led an apt candidate for unconditional affirmation. But this line of thought excessively intellectualizes the attitudes that are involved in the unconditional affirmation of your own life. To adopt this attitude is not merely to accept that your life has achieved something that is worthwhile, but to value the things it has achieved, in a way that enables you to find in them sources of meaning and significance. This is part of what is involved in saying that a given set of values has the status of a ground project or an

---

48. In my paper "Constructing Normativity," *Philosophical Topics* 32 (2004), pp. 451–76, sec. 3, I question whether reflective agency requires that agents should positively endorse their contingent practical identities; my suggestion there is that sufficiently "confident" agents might be able to act on the values that shape their practical identities, even if they cannot provide a rational vindication of those identities from a more abstract point of view. The proposal currently under consideration is different, however. The question here is not whether one can act confidently on one's practical identities without reflectively endorsing them, but whether one can adopt an attitude of unconditional affirmation toward one's life if one is not willing to endorse the identities that ground that very attitude. This stance seems to me to be reflectively unstable, in a way that generates genuine pressure on agents to affirm the projects and identities that are normative conditions of their ability to affirm their own lives.

aspect of your practical identity.[49] This existential dimension of pro-jects and identities is what will be threatened if you are not prepared to endorse them when you make them objects of direct reflection. If you sincerely prefer on balance that your life should have lacked a given project or practical identity, you thereby distance yourself from it in a way that undermines its potential role as a basis for affirming your life. Unconditional affirmation of your life will be stable under reflection, then, only to the extent you are also prepared to affirm un-conditionally the normative basis of the attitude you take toward it. You are in this way pragmatically committed to endorsing your prac-tical identities or ground projects, insofar as they are normative con-ditions of the affirmative attitude you adopt toward the life you have actually led.

But if you are committed to affirming unconditionally your pro-jects and practical identities, then you must affirm as well *their* necessary historical and constitutive conditions. This follows from the nature of unconditional affirmation, which as we have seen has a built-in tendency to spread backward to the things that make possible its immediate object. So if we are thus committed to affirming our projects and practical identities, we will be committed in addition to affirming the things that historically condition them or that are con-stitutively bound up with them. If I prefer, unconditionally and on balance, that I have the projects and practical identities that shape who I actually am, I therefore prefer on balance that those events and circumstances should have occurred that were necessary for me to acquire the projects and practical identities that I have. This is a fur-ther instantiation of the affirmation dynamic that we have already encountered in other contexts.

With these points in place, we are now in a position to see that there are a number of other situations that agents might find themselves in

---

49. I return to this theme in sec. 5.1 below.

that resemble the situation of the mother in the case of young girl's child. One interesting class of situations involves disabilities of various kinds. People who have lived for a significant period of time with a serious incapacity may find that the most important sources of meaning in their lives are shaped by their incapacity. They may have been born deaf, for instance, and led rich lives that involved complete immersion in the forms of communication and sensibility that are available only to people who similarly lack the ability to hear. Their ground projects will then essentially be the projects of someone who is deaf, and this will importantly shape their practical identity. Similar things might be said about amputees who go on to become world-class athletes, competing successfully in the Paralympics and devoting themselves to making similar opportunities available to others who have lost a limb. For agents in these situations, the attachments that ground their ability to take an affirmative attitude toward the life they have actually led will be to activities that presuppose the disabilities that have been visited upon them. Their ability to affirm their lives unconditionally will be stable only if they can also affirm unconditionally the projects and identities that make that attitude possible, and this in turn will commit them to affirming their disabilities when they look back in thought on the lives they have actually led.

I don't want to say that this will necessarily be the situation of anyone who has the kind of disabilities that are at issue here. Presumably there are plenty of people who, though they suffer from disabilities of various kinds, do not come to identify with them in the way of the agents described in the preceding paragraph. Perhaps they are able to cope well enough with the challenges they face, and live lives that are full of rewarding and valuable projects and relationships. But the things that give meaning to their lives are not primarily activities that presuppose the forms of disability that they have experienced. For people in this position, the normative bases of the affirmative attitude that they adopt toward their own lives are not projects or forms of identity that presuppose their disability. So they might well regret on balance the disabilities that they have had to live with, even while they adopt an attitude of unconditional affirmation toward the life they have actually lived.[50]

My point, however, is that we can easily imagine people with significant disabilities whose attitude toward them is different. In particular, agents whose disabilities condition the projects that most importantly imbue their lives with meaning might well find that their affirmative attitude toward the lives they have led commits them to affirming their disabilities as well. They cannot wish on balance that they hadn't suffered from the conditions that disable them, since that would entail the absence from their lives of the very things that enable them to affirm those lives in the first place.

From the fact that such agents have good reason to affirm their own disabilities, however, it doesn't follow that the condition that they affirm is generally a valuable one, something that in other contexts we have reason to promote or to encourage or to choose for people when there are alternatives available for them. Consider in this connection parents whose own practical identities are significantly conditioned by their deafness and who face a decision about whether to have cochlear implants made available to their deaf children, thereby giving the children the capacity they would otherwise lack for spoken language and for effective oral communication with people who are not themselves hearing-impaired. The parents in this situation might, for reasons of the kind I have been elaborating, be committed to affirming their own incapacity to hear, insofar as this

---

50. One difference between this kind of case and that of the young girl's child is that the affirmative attitudes at issue take impersonal conditions as their objects, rather than voluntary actions that the person earlier performed. As I noted in sec. 2.3 above, retrospective preferences have a less straightforwardly agential character in cases of this kind, on account of the more complicated counterfactual conditions that are embedded in them. I return in chapters 5 and 6 to cases in which we are committed, in virtue of our affirmation of our lives, to affirming the objectionable impersonal conditions that our attachments presuppose.

conditions normatively the affirmative attitude they adopt toward the lives they have actually lived. But this does not mean that they have good reason to wish the same condition on their offspring. There is no inconsistency whatsoever involved in being glad that one has suffered a given disability oneself, when one looks back on the life one has led, even while one chooses that one's children should not experience the same condition in the life that they are just embarking on.

The parallels should be apparent with the case of the young girl's child that was extensively discussed in earlier sections of this chapter. There we saw that the mother's retrospective affirmation of her decision to have a child as a teenager did not amount to a justification of it, something that entails that it was after all the right thing for her to do. The deliberative context she inhabits when she looks back on the decision is different from the context of the agent who made the decision at the earlier point in time, and we can consistently say that she has reason to affirm the decision from the retrospective point of view, even if it was a decision that she ought not to have made at the earlier point in time. Similarly, the persons whose life projects presuppose their own deafness may have compelling reasons, of the kind we have sketched, to affirm that condition on balance when they look back on the life they have led. But it does not follow from this that it would not have been better for them, as they were starting out in life, to have been given capacities to hear that were sufficient to enable them to participate fully in the world of spoken human language. Nor does it follow that they have reason to deprive their own children of these same capacities by refusing to equip them with cochlear implants at a stage in their development when they could easily develop facility with spoken language. The deaf adults' deliberative situation, when they look back in reflection on the life that they have actually led, is simply different from the deliberative situation they face when they have to decide about the opportunities that their children should be afforded at the point when the children are starting out in life.

There has notoriously been some resistance within the adult deaf community to the new technologies that are giving hearing-impaired people the ability to participate in the world of oral communication. I would suggest that at least some of this resistance might rest on confusions of the kind I have attempted to uncover, between the retrospective point of view of adults whose defining life projects presuppose their deafness and the situation of children who are just starting out in life. What should be acknowledged on all sides is that deafness can be bound up constitutively with forms of activity that are distinctively valuable, capable of imparting meaning to a human life, and thereby providing a basis for agents to affirm their lives when they look back on them in reflection. Signed language is a human cultural achievement, and those who participate fully in this culture experience forms of intimacy and understanding and human exchange that are not accessible to the rest of us. The value of these activities, however, does not mean that they should be forced on people who are just starting out in life, and who could potentially be given the means to participate fully in the different forms of communication and exchange that most human beings are capable of. The tendency to think otherwise seems to reflect a confusion similar to the one that leads us to interpret the mother's affirmation of her decision to conceive a child when she was a teenager as a retroactive justification of that decision.[51]

In saying this, I don't mean to deny that there might be some considerations that count as genuine reasons for hesitating before having

---

51. My conclusions here are broadly in line with those defended by Elizabeth Harman in "'I'll Be Glad I Did It' Reasoning and the Significance of Future Desires," *Philosophical Perspectives* 23 (2009), pp. 177–99. Among other things, Harman too sees explicit parallels between the case of the deaf infant and the case of young girl's child. I go beyond Harman in situating the discussion of these and other cases in the context of a much more detailed analysis of affirmation, regret, and their corresponding commitments.

one's hearing-impaired infant outfitted with cochlear implants. There are, as with any serious medical intervention, significant health risks associated with the procedure whereby an electrode array is inserted into the patient's inner ear. In addition, parents who are themselves deaf may worry about the effects on the quality of their relationship with their offspring of an operation that will enable the offspring to communicate orally. A certain estrangement and loss of intimacy might rightly be feared. Parents might additionally worry that their children will be left in a kind of limbo by the acquisition of cochlear implants, having significant residual impairments that prevent them from participating fully in hearing-based exchange but too much functionality to benefit from the solidarity of the larger deaf community. Finally, adult participants in that community might reasonably be saddened by the prospect that the distinctive forms of culture that they have contributed to, and that have given their own activities meaning and significance, could gradually wither and even die out. None of these considerations seem to me to represent a genuinely compelling reason to withhold cochlear implants from a congenitally hearing-impaired child who could learn to speak and to hear as a result of them.[52] But the immediate point at issue is that they are distinct from the considerations mentioned above concerning the deaf parents' attitude toward the hearing impairment that has conditioned their own ability to affirm their lives. Their disability may be a normative condition for the affirmative attitude they adopt toward their own lives, and this might give them a strong reason to embrace the disability when they look back on it retrospectively; but these considerations are not in themselves reasons for seeing to it that the disabling condition is imposed on others when reasonable alternatives are available.

---

52. For a sensitive account of one family's attempt to negotiate the issues that bear on such decisions, see Jennifer Rosner, *If a Tree Falls: A Family's Quest to Hear and Be Heard* (New York: Feminist Press, 2010).

The attitudes of disabled adults toward their own conditions have significance for decision contexts of the latter kind, but it is an indirect significance. As we have seen, the forms of activity that they participate in can be distinctively valuable, providing a genuine independent basis for them to affirm the lives that they have led. In negotiating decisions about the actual and potential disabilities of infants (and also of children who are not yet born), we need to be careful to acknowledge the values that are realized in life by adult persons with precisely the disabilities in question. It is not just that those individuals have lives that are well worth living on the whole; at least some of the activities that make their lives worth affirming, from their own point of view, will be activities that presuppose the very disabilities we might want younger people to be able to overcome. There is no theoretical inconsistency between acknowledging the value of activities that essentially involve a given disability on the part of the adults who already have the disabling condition and seeking to eradicate the same condition in future generations. But efforts of the latter kind can, if those involved in them are not careful, easily appear to express a disrespectful or disparaging attitude toward disabled adults and the conditions that help to give meaning to their lives. This is an expressive effect that we should strive to avoid, especially when devising public policies to regulate decisions about disabilities that might potentially affect actual and future children.[53]

A further set of situations that involve a similar structure of attitudes arises under social conditions of injustice and oppression. Consider ordinary citizens who have grown up and lived much of their adult lives in societies such as the German Democratic Republic (GDR) or contemporary Saudi Arabia. I take it as given that these are at least moderately oppressive political cultures, which

---

53. This is an important theme in McMahan, "Preventing the Existence of People with Disabilities."

fail to accord equal basic rights and liberties to many of their citizens. I assume, further, that many of the people who lived and who live in such cultures, even if they have been personally disadvantaged by the prevailing political systems, have relationships and activities that impart meaning to their lives, and that constitute a powerful basis for retrospectively affirming those lives when they look back on them. Indeed, for at least some citizens of these regimes the bases of affirmation might well be things that are directly conditioned by the oppressive political structures under which they live. Think in this connection of the forms of friendship and social solidarity that people achieve precisely through their common awareness of oppression and through the efforts they might together undertake to find politically acceptable ways of resisting or at least acknowledging it. These are values that might provide a basis for affirming the life one has actually led in a society such as the GDR. Or consider the lives of ordinary women in the Wahhabist culture of Saudi Arabia, which systematically deprives them of professional and social opportunities that are freely available to men in their society. It isn't implausible to suppose that such oppressive structures might also foster distinctively valuable expressions of intimacy and class consciousness among the oppressed, which help to impart meaning to some of their lives, even though they are connected to forms of social organization that are indisputably unjust.

If the argument of this section is on the right lines, then some of the agents in these situations could easily find themselves committed to affirming the oppressive structures that affect their own lives, precisely because of the role of those structures in shaping their ground projects and their practical identities. They have compelling reason to endorse unconditionally the things that ground their affirmative attitude toward the lives they have actually led, and this in turn commits them to affirming the social conditions that made those things possible in the first place.[54] This is a theme to which I shall return in chapter 5 below. Once again, however, it doesn't follow from these points about the retrospective point of view that the social conditions in question acquire a justification through their role in the lives of the people in this way affected by them. The structures remain unjust and oppressive, and in consequence they are ones that people have good reason, going forward, to resist and to attempt to change, whenever that is possible.

As in the case of disability, however, the role of oppression in the retrospective standpoint of those affected by it has an indirect normative significance for those who are working to bring about social and political transformation. The challenge is to find ways of acknowledging that the structures they are attempting to overthrow are connected to forms of meaning that sustain at least some of the ordinary agents who have been forced to make a life under them. Political change is in practice often a very messy process, carried forward by enthusiasms that border on the fanatical and that are correspondingly oblivious to nuance. But there is no significant political transformation that does not also involve some loss. As agents of change, we owe it to those who have been subjected to the conditions we are attempting to fight to try to understand and to respect the values that those conditions might also have brought into existence.

---

54. This kind of attitude, on the part of at least some of those who lived under the GDR regime, finds ironic expression in "Ostalgie," the gauzy and slightly sentimental representation of ordinary life in East Germany, from the perspective of the events that have happened in the wake of reunification. See, for example, Leander Haußmann's film *Sonnenallee* (1998) or Wolfgang Becker's *Good Bye, Lenin!* (2003). Two points of clarification: First, in saying that some denizens of oppressive regimes might be committed to affirming the political conditions that shaped their lives, I of course don't mean to deny that many other citizens—including, above all, those most directly victimized by the regimes—will have overwhelming reason to reject those same conditions when they look back in reflection. Second, even for those who find they are committed to affirming the oppressive political and social conditions under which they have lived, there is a real question about whether those conditions are really worthy of being affirmed, on balance. This is a question to which I come back in the two chapters that follow.

Chapter 4

Luck, Justification, and Moral Complaint

In "Moral Luck," Bernard Williams famously argued that our decisions could be justified or "unjustified" retroactively by the course of events that they set in motion.[1] Those events fundamentally shape the standpoint from which we look back on the earlier decision, in ways that it may have been impossible for us to anticipate at the time when the decision was originally made. If we are lucky, the later standpoint will be one from which we cannot regret the earlier decision, so that the decision is vindicated by the course of events. But it is possible for things to develop in a way that leaves us only with regret about the earlier decision, and in that case the decision may turn out retroactively to have been "wrong" and "unjustified" (p. 25).

There is much that is both interesting and puzzling in this picture of the susceptibility of justification to a certain kind of resultant luck.[2] I want to focus on a basic question that the picture raises about the relation between justification and regret. Williams suggests that our retrospective attitude toward a decision we have made can determine

---

1. Bernard Williams, "Moral Luck," as reprinted in his *Moral Luck: Philosophical Papers, 1973–1980* (Cambridge, U.K.: Cambridge University Press, 1981), pp. 20–39. Page numbers given in parentheses in the text of the present chapter will refer to this article.
2. This is Thomas Nagel's label for luck in the way things turn out as a result of our actions; see Nagel, "Moral Luck," as reprinted in his *Mortal Questions* (Cambridge, U.K.: Cambridge University Press, 1979), pp. 24–38.

whether that decision was or was not justified after all.[3] There is a certain plausibility to this idea: regret and the lack of justification often go hand in hand, and there is something odd about the thought that a decision was the wrong one to make if we are unable to regret it ex post facto. But the idea is nevertheless mistaken. As we saw in the preceding chapter, regret and lack of justification do not reliably track each other, and the fact that an agent is unable fundamentally to regret a decision does not entail that it has acquired a justification.

The present chapter explores the implications of this point for the argument of "Moral Luck." I begin by sketching the situation of Gauguin, as Williams describes it, explaining why it seems implausible to think that his later standpoint amounts to a retrospective justification of his action (section 4.1). I then turn to a more detailed analysis of Williams's argument, focusing first on the nature of the affirmative attitude that Gauguin takes toward his life as a successful artist (section 4.2) and then on the basic idea that this affirmative attitude yields a rational justification for what he did (section 4.3). It turns out that Williams's argument makes large assumptions about issues that are inherently somewhat obscure; looking closely at the details of the argument will lead to an improved understanding of what it is to affirm one's own life, and of the different ways in which outcomes might potentially be thought to justify an event or decision that occurred in the past. I conclude (section 4.4) with a discussion of ambivalence. I suggest that even from the retrospective point of view, the successful Gauguin might have powerful reasons for regretting

---

3. I take this to be the main point of his challenging article. The moral luck that Williams is primarily interested in is not so much the susceptibility of narrowly moral assessments to luck of various kinds, but the way the significance of morality for an agent can be conditioned by resultant luck. Thus in the case of Gauguin, which will be my main focus in this chapter, the success of his artistic projects is said to justify retrospectively his earlier actions, without rendering those actions morally all right. See Bernard Williams, "Moral Luck: A Postscript," as reprinted in Bernard Williams, *Making Sense of Humanity and Other Philosophical Papers, 1982–1993* (Cambridge, England: Cambridge University Press, 1995), pp. 241–47.

the earlier decision that he made, despite its role as a condition of the values that his life has come to embody. His unconditional affirmation of his life would then commit him to affirming things that are not really worthy of this attitude. This possibility will provide the larger framework for my investigations in the final two chapters of the book.

4.1. WILLIAMS'S GAUGUIN

Williams's central example of moral luck is his reimagining of the case of Gauguin. We are to consider a young man, loosely modeled on the historical figure of Paul Gauguin (p. 22), who decides to leave his family behind in Paris in order to pursue his artistic ambitions on a South Sea island.[4] The situation is one in which he cannot in the nature of the case know in advance how the decision will turn out; this is the element of what Williams calls epistemic luck, relative to the considerations that were available to him at the moment when the decision was made (p. 25). But the events that the decision set in motion will ultimately determine retroactively whether the decision was in fact justified (pp. 35–36).

Thus, if the imagined Gauguin is an artistic failure, then there will be nothing in his life to set over against the fact that he wronged his family in his youth. He will be left only with regrets, and this fact will function to render the decision unjustified. If on the other hand he turns out to be an artistic success, then he will be unable, looking back, to regret his earlier behavior. His success will determine that he takes an affirmative attitude toward his life as it has actually gone, and this will preclude his regretting the earlier decision that was a

---

4. The actual Gauguin, it seems, was already estranged from his Danish wife and his children by the time he left for Tahiti in 1891; on this and other aspects of the biography of the historical Gauguin, see, for example, David Sweetman, *Paul Gauguin: A Life* (New York: Simon & Shuster, 1995).

necessary condition of its turning out as it did. His decision will in this case be justified ex post facto by his success. Not morally justified, of course: Williams concedes that Gauguin's imagined success might not silence the complaints about his treatment of them that might be brought by or on behalf of his children and partner (pp. 23–24, 39). But his inability to regret his decision will entail that his earlier immorality was not in fact a serious rational or deliberative failing, as it may have seemed to be at the time.

In light of the discussion in the preceding chapters, however, we are in a position to question the framework that Williams's argument presupposes. In particular, we have seen that the inaccessibility of a decision to all-in regret on the part of the agent who looks back on it does not in general entail either that the decision was justified or that the agent has come to believe it was justified. Regret of this kind, in virtue of its totalizing character, is too undiscriminating an instrument to track or determine facts about agential justification. Thus in the case of the young girl's child, it was wrong for the mother to conceive a child when she was not in a position to attend adequately to its developmental needs. This is something that she ought not to have done, and it is also something that she lacked a justification for doing. These facts are not affected by the change in her deliberative situation that was induced by the arrival onto the scene of her daughter. What is affected by that development are a different set of facts, about the accessibility to the young girl of regret for her earlier decision. She now loves her daughter, and she has correspondingly powerful reasons for affirming that the daughter exists. The unconditional nature of her affirmative attitude toward her daughter entails that she also affirms the historically necessary conditions of her daughter's existence, including her decision to have a child in the first place. Hence she cannot experience all-in regret about that decision, despite the fact that it was and remains without justification.

This example, however, looks structurally similar to Williams's description of the situation of Gauguin. The artist, like the mother, looks back on his earlier decision from a perspective that seems to preclude all-in regret. His artistic success determines him to affirm the path he has taken in life, including the momentous decision that was a necessary condition for its realization. But if he affirms that decision retrospectively, he cannot wish on balance that it had been otherwise, and so he cannot be subject to all-in regret about it. Williams wishes to argue that the decision has acquired an ex post facto justification in virtue of Gauguin's inability to regret it. But for reasons we have explored in other cases, the argument doesn't go through. From the fact that Gauguin is unable to experience all-in regret about his decision to leave his family in the lurch, it simply doesn't follow that the decision has acquired a justification. It can remain the case that he ought not to have treated his family in this way, and that doing so was something that he lacked a sufficient justification for, even though he is no longer able to regret that he acted in that way.

This is my initial response to Williams's main argument in "Moral Luck," based on the conclusions arrived at earlier in this book. In the remainder of the present chapter, I want to extend and deepen the response, by working carefully through the details of Williams's extremely influential discussion of the Gauguin case. There are, of course, several salient differences between the cases discussed in the preceding chapter and the example of Gauguin; we should begin by looking closely at these differences, to see whether they might defeat the initial parallel I have proposed between the two situations.

The first of these differences concerns the element of luck. Williams's larger aim in "Moral Luck" is to question the Kantian conception of morality as a form of assessment whose reach is immune to the effects of luck. As we saw in chapter 2, his alternative picture is one in which human agency is embedded in a larger world of causal processes, in a way that limits our ability to anticipate or control its ultimate nature and effects (pp. 29–30). Momentous decisions such as those of Gauguin and Anna Karenina (another figure discussed in "Moral Luck", pp. 26–27) are especially dramatic examples of this simple truth, cases in which an agent's choices set in motion causal processes whose final shape cannot be known at the time when they are made, where those processes in turn determine the standpoint from which the agent will later look back on them. Thus in the Gauguin case, the question of the justification of his decision to decamp for Tahiti is meant to be one that is hostage to fortune. He cannot know, at the time when the decision was made, whether it will turn out to have been justified, because he is not yet in a position to anticipate the position from which he will eventually look back on it in reflection.

This is a respect in which Gauguin's situation differs strikingly from that of the young girl. In the latter example, it is already perfectly clear at the time when the girl's decision was made that it is a decision she will herself be unable fundamentally to regret. We know this, because the effects that the child will have on her normative situation are perfectly predictable. It is a general truth that people who stand in maternal relationships tend to affirm unconditionally the children they are thus attached to, and that they have powerful agent-relative reasons for adopting this affirmative stance.[5] So it was in no way a matter of luck, relative to the girl's epistemic situation at the time of her decision to conceive, that she would be unable to look back on the decision with all-in regret. On the contrary, that she

---

5. As I noted in chapter 3, attachments provide agent-relative reasons that are perspectival, insofar as they are primarily reasons only for agents who actually have the attachments in question (standing, e.g., in a relationship of love with an actual person). But it is a general truth, accessible nonperspectivally to anyone, that people who have attachments also have corresponding agent-relative reasons that they wouldn't otherwise have. This is the general truth that the child is able to grasp before giving birth to her daughter.

would eventually find herself in this position is something that could easily have been anticipated in advance.

This difference between the cases, however, does not undermine the parallel between them that I have been trying to draw. The crux of Williams's argument in the Gauguin case is that the mature artist's inability to regret the decision he looks back on amounts to a retroactive justification of it. This is the assumption that drives the argument, and that makes the phenomenon of moral luck possible in the first place. Epistemic luck enters the picture because the young Gauguin cannot know, at the time when he departs Paris for Tahiti, what the effects of this decision are going to be. In particular, he cannot know whether the life he is embarking on is one that he will be destined to affirm when he looks back on it, which in turn will determine whether he is able to regret the decision that made that life possible in the first place. But these considerations about luck would be uninteresting in the absence of the assumption that justification and the inability to regret go hand in hand.

The young girl's child case is significant for Williams's argument, because it serves to call this crucial premise into question, and in a way that avoids entanglement in adventitious issues about the nature and role of epistemic luck. We know in advance that the young girl will be unable fundamentally to regret her decision to conceive a child. But if immunity to all-in regret does not yield a retrospective justification in cases of this kind, it will equally fail to do so in cases in which the immunity to regret results from causal processes whose outcomes could not be anticipated at the time of the decisions that set them in motion.

There is another difference between the prospective life cases and Williams's Gauguin example that deserves comment. In the former cases, the immunity to regret of those who are implicated in them results from the fact that the putative target of all-in regret is a necessary condition of a distinct state or fact that those agents have powerful reason to affirm. The mother cannot regret in this way her decision to conceive when she did, because she now loves the child and celebrates the child's existence, and these objects of affirmation require that she acted as she did. Similarly, the child herself cannot feel all-in regret about her mother's choice, since she affirms her own life, and she would not exist if her mother had acted otherwise. In the Gauguin case, by contrast, it is unclear whether there is the same structure in place.

One reason for this is that the kind of affirmation that is at issue for the mature Gauguin is elusive. In the example of the young girl's child, it is easy enough to understand the element of affirmation that is involved. It is, in the first instance, affirmation of an individual human being, the child, and of that individual's life; this is something that both the mother and the child are attached to, in a way that gives them compelling reason to affirm unconditionally that the child exists. But what exactly is it that Gauguin, looking back on his life, is supposed to affirm, and what is the relation between the affirmative attitude he adopts and his artistic success? We need to look more closely at Williams's argument before we will be in a position to answer these questions.

Williams himself is impressed by the fact that Gauguin is identified with the particular artistic project on which he launched himself when he set off for the South Sea Islands. The project partly constitutes his mature point of view, and this in turn seems to imbue it with importance when he looks back on his life from that point of view. Thus, in a crucial passage from "Moral Luck," Williams writes that the project of an agent in Gauguin's situation

> is one with which the agent is identified in such a way that if it succeeds, his stand-point of assessment will be from a life which then derives an important part of its significance from that very

fact; if it fails, it can, necessarily, have no such significance in his life. If he succeeds, it cannot be that while welcoming the outcome he more basically regrets the decision. If he fails, his standpoint will be one for whom the ground project of the decision has proved worthless, and this (under the simplifying assumption that other adequate projects are not generated in the process) must leave him with the most basic regrets. So if he fails, his most basic regrets will attach to his decision, and if he succeeds, they cannot. That is the sense in which his decision can be justified, for him, by success. (pp. 35–36)

A key thought in this passage is that Gauguin, if he succeeds in his artistic project, will "welcome the outcome" of his earlier decision to embark on that project. The outcome in question is presumably his own life as an artist, a life whose content and significance are essentially bound up with his artistic activities. This suggests that the immediate object of affirmation for the successful Gauguin will be the life he has led, including the artistic projects that the life contains.

The connection between success in these projects and affirmation of the life they contain requires further unpacking, however. One assumption at work in Williams's argument seems to be that success in his projects is a condition that needs to be satisfied if Gauguin is to have reason to affirm the life he has led. That life is organized around the activities of painting to which Gauguin has dedicated himself. So if the project in which those activities consist is a failure, there will be no normative basis in them for affirming the life that results. At issue, of course, is not success or failure of a commercial nature but *artistic* success or failure: whether, that is, Gauguin's activities are valuable as the activities of one who is dedicated to painting as an art (something that will depend at least in part on the artistic quality of the paintings that he produces), or whether, instead, those activities are "worthless" along the same dimension.[6] In the latter case, Williams seems to assume, there will be no basis in Gauguin's later standpoint of assessment for affirming the life he has led, and this in turn will leave him with nothing but "the most basic regrets" about the decision to embark on that life. (At least that will be the case so long as there are not other successful projects that provide a basis for an affirmative attitude toward his life.) The crucial assumption at work here is that it is the value of our projects and attachments that determines whether we have reason to affirm the life we have led when we look back on it in reflection; this is an idea that was encountered in section 3.4 above, and I shall come back to it below.

A second assumption that seems to be at work in Williams's argument is that, other things being equal, artistic success is sufficient for Gauguin's adoption of an affirmative attitude toward his life. If he manages to cross some threshold of value in his activities as a painter, then he will welcome the outcome of his decision to undertake those activities, and this attitude will also be a reasonable one for him to adopt. The idea is presumably not that affirmation of one's life is a psychological necessity for somebody in the position of the successful Gauguin. One can achieve great things through one's artistic activities and yet fail to affirm the life one has led, because (for example) one has fallen into a state of deep and persistent depression (a possibility well illustrated by the history of artistic and intellectual activity in Western culture). The idea, rather, is that artistic success provides a sufficient *normative* basis for the affirmation of one's own life, injecting it with the kind of meaning that gives one a powerful reason to be glad to have lived.

---

6. In a different context, Williams describes the failure scenario as follows: "Gauguin did everything he might do to develop his work but in the end neither he nor anyone else thought it was worth much," in "Unbearable Suffering," in Bernard Williams, *The Sense of the Past: Essays in the History of Philosophy*, ed. Myles Burnyeat (Princeton, N.J.: Princeton University Press, 2006), pp. 331–36, at pp. 336–37.

There are two qualifications that should be registered regarding this idea, however. First, to say that artistic success is a sufficient normative basis for Gauguin to affirm his life is not to contend that it is necessarily sufficient on balance for such affirmation. It might be sufficient in itself to justify affirmation, abstracting from other normative factors that might be in play, without being a sufficient basis for affirmation once those other factors have been taken into account. I shall come back to this possibility in the final section of the present chapter, considering the reasons for regret that might potentially obtain in Gauguin's retrospective situation, and how those reasons interact with his important reasons for affirming the life to which his earlier decision gave rise. In the meantime, we may assume that Gauguin's artistic success is at least a pro tanto sufficient basis for him to affirm his life.

Second, there is a qualification to enter about the psychological necessity of affirmation in the Gauguin case. As I noted above, it is not impossible even for those who have good reasons to affirm their lives to fail to adopt such an attitude in practice. But most people do, of course, affirm their lives. What exactly this comes to is a difficult question, which will occupy us in section 4.2, but it is undoubtedly the default stance of most of us as we look back on the lives we have led. If we affirm our lives, however, and if a given decision or choice was a condition of the life that we now affirm, it seems that our affirmative attitude will embrace the decision or choice itself. At least this is true if the form of affirmation at issue is unconditional, in the terminology introduced earlier in this book. As we have seen, there are cases of merely conditional affirmation, in which one welcomes an event or situation without welcoming in the same way the necessary conditions of the event or situation. To return to an example from chapter 2, I might be glad for the heroic actions of the firefighters who rescued my children while regretting on balance the fire that made it necessary for them to come to our assistance. Williams must be assuming, then, that Gauguin's actual attitude toward his life is one of unconditional affirmation, the kind of affirmation that spreads backward to encompass the necessary historical conditions of its proper object, via what I have called the affirmation dynamic. On this assumption, Gauguin affirms on balance the life he has led as a successful artist, and this commits him to affirming as well the decision to decamp for Tahiti, which was the historical condition that set that life in motion.

This helps us to get a grip on some of the assumptions that are at issue in Williams's discussion of the Gauguin example. But important questions remain.

4.2. AFFIRMING ONE'S LIFE

The successful Gauguin looks back on his life from a standpoint that is partly constituted by his artistic projects, affirming that life because of the values that are realized in it. Williams says about this Gauguin: "[I]t cannot be that while welcoming the outcome he more basically regrets the decision" that led to the outcome (p. 35). On the interpretation I have proposed, this comment rests on some plausible assumptions about the unconditional character of the successful Gauguin's affirmative attitude toward the life he has led. But the role of his artistic success in relation to this affirmative stance remains somewhat obscure.

To clarify this role, it will help to examine more closely the affirmation dynamic as it plays out in the case of Gauguin. Thus, even if we assume that Gauguin's attitude toward his life is one of unconditional affirmation, it isn't obvious that he is thereby committed to affirming the decision that actually led to it. Here it may be instructive to return to the example of the young girl's child. In this case, there is an extremely tight connection between the direct object of affirmation and the decision that is its historical condition. What is affirmed is the individual human being that the young girl brought into the world and the life of that individual human being. The young girl's decision to have a child when she did is a necessary condition for this object of affirmation, because the individual person simply wouldn't have existed if the girl had decided to postpone conception by more than a few weeks. At least this is the case so long as we abstract from the possibility of deploying techniques of assisted reproduction, such as the cryopreservation of the young girl's fertilized egg cells, techniques which we can reasonably assume not to have been real options for the girl in this particular scenario.[7]

Things seem different in this respect with Gauguin, however. The thing that he is imagined to affirm, as he looks back from the perspective of artistic success, is the life he has led, the life of the individual person he is. If he had decided to remain in Paris, then the life he looks back on would have been different in certain important respects. But it would still have been his life, the life of an individual with his identity. The decision not to travel to Tahiti would not have had the effect that Gauguin would not have existed, or that there is no such thing in the world as Gauguin's life. In this regard, the Gauguin example differs from the case of the young girl's child, where the decision to postpone pregnancy would have made it the case that the individual human being who is the locus of affirmation didn't come into existence in the first place.

This is a difference between the cases, to be sure, but it might be argued that it is not a relevant difference. Gauguin's situation is perhaps most closely analogous to that of the child in the example of the young girl. She affirms her life, as she looks back on it, and this commits her to affirming her mother's decision to conceive when she did,

---

7. There would of course have been no point in deploying such techniques with a fourteen-year-old girl, nor would any fertility clinic have been willing to take her on as a patient. And we can stipulate, for good measure, that she would not have had the resources to pay for the procedure even if it had been available to her.

since that is a necessary condition of her having a life to affirm. Gauguin, too, affirms his life as he looks back on it, and Williams's suggestion is apparently that this commits him to affirming his decision to leave for Tahiti. It is true that if he had not made that decision, he would still have existed and had some life or other, which would have been a possible object of affirmation from whatever retrospective point of view he eventually came to occupy. But that life, though his, would not have been the life that is the direct object of affirmation under the circumstances he actually inhabits. The point is that the decision to leave Paris in his youth was a necessary historical condition for the life that he actually led; *that* life would not so much as have existed if he had taken a different path when confronted with the choice between staying in Europe and departing for more exotic climes. Perhaps this is enough to preserve the analogy. He affirms the life he actually led, retrospectively, and so he is committed to affirming the decision that led to it, since a different decision would have had the effect that the thing he affirms does not exist (albeit for different reasons than those that apply in the case of the young girl's child).

This interpretation of the argument, however, seems to prove too much. It is plausible enough to say that if Gauguin had decided to remain in Paris, the life he would have lived would have been different from the life he actually lived, which played out on a South Sea island away from his wife and children. But of course his life would also have been different if (for example) he had had a banana for breakfast rather than a plate of sausages on the fifth day of the voyage from Paris to Tahiti. Do we want to say, then, that his affirmation of the life he has actually led commits him to affirming his decision about what to have for breakfast on day five of the trip? I assume that this would be an implausible result, and one that Williams himself would wish to reject. The decision to depart Paris for the South Sea Islands appears to have a significance for Gauguin's retrospective reflections that is not shared by the decision about what to have for breakfast on a random morning during his voyage.

One might reject this assumption if one operated with a Nietzschean conception of affirmation, according to which one can affirm an aspect of one's current life only if one is prepared to affirm the entire course of world events of which it is a tiny part, willing, as it were, the eternal recurrence of those events as they have in fact played out.[8] But this is not an uncontroversial conception, as we saw in chapter 2, nor does Williams himself invoke anything like it in the immediate context of his argument about moral luck. A more intuitive view would be that Gauguin's affirmation of his life leaves room for regret about at least some of the things that he did in the course of it. But then we need a way to distinguish between those aspects of his actual life that Gauguin's affirmation of it commits him to affirming and those aspects that are possible objects of regret on his part.

One possible way to draw this distinction would be by appeal to a theory of the identity conditions for a human life. Such a theory would classify some aspects of our lives as essential to them, such that the absence of those features would entail that the life no longer exists. Changes in other, peripheral features, by contrast, would be compatible with the continued existence of the life to which they belong. The hope would be to develop a principled way of explaining why the object that Gauguin retrospectively affirms would not have existed had he stayed in Paris, whereas a different decision about what to eat for breakfast on his way to Tahiti wouldn't have had the same effect.

But this isn't a very promising line to pursue. Human lives are not individual substances, but rather distended events or series of events. Such unity as they have derives primarily from the identity of the

---

8. Compare the discussion of Nietzschean affirmation in section 2.4 above. I return to Nietzsche's idea of eternal recurrence in chapter 6.

persons who live the lives. Thus "Gauguin's life," to a first approximation, is that set of events that have in common that they were either
things that Gauguin did or things that Gauguin experienced while he
was alive.[9] But an artificial entity of this kind does not tolerate a distinction between essential and peripheral features or properties. The
only thing that is strictly essential to Gauguin's life is Gauguin himself, the individual person whose identity provides a principle of
unity for the events that constitute the life. But if that is right, then a
decision to remain in Paris would not have had the consequence that
Gauguin's life would not have existed. The only thing that would have
had that consequence is an occurrence that would have affected the
existence of the individual Gauguin, such as a decision on the part of
his parents not to have a child at the time when he was in fact
conceived.[10]

These reflections suggest that we need a different way of understanding the nature of the affirmative attitude that the successful

9. This approach will make the unity of a person's life hostage, to some extent, to philosophical
views about the identity of persons over time. But that, it seems to me, is as it should be. If
facts about personal identity turn out to be comparatively superficial, insofar, e.g., as they
are constituted by facts about the scalar relations between experiences and states at discrete
times, then the unity of a human life will turn out to be comparatively superficial as well.

10. It is sometimes said that the characteristic unity of a human life is the unity of a narrative;
see, e.g., J. David Velleman, *How We Get Along* (Cambridge, U.K.: Cambridge University
Press, 2009), esp. chap. 7; also Alasdair MacIntyre, *After Virtue: A Study in Moral Theory*, 3rd
ed. (Notre Dame, Ind.: University of Notre Dame Press, 2007), esp. chap. 15. Appealing to
this idea, we could perhaps distinguish the decision to remain in Paris from the decision to
eat a plate of sausages for breakfast as follows: the former decision would have undermined
the narrative unity that Gauguin actually achieved in his life, whereas the latter decision
would not have had that effect. Note, however, that narrative unity functions here not as
a condition for the existence or identity of a human life but as a normative standard for
its assessment. The idea is that we act rightly, or live better lives, to the extent we do things
that imbue the lives we lead with the unity of a good story. Applied to the Gauguin case,
we have the result not that Gauguin's life would not have existed if he had chosen to stay in
Paris but that its distinctive value wouldn't have survived under that condition. This comes
close to the interpretation that I shall go on to propose later in the present section (though
I am skeptical that the value achieved by human lives is always well thought of as a form of
narrative unity).

Gauguin adopts in Williams's example. I now want to propose an interpretation that draws heavily on the discussion of the affirmation dynamic from section 3.4 of the preceding chapter. Let's begin with the immediate object of Gauguin's affirmative attitude, which is Gauguin's own life, a life that consists in a series of events whose unity derives from their relation to him. To affirm one's life, in the relevant unconditional sense, would seem to be to prefer on balance that the series of events of which the life consists should have occurred when one looks back on it in reflection. But what is the implicit contrast class for these purposes? Is it that one prefers one's life to alternative scenarios in which some of the events of which it consists did not occur? This is the interpretation that has created our recent difficulties. For either one holds that affirmation involves a blanket preference for one's actual life over *any* alternative course that it might have taken, which leaves no space at all for localized regret (e.g., about the fact that Gauguin ate the sausages on day five of the trip, even if they made him violently sick), or one needs a principle for distinguishing between essential and peripheral parts of the life one has led, so as to support the view that one prefers one's actual life only to those alternative series of events that involve changes in its essential constituents. But it seems there is no plausible way to draw this distinction on metaphysical grounds, simply by appeal to the nature of the object that is affirmed.

I would therefore propose that we consider a different way of understanding the implicit contrast class. To affirm one's life, on this interpretation, is to prefer on balance that the series of events that constitutes the life should have occurred, as against the alternative that one should not have lived at all. To this it will immediately be replied that it sets a very low standard for application of the notion of the affirmation of a life. The successful Gauguin presumably prefers the actual course his life has taken, looking back on it, to the alternative that he should not have lived in the first place. But nearly all of us will say the same thing, including those in a position analogous to that of the failed Gauguin. So long as a human life satisfies the conditions that make it minimally worth living, the agent who lives the life will most likely cling to it, preferring retrospectively to have lived their life to a scenario in which they did not live at all. There doesn't appear to be anything special or distinctive about an agent such as the successful Gauguin, whose projects come to fruition in a way that seems connected to the affirmative attitude he takes when he looks back on the life he has led.

I agree that the proposal under consideration sets a low bar for affirming one's life. But this seems to me to be appropriate to the case at hand. The fact of the matter is that most of us do affirm our lives, both as we live them and in retrospective reflection about the course they have taken. Whether our lives justify this kind of affirmative attitude—whether, that is, they are worthy of being affirmed by us in this way—is a separate question, and one that we shall come back to later. But for most of us, affirmation, I take it, is the default attitude we adopt to our own lives.

What distinguishes the two Gauguins, the successful and the failed one, I would suggest, is not whether they adopt an affirmative attitude toward the lives they have lived as they look back in reflection, but the basis for the affirmative attitude that they adopt.[11] In the case of the successful Gauguin, that basis will be, in large measure, his artistic project. He affirms the life he has led because of the innovative works of art that he has created through that project, as well as the valuable activities that gave rise to them. The project will thus be

---

11. Williams's other central example of moral luck is that of Anna Karenina, who of course isn't able to affirm her life when she looks back on it from the perspective of her failed project; see "Moral Luck," pp. 26–27. My present point is just that it isn't essential to Williams's argument that the agent of a failed project should regret having lived the life they led. They might have other grounds, besides the project that has failed, for being glad to have lived, and they might even cling to the life they have led in the absence of compelling grounds for doing so. I return to the latter possibility later in this book.

what he has primarily lived for, and it constitutes his standpoint of retrospective reflection, insofar as it provides the values that he appeals to when he looks back approvingly on the life he has led.[12] It has the status of a "ground project" or a "categorical desire," and it forms a crucial part of what Christine Korsgaard would describe as Gauguin's "practical identity."[13] But if his successful artistic project provides the grounds on which Gauguin affirms his life, and if he is aware that it has this kind of significance for his retrospective attitudes, then he will affirm the project itself unconditionally, preferring that the project should be part of his life than that it should not. This is a further example of the process that was discussed in section 3.4, whereby the affirmation dynamic extends to the normative conditions of the things that we unconditionally affirm. Gauguin's actual attachment to his life in this way involves a commitment to affirm the things in the life that make it worthy of his affirmative attitude to it.

Assume, then, that the successful Gauguin affirms unconditionally the artistic activities that he was able to carry out during his sojourn in the South Pacific. This will arguably commit him to affirming in turn his earlier decision to leave for Tahiti, because that is the necessary historical condition for the successful artistic project that he now affirms.[14] It is not that Gauguin prefers his actual life to any alternative life that he could imagine (including the alternative that he should have remained in Paris). Rather, he prefers the life he has actually lived to the alternative that he should not have lived at all;

---

12. Compare "Moral Luck," p. 36, where Williams writes that the outcome of the decision in a case such as Gauguin's "importantly conditions the agent's sense of what is significant in his life, and hence his standpoint of retrospective assessment."

13. The notions of a "ground project," a "categorical desire," and a "practical identity" are discussed in sec. 3.4 above, which includes references to relevant works by Williams and Korsgaard. I come back to these themes in sec. 5.1 below.

14. Compare the suggestion discussed in sec. 3.4, that disabled adults might similarly be committed to affirming their disability, insofar as it is necessary for the actual projects and activities that provide a normative basis for their affirmative attitude toward their own life.

this requires him to affirm his earlier decision, on account of its essential role in relation to the values that enable him to look back favorably on his life in the way that he does.

The situation of the failed Gauguin is different in precisely this respect. Even if he in fact still affirms his life as a whole, preferring that life, as he has actually led it, to the alternative that he should not have lived at all, his artistic activities will not provide the basis for such a preference. They are, in this scenario, without positive value, and hence they are incapable of contributing to the justification of his retrospective preference to have lived.[15] On the "simplifying assumption" that the artistic project has not conditioned something else in Gauguin's life that provides a basis for affirming it, the only reasonable attitude for him to adopt toward that project will be one of all-in regret. But if he rejects the project, then he must regret on balance the decision that gave rise to it in the first place; the decision was always subject to important moral objections, and it now turns out that the only thing that might possibly have redeemed it has not come to pass. The failed Gauguin is thus left with "the most basic regrets"—if not about his life as a whole, then at least about the decision to leave his family in Paris that is at the center of Williams's discussion in "Moral Luck."

This seems to me the most promising way to understand Williams's argument. The interpretation rests on an independently plausible conception of affirmation and its bases, defended in chapter 3, which avoids the difficulties that plague the other accounts we have canvassed. With this interpretation in place, we now need to return to Williams's contention that the successful Gauguin is committed to affirming the decision to pursue his artistic project in Tahiti. The idea

---

15. Compare Williams, "Unbearable Suffering," p. 337, where he writes of the scenario under which Gauguin's project proves to be an intrinsic failure: "[I]t was precisely the meaning of his life that was destroyed in the refutation of the project."

seems to be that, since Gauguin affirms unconditionally the artistic project that is the ground of his affirmative attitude toward his life, he has to affirm the decision when he looks back on it, because of the role that the decision plays as a condition of his defining life project. But was the decision strictly *necessary* for the artistic identity that Gauguin now affirms? No doubt his career would have taken a very different course if he hadn't left his family to travel to Tahiti. But he might still have had artistic projects worth affirming under this scenario, ones that are continuous with his actual projects, insofar as they result from the application of his talents and ambition to a different range of challenges and opportunities. This might be enough to open space for even the successful Gauguin to experience all-in regret about his decision to leave his family in Paris, compatibly with the element of affirmation that Williams ascribes to the artist in this case.

It is true that Gauguin might well have had a basis for affirming his life had he chosen to remain in Paris with his family; and it is true, too, that this basis might have been provided (at least in part) by the artistic activities and accomplishments that would have marked his life under this alternative scenario. But these points are not sufficient to undermine Williams's contention that Gauguin is committed to affirming the decision when he looks back on it from the perspective of his later artistic success. What he unconditionally affirms, from that point of view, is the life he has actually led, including the artistic projects that he has in fact undertaken in that life. But those projects do appear to have been historically conditioned by his decision to leave Paris for the South Sea Islands. That Gauguin might have had other artistic projects had he remained in Paris, ones whose value would have provided him with a basis for affirming the life he would then have led, does not undermine Williams's contention about the commitments of the actual Gauguin.

This interpretation of the argument does not rest on assumptions about the identity conditions of Gauguin's life but on assumptions about the character of the ground project that provides him with a basis for affirming his life. The idea is that, whatever else may be true about the situation Gauguin would have found himself in had he remained in Paris, that situation would not have included the projects that he has actually built his life around. Even in the absence of a general theory about the essential features of individual projects, this idea seems highly intuitive: what is distinctive and valuable in Gauguin's actual artistic output seems too closely bound up with his experiences in the South Pacific to make it plausible that he could have had anything quite like the same achievements if he had remained in Paris.[16] The kind of artistic success Gauguin has realized in his life is in this way genuinely conditioned by the fateful decision that he looks back on in reflection.

Our views about this case rely, it seems to me, on intuitions about the values that inhere in an agent's projects. Gauguin's artistic project is an organized set of activities that he engaged in over a period of time. The project provides him with a basis for affirming his life, insofar as there are values that inhere in its constituent activities, where those values are in turn ones that Gauguin is attached to emotionally. The question of whether the agent would have sustained the same project under a given set of counterfactual circumstances can thus be understood as the question of whether the values that are realized through the agent's actual activities would have survived under those circumstances. Thus, even if Gauguin had been both active and successful as an artist back in France, it simply isn't plausible to assume that the works of art that he would have created through

---

16. The historical Gauguin seems to have found life in Tahiti disappointingly Europeanized, and the paintings that resulted from his stay there reflect his fantasy of life on the island more than the discouraging reality he encountered. Even if we hold this aspect of his biography fixed in considering Williams's argument, it remains plausible to assume that Gauguin would not have produced the kinds of paintings that he did produce in the most important phase of his career if he hadn't been working on them in the South Pacific.

those activities would have been the same as the valuable works that were brought about through his actual activities in Tahiti. Many of his techniques as a painter might have been in place by the time he decided to depart for the island, but the subjects of his paintings would have been massively different if he had chosen to apply those techniques in a studio on the European continent. They would therefore have lacked elements that contribute crucially to making his actual output so interesting and important, such as the appropriation of "primitive" Oceanic motifs to express a personal fantasy of Polynesian culture. By contrast, there is no reason to believe that the values embodied in his art would have been affected one way or another if he had made different decisions about what to have for breakfast on one or several mornings during his journey to Polynesia.

Of course, our judgments about counterfactual matters of this kind are fallible, and it is often difficult to know exactly what would have happened if things had been different than they actually were in some respect or other. It is certainly conceivable that even a superficially inconsequential decision, such as Gauguin's choice to eat sausages for breakfast one morning, might in fact have been necessary in some obscure way as a condition of his eventual artistic achievements.[17] But there is no reason for Gauguin to believe that this is the case when he looks back on his life, whereas there is extremely good reason for him to believe that his artistic ambitions would not have come to fruition in the way they did if he had remained in France. What makes all-in regret about his earlier decision inaccessible to Gauguin is his standpoint of later assessment, and that standpoint is shaped in part by epistemic facts about what he has reason to believe (e.g., about the truth of various counterfactuals concerning his own biography).

Another complication is due to the fact that there is a certain indeterminacy when it comes to specifying the values that are realized

17. I return to this possibility in chapter 6.

in a given agent's activities. Gauguin's actual artistic accomplishments, I think it safe to say, would not have come about had he not decided to leave for Tahiti. But how much hypothetical deviation from the precise trajectory of his actual artistic existence can be tolerated before we conclude that the values that he brought about would no longer have been present in his work and life? Suppose, for instance, that he had gone to Tahiti, but that he had not taken up while there with Teha'amana, the teenage girl on whom the native women in many of his most famous paintings were in fact modeled. His artistic output would certainly have been somewhat different in this scenario; that is to say, some of the paintings he produced in this phase of his career would have differed from their counterparts in his actual oeuvre, at least in the facial and other features of the idealized figures that appear in them. But it isn't clear that the result would have been a set of paintings that are significantly different from his actual output in their aesthetic qualities and importance.[18] The question whether the artistic values he has realized would have survived under this counterfactual circumstance may therefore have no determinate answer that is epistemically accessible to us. But Williams's argument does not presuppose that there should be epistemically determinate answers to all counterfactual questions of this kind. All that it requires is that there are some cases, such as that of Gauguin's decision to leave Paris, in which we have good reason for believing that an earlier action or event was necessary for the realization of our later projects,

18. Of course, the paintings he might have produced had he stayed in France would also have been similar to his actual output in at least some of their aesthetic qualities and values; they might, for instance, have made similar use of bold colors and simplified forms to depict figures from Christian iconography in Breton settings (as some of his actual paintings from the period before his departure to Tahiti did). There would have been values in these paintings that are continuous with the values of his actual oeuvre, but there would at the same time also have been significant aesthetic values that are entirely missing in these works. There may be no definite answer to the question of how much divergence from actuality his paintings could have displayed before we would say that they no longer embody the values he actually achieved in his work; this is the indeterminacy to which I refer in the text.

including the values that most centrally ground our affirmative attitude to the life we have lived.

A final point to note about this part of Williams's argument is that the values realized in Gauguin's artistic activities play a different role in the retrospective and prospective points of view. When he looks back on his life from the standpoint of his eventual achievements as a painter, he will find that he affirms those achievements unconditionally, in a way that commits him to affirming the earlier decision that enabled them. But those same values do not similarly dominate his standpoint of assessment when he looks ahead on his life from the perspective of the earlier decision. He might have good reason to believe that there are significant artistic values that he will only be able to realize if he turns his back on the setting of his European existence. But for all he knows, there may equally be a quite different set of artistic values that he will realize if he remains in France and pursues his projects there, values that would be comparably significant if he were to live a life that is devoted to them. So long as this is the case, the identity of the values that he would bring into existence by choosing one path rather than the other has no significance at all for his deliberations about what to do.

What might matter prospectively would be considerations of a different kind, namely, reasons for believing that Gauguin can only achieve great things as a painter if he abandons his family to take up a new life in the South Sea Islands. Perhaps something like this was in fact true of Gauguin, as it may be of other artists who feel compelled to flout bourgeois expectations in pursuit of their creative visions. But it seems likely that there is also some romanticization and self-indulgence at work in the uncritical acceptance of assumptions of this kind about the situation of important artists and intellectuals. Even if their actual achievements give them (and us) good reason to affirm the sometimes dubious choices they made as their artistic biographies played out, there might have been equally good reason to affirm their achievements if they had found different and less dubious ways to develop their talents.

4.3. AFFIRMATION, JUSTIFICATION, AND MORALITY

For the reasons canvassed in the preceding section, I shall grant Williams's assumption that the successful Gauguin cannot feel all-in regret about his earlier decision if he takes a fundamentally affirmative attitude toward the artistic identity that that decision gave rise to. His decision was a necessary historical condition for the values that shape his later point of view and ground his affirmative attitude toward the life he has actually led. This provides a powerful basis for affirming the decision itself, which in turn precludes Gauguin from feeling all-in regret about it.

My basic claim in this chapter is that even with these assumptions in place, it doesn't follow that Gauguin's decision is justified by its eventual success. There was a decisive moral objection to what he did, and it therefore remains the case, looking backward, that he ought not to have followed the course that he chose. That he is unable to experience all-in regret about the decision is a function of his retrospective standpoint, deriving in particular from the reasons he has for affirming his life and the projects that give it meaning. But the question of the justification of the decision has to do with his deliberative situation at the time when the decision was made. Nothing in Gauguin's subsequent history serves to undermine the significant objections to abandoning his family that obtained at the earlier point in time, and we should therefore resist the conclusion that his later affirmation of the decision constitutes a retroactive justification of it. In this respect, the case of Gauguin is exactly like the case of the young girl's child.

The notion of a retroactive justification is a peculiar one; it will be helpful at this point to look a bit more closely at this notion, to see if we can understand better Williams's alternative interpretation of the Gauguin case. The conception of justification that is at issue, Williams suggests, is connected to rationality (p. 22). Gauguin's success can provide him with a rational justification for his decision to pursue his art in Tahiti, even though he couldn't have known that he would be successful at the time when he made the decision. Failure, by contrast, would show the decision to be "unjustified," and in that scenario it will turn out to have been "wrong" (p. 25). At least this will be the case so long as the outcome involves what Williams calls "intrinsic" as opposed to "extrinsic failure" (pp. 25–27, 36). The latter would be the result of circumstances that thwart Gauguin's ambitions, but without "discrediting" the project that he was launched on; an example would be a case in which Gauguin's ship capsizes while he is on the way to Tahiti. With intrinsic failure, by contrast, "the project which generated the decision is revealed as an empty thing, incapable of grounding the agent's life" (p. 36). In the terms I have proposed, it turns out not to realize the kind of value that could provide a normative basis for Gauguin to affirm his life when he looks back on it in thought.

In situations of intrinsic failure, Gauguin's decision is shown to be "wrong" and "unjustified." In the success case, by contrast, the decision is justified retrospectively; we might provisionally put this by saying that it turns out to have been the "right" thing to do, or what Gauguin "ought" to do, though Williams himself doesn't express the point in this vocabulary.[19] It is clear, however, that the notion of justification

---

19. As we saw in the preceding chapter, there are cases in which we might say that an agent was justified in doing X, even though doing X wasn't really what they ought to have done; the case of the broken promise that saves someone from being killed in a plane crash is a possible example. In that example, however, it is notable that the consideration that puts pressure on us to modify our conclusion retrospectively about what the agent ought to have done is one that would have undermined the moral objection to it, if the consideration had been

that is at issue, and the concepts of "right," "wrong," and "ought" that go together with it, are not to be given a distinctively moral interpretation. As I noted above, Gauguin's departure for Polynesia may be supposed to have wronged the family that he left behind. They had "claims" on him to support and attention, claims that Williams imagines Gauguin not to have been indifferent to, and we are to suppose that Gauguin's neglect of those claims had "grim" consequences for his wife and children (pp. 22–23). They therefore have a very compelling grievance about the way Gauguin has treated them, and a corresponding basis for resentment and reproach that take his decision as their object. Williams quite reasonably observes that Gauguin's artistic success will do nothing to silence or undermine these objections to his decision on the part of the individuals whose claims he has failed to honor (pp. 21–22, 38–39).[20] The retrospective justification that artistic

accessible to the people affected at the time of action. By hypothesis, Williams's Gauguin case is different in precisely this respect. This suggests that justification and "ought" will go hand-in-hand in this case, so that if Gauguin's departure for Tahiti is justified retroactively by his success, the result should also be to make it true that that is what he ought to have done. The "ought" at issue here, just to be clear, would be the practical "ought" that is connected to the agent's reasons for action, not the "ought" of moral obligation that can potentially come apart form the practical "ought" (as it seems to do, on Williams's account, in the successful Gauguin case); for this distinction, see Bernard Williams, "'Ought' and Moral Obligation," in his *Moral Luck*, pp. 114–23. At the end of the current section, I return to the question of the connection between justification and "ought," proposing a weaker interpretation of the notion of justification at work in Williams's argument that doesn't entail that the action that is justified is the action that agent ought (in retrospect) to have performed.

20. On a view to which I am attracted, the emotional acknowledgment of these complaints by his family members would amount to their blaming Gauguin for what he did to them; see, e.g., my "Dispassionate Opprobrium. On Blame and the Reactive Sentiments," in R. Jay Wallace, Rahul Kumar, and Samuel Freeman, eds., *Reasons and Recognition: Essays on the Philosophy of T. M. Scanlon* (New York: Oxford University Press, 2011), pp. 348–72. It is natural to assume that blame in turn presupposes that the person who is its target ought not to have acted as they did; see, e.g., my "The Argument from Resentment," *Proceedings of the Aristotelian Society* 107 (2007), pp. 295–318. So if Williams were to agree that the family members are entitled to blame the successful Gauguin for abandoning them, he might seem to be committed to thinking that his decision to do so was not justified. But Williams rejects this assumption about the normative commitments of blame; see, e.g., his "Internal Reasons and the Obscurity of Blame," as reprinted in his *Making Sense of Humanity*, pp. 35–45.

success provides consists not in the removal of the complaints that were already in place about his decision but in Gauguin's acquiring something to "lay against" those complaints, as it were on the other side of the ledger (p. 38).

From the fact that Gauguin's retrospective justification does not undermine the objections of his family members to his decision to abandon them, Williams says, it does not follow that the justification is not a moral one (pp. 38–39). There are cases, such as those that involve the problem of "dirty hands" in politics, in which actions are justified morally by their effects without the justification serving to silence the complaints about the action that might be brought by the people who were its victims (the individuals whose rights were trampled, for instance, to avert some general catastrophe).[21] But Williams suggests that the Gauguin scenario is not a case of this kind. The artistic success that provides him with a basis for affirming his decision retroactively is not itself a straightforwardly moral consideration (even if, as Williams notes, it is a consideration that has some significance for moral reflection; pp. 37–38). It operates, as I noted earlier, to provide a rational justification for Gauguin's decision. If this is right, however, then the element of distinctively *moral* luck in cases of this kind cannot be understood as a matter of the acquisition by the agents in them of a moral justification for actions that were originally subject to moral objections. "It lies rather," Williams writes, "in the relation of their life, and of their justification or lack of it, to morality" (p. 39).

On this interpretation of the example, Gauguin acted immorally when he ignored the claims of his family in order to pursue his artistic

---

21. This is Williams's way of glossing the "dirty hands" cases, in "Moral Luck," pp. 38–39; see also Bernard Williams, "Politics and Moral Character," as reprinted in his *Moral Luck*, pp. 54–70. I myself prefer to think of the dirty hands cases in terms of entrenched moral conflict, as cases in which there are significant grounds for complaint on the part of individuals affected by our conduct whatever we end up deciding to do. On this approach, there is no single action that would be fully justified in moral terms under the circumstances.

ambitions in the South Sea Islands, and this feature of the case is not affected by what happens after he sets out on his journey. His good fortune, relative to his epistemic situation at the time when he made the decision, lies in the value that his artistic projects eventually come to acquire, which is something he was not in a position to anticipate with confidence when the decision was originally made. That value has the effect that Gauguin's decision is rationally justified; it becomes the "right" thing to do in the situation he confronted, or what he "ought" to have done after all (in the terms that I have proposed for thinking about questions of rational justification in this case). The effect of this retrospective justification is to undermine the rational significance of Gauguin's immorality for him. His offense against moral requirements turns out not to render his action unjustified, or to count decisively against it; the action may be morally wrong, but it is not on that account the wrong thing for him to have done (the wrong thing "full stop," as we might put it). This in turn calls into question the common assumption that morality is supremely important for human action, a body of considerations that trump (or are at least on a par with) any of the reasons that might conceivably conflict with them.

The conception of rational justification that figures in this argument is distinctively perspectival. It is a conception that is tied to Gauguin's personal point of view; whether his action is justified or not, after all, is meant to be a question not of whether we (or his family members!) are glad that he performed it but of whether he himself takes an affirmative stance toward it. What matters, on this conception, is Gauguin's own "standpoint of assessment" (p. 35), which need not be the standpoint that other agents or observers adopt in thinking about what he has done.[22] But while rational justification, as Williams

22. I think this is what Williams is driving at when he says of Gauguin that "his decision can be justified, *for him*, by success," "Moral Luck," p. 36 (italics mine). It is a justification for him rather than for others, insofar as the justification isn't sufficient to undermine the grievance that others who are affected by the decision have against him on account of it. And it is a

conceives of it, is in this way perspectival, there is another way in which it is not. The argument of "Moral Luck" apparently privileges Gauguin's retrospective point of view, as compared to the standpoint he occupies at the earlier moment when he was confronted with his original choice. A natural way to understand the argument, at any rate, is along these lines: There is a single and determinate answer to the question of whether Gauguin's decision was or was not justified rationally. What fixes that answer, however, is the standpoint of later assessment that Gauguin will occupy only after his artistic experiment has for the most part run its course. It is true, once and for all, that the decision was justified in light of Gauguin's artistic success, and this is the case because the standpoint that is shaped by that success precludes regret on his part when he looks back from it on the decision he has made. The element of epistemic luck in the case derives from the fact that Gauguin cannot know, at the time he makes his decision, whether it is really justified, because he cannot then anticipate how the decision will affect the standpoint of assessment from which he looks back on it.

A more thoroughly perspectival approach, however, would reject the privileging of the agent's later standpoint that Williams apparently takes for granted. Consider, for instance, relativist views about the judgments that express conclusions of rational justification in cases of this kind. One kind of relativist about truth, for instance, might hold

---

justification for him, insofar as its presence or absence depends on his own standpoint of assessment when he looks back on the decision. But if that standpoint is such as to preclude regret on his part, then I believe Williams would conclude that the decision was after all rationally justified full stop (not merely justified "for him"). This is a conclusion that even his family members should accept, if they are thinking clearly about his situation, though their acceptance of it would not suffice to undermine their objections to his treatment of them. (Though Gauguin's decision might turn out to be justified rationally by his later inability to regret it, his family presumably continues to be justified in regretting that he made the decision, and in wishing that he had acted otherwise; I return to this aspect of the situation in sec. 4.4 below.)

that a single claim about the justification of Gauguin's action could be false relative to Gauguin's earlier standpoint of assessment and true relative to the later standpoint.[23] Thus, it might be false that Gauguin ought to leave his family for an artistic life in Tahiti, assessed from Gauguin's standpoint at the time of action, and true that he ought to do so relative to his later standpoint of assessment. A still different kind of relativist might maintain that there isn't a single claim that is at issue in cases of this kind, but rather two claims, which are implicitly indexed in some way to features of the two different standpoints. The judgment that it was right for Gauguin to leave for Tahiti (given Gauguin$_1$'s point of view) could be false, for instance, while the different judgment that it was right for Gauguin to leave for Tahiti (given Gauguin$_2$'s point of view) is true. Both of these approaches allow that the truth of judgments about the justification of Gauguin's decision is in some sense relative to Gauguin's later standpoint of assessment. But they do this without privileging the later point of view: the same judgment (or a semantically contextualized counterpart of it) might be false relative to Gauguin's earlier standpoint of assessment.

Williams doesn't say very much in the context of this discussion about the semantics and truth conditions of judgments expressing rational justification. Indeed, he seemingly goes out of his way to avoid giving us examples of the kinds of judgments that might be at issue. (As I noted earlier, he says that Gauguin's decision will be "wrong" and "unjustified" in the event that he is unsuccessful; but he does not tell us that it will be "right" in the success scenario, or a decision that Gauguin "ought" to have made.) The image of a "retroactive" justification suggests that the later standpoint reaches back in time to affect the truth of a judgment about the decision that might have been made at the moment when the decision was made. Perhaps

---

23. Compare Niko Kolodny and John MacFarlane, "Ought: Between Objective and Subjective" (unpublished manuscript).

it is timelessly true that the decision was justified, in virtue of facts about Gauguin's standpoint of assessment after his projects have come to fruition; it is just that Gauguin cannot know that the judgment is true at the time when he makes the decision to which it refers, since he doesn't then know what his later standpoint of assessment will be. Alternatively, if we accept a more relativistic framework, we could say that it isn't *yet* either true or false that the decision is justified when that decision is assessed from Gauguin's earlier standpoint, but that it becomes true later, when assessed from the standpoint of his eventual artistic success.[24] Both of these alternatives preserve the privileged role that Williams assigns to Gauguin's later standpoint of assessment when thinking about the question of the justification of his decision.

But why should we privilege the later standpoint in this way? What grants this standpoint its apparent authority for the question of rational justification? Williams's argument, if I understand it, is that the latter standpoint derives its significance in this context from the fact that it determines what Gauguin is ultimately able to affirm and to regret when he looks back on the decision he has made. It is because Gauguin is then precluded from regretting the decision that it is (or becomes) justified for him to have made it.[25]

---

24. Compare the relativist treatment of the truth of future contingent judgments proposed by John MacFarlane in his "Truth in the Garden of Forking Paths," in Manuel García-Carpintero and Max Kölbel, eds., *Relative Truth* (Oxford: Oxford University Press, 2008), pp. 81–102. This approach privileges the standpoint of later assessment, insofar as it is that standpoint that ultimately determines the assignment of a determinate truth value to claims about whether Gauguin's earlier decision was justified.

25. It might be suggested that the successful Gauguin's inability to regret his earlier decision isn't the consideration that makes the decision justified, but merely an indication that some other consideration obtains that does this work. One might suppose, e.g., that it is the objective artistic value of Gauguin's paintings that eventually justifies his decision, not the facts about his inability to regret the decision that are based in the significance of that value from his own retrospective point of view. But this isn't what Williams says; compare the end of the long passage from p. 36 of "Moral Luck" quoted above in the text: "So if [Gauguin] fails, his most basic regrets will attach to his decision, and if he succeeds, they cannot. That is the sense in which his decision can be justified, for him, by success."

If this is the argument, however, then we have already seen that its central premise is dubious. There is simply no good reason to suppose that questions of rational justification and questions of rational regret will track each other systematically in the way that Williams apparently relies on. Whether Gauguin's decision was justified, or rationally justified, is a question of what he had reason to do at the time when the decision was made. There was, as we have already seen, a powerful objection to the option of trying his artistic luck in Polynesia, which is grounded in the claims that his family members have on him for attention and support. On the other side, there are the artistic values that he hopes to realize through his activities as a painter in a highly exotic setting. These prospective values have some rational force; they are considerations that count in favor of leaving behind his European life and striking out in a new direction. In the context of the decision, however, they do not seem sufficient to defeat the moral objections against this course of action. Nor does this conclusion rest on Gauguin's (or our) uncertainty at the time about how valuable his artistic accomplishments will eventually be. Even if we postulate that Gauguin's achievements in Tahiti would constitute a major contribution to the tradition of European painting, this consideration is still not such as to defeat the powerful reasons against abandoning his family. His parental obligations are extremely weighty, and their significance in his deliberative context is not undermined by the fact that there are distinctively artistic values in play on the other side.

Of course I may be wrong in this assessment of what Gauguin has most reason to do. It is a live question whether moral claims or obligations always trump the considerations with which they might conflict, and, if not, whether the aesthetic issues that are implicated in the Gauguin case are of the kind that might suffice to defeat them. Williams himself has argued that our ground projects place limits on what we can rationally be required to do, and that the normative force of moral considerations is undermined when they conflict fundamentally with the things that give us reason to go on in life in the first place.[26] But that is not the argument that he makes in "Moral Luck." The claim here is not about the rational force of moral vs. other considerations in the deliberative situation that confronts Gauguin in Paris but about the retroactive significance of his later standpoint of assessment, after he has become a massively successful artist. In particular, Williams contends that the inability of the later Gauguin to experience all-in regret about the decision he has made amounts to an ex post facto justification of the decision. This is the contention that I am taking issue with. I maintain that Gauguin's normative situation, at the later standpoint of assessment, is very different from his normative situation at the earlier time of decision. His normative situation as he looks back on his life is determined by the question of what he has reason to affirm and to regret, not what he has reason to do. At that point in time, the question of whether to leave Paris or to remain with his family has already long been settled; the only issue that arises is whether to be glad that he decided as he did, or whether instead he has reason to wish that he had acted otherwise at the time. I have accepted that the successful Gauguin will have powerful reasons to affirm the decision that he made, and that all-in regret for that decision will therefore be inaccessible to him when he looks back on it in reflection. Nothing interesting follows from this, however, about what he had reason to do when he was actually confronted with the decision about whether to stay in Paris or to leave. This is the primary moral of our earlier discussion of the case of the young girl's child.

An independent reason for questioning Williams's notion of retroactive justification, as we have provisionally been interpreting it, has to do with its curiously symmetrical character. The primary alternative that he was confronted with in Paris was to remain with his

---

26. See, for example, Bernard Williams, "Persons, Character, and Morality," as reprinted in his *Moral Luck*, pp. 1–19.

family, perhaps finding a way to pursue his artistic interests while honoring the claims they had on him to paternal support. If he had chosen that path, however, then it is very plausible to suppose that it would also eventually have put him in a position from which he would be unable to regret the decision he has made when he looks back on it. This is the case, at any rate, so long as the life he leads with his family involves significant domestic values, where these in turn provide him with a basis for affirming the life he has actually led. Under these conditions, the very same retrospective structure will be in place that is at work in the case of the artistically successful Gauguin. There will be values that are realized through his activities, which he affirms on account of their significance for the life he has led; this will give him powerful reason to affirm the decision to remain in France, since doing so was (we may suppose) a historically necessary condition for the achievement of those domestic values in his life.

The upshot is that, if the decision to leave for Tahiti is justified retroactively by Gauguin's success, the decision to remain with his family could also have been justified retroactively in precisely the same way. But this result—a potential flood of rational dilemmas— would put too much strain on the conventional notion of justification. Ordinarily we think that if an action is justified, or the right thing for the agent to do, then it would have been wrong or a mistake of some kind for the agent to do something else instead. Similarly, if it is true that the agent ought to do X, then it is not the case that the agent ought to do not-X. But these entailments, which express what we might think of as the "exclusivity" of practical justification, do not seem to hold on Williams's account of the notion. From the alleged fact that Gauguin's success makes his departure for Tahiti the right thing to have done, it doesn't follow that it would have been wrong, or a mistake, for him to stay in Paris instead. For if he had done so, there is a good chance that his action would have been justified in just the same way that his actual decision turns out to be.

The difficulty here is caused by our interpretation of justification in terms of something like a rational requirement. Is there an alternative? I believe that a weaker notion of justification is available, one whose contours better match the shape of Williams's argument. Thus, a consideration might be said to justify an action not by providing a conclusive reason for performing it but by removing or disabling an apparent objection to it, rendering it true that the action is something that it would be "all right" for the agent to do. In the latter case, justification could be understood as a matter of rational permissibility rather than rational requirement, and this does not appear to be an exclusive notion. Thus, in the Gauguin case, his artistic success might retroactively justify his action, insofar as it disarms the normative significance of the moral grievances that his family members still have to his decision to abandon them. The action becomes something that it was all right for him to do after all, despite the considerations that appeared to speak against it. But it can be true that it was all right for him to take this path, even if it would also have been all right in the same sense for him to remain back in Paris, attending to his projects in a way that did not flout his domestic obligations. This interpretation would have the additional advantage of explaining why Williams highlights the negative judgments when discussing the conception of rational justification at work in his argument. As we saw above, he notes that Gauguin's decision would have been rendered "wrong" or "unjustified" by his artistic failure, but he is oddly reluctant to provide examples of the kinds of positive judgments of justification that would be made true by his artistic success. The reason might well be that retrospective justification, as he understands it, involves the removal of an objection that would otherwise obtain against an action, where this weaker form of justification does not entail that the action was the right thing to do, or something the agent ought after all to have done.

This interpretative suggestion does not help, however, with the larger criticism that I have been developing of Williams's argument.

The notion of rational permissibility, like that of rational requirement, is tied to the deliberative situation of an agent at the time of
action. It is a question of what the agent had reason to do in that situation, in particular whether the balance of reasons is such that there
are one or more options available to the agent that are not subject to
decisive objections, even if they are not things that the agent absolutely ought to do. When we think of Gauguin in the deliberative situation he confronted back in Paris, it seems implausible to suggest
that it would be all right for him, in this weak sense, to ignore his
family obligations and to leave his children to their "grim" fate.
Gauguin's normative situation, when he looks back on the decision,
is a very different one, and from the fact that he might then have reason to affirm the earlier decision he made, it doesn't follow that the
rational objections to it have been undermined.

4.4. DEEP AND SHALLOW AMBIVALENCE

Against this suggestion, it might be asked whether there is any point
to a backward-looking concern with justification—in the sense
either of rational permissibility or of rational requirement—if it can
come apart in this way from the agent's fundamental regrets. Williams, at any rate, raises a question along these lines in the course of
his argument in "Moral Luck" (pp. 32–33). It makes sense to care
about your deliberative mistakes if they led to outcomes that you
now have reason to regret, or if situations are apt to arise in the future
that you are likely to cope with better by attempting to avoid similar
mistakes. But the kinds of life decisions that we have been considering do not have these features. Gauguin cannot (by hypothesis)
feel all-in regret on account of his choice, nor is he likely to encounter future life choices to which the lessons of his earlier decision
might be applicable.

But the point of the retrospective concern with justification is not necessarily tied to effects of these kinds. It can equally reflect an ongoing aspiration to face up to the facts about one's biography as an agent, and to make sense of those facts in light of a broader pattern of normative thought and judgment. Consider in this connection the case of the young girl that we considered in the preceding chapter. There are powerful reasons of both a prudential and a moral nature why the girl should have put off motherhood for several years. Nothing in the girl's subsequent history undermines or negates those reasons, and continuing to acknowledge them is therefore the only truthful way to understand her own past.[27] It is also importantly connected to her understanding of the normative situations of other agents. Presumably the mother will think that young teenage girls generally have good reason to postpone motherhood when they are in situations like the one that she confronted. To endorse this conclusion while refusing to make the same judgment about her own case would introduce an intolerable incoherence into her outlook. These are considerations that make it sensible for her to continue to be concerned about issues of justification when she looks back on her life from the vantage point of the projects and relationships that her earlier decisions gave rise to.

Precisely analogous points apply to the case of Williams's Gauguin. Here, too, there were important considerations that told against the deliberative option of leaving his family in the lurch to pursue his passion as a painter. The force of those considerations is such that it was not all right for him to embark on that course of action, and nothing in his subsequent history affects the truth of this essentially deliberative conclusion. Gauguin might not be able to regret his decision when he looks back on it from the point of view of his later success, but an honest and realistic accounting of his life

27. Recall the realism condition on our attitudes from sec. 2.4 above.

needs to acknowledge that it was nevertheless something that it was not all right for him to have done.

It is a salient feature of both of these examples that the objections to the agent's earlier actions are in part of a moral nature, grounded in the claims of other parties whose lives are affected by what the agents have done. A retrospective failure to acknowledge the strength of those objections would therefore involve an attitude of continuing disregard for those claims on the part of the mother and Gauguin, which goes beyond the disregard that was expressed in the original actions that those agents look back on in reflection. This contributes to our sense of the importance of affirming the strength of the deliberative objections to the earlier actions in those cases. But the retrospective concern for justification has a point even in situations in which specifically moral objections are not at issue. Recall the example that was briefly discussed in section 3.3 above, in which an agent foolishly squanders his retirement savings on a gambling spree and ends up winning a fortune through a stroke of remarkable good luck. (We are unrealistically to suppose, as before, that there are no moral claims at issue in this case, so that the objections to what the agent did were of a purely prudential nature.) Even here, it seems to me, it is important for the agent to continue to acknowledge the powerful deliberative objections to his action as he looks back on it without regret. It was a deeply stupid thing to do, and nothing in the course of events it set in motion changes this fact about it. A truthful understanding of his own life needs to accommodate this important fact about one of the seminal choices that shaped it; he owes it to himself to face up to this aspect of the life he has lived, even if he does not owe such an acknowledgment to other people, in the way the mother and Gauguin might be said to do.

As we saw in chapter 3, the acknowledgment of such deliberative failures can be expected to leave an emotional residue in the outlook of the people who contemplate them in reflection. At the very least, such persons will normally be subject to regrets (where these are understood as pained feelings that accompany the acknowledgment that one has done something that was not all right), which might persist even in the absence of what I have called all-in regret. Thus, the person who has won big at Vegas will tend to cringe when he thinks of the stupid risk he took with his life savings, despite the fact that he does not wish on balance that he had done otherwise at the time. In the more interesting cases that involve moral objections to an earlier action, the emotional residue that corresponds to their acknowledgment is apt to be correspondingly more significant. With Gauguin, for instance, we would expect some persistent tendency to guilt, of just the kind that we earlier saw to be appropriate on the part of the mother in the case of the young girl's child. This sentiment precisely corresponds to the complaint that the members of his family have about the grim situation he put them in when he abandoned them. Moreover, it can coexist with the absence of all-in regret, reflecting an ambivalence of retrospective attitude that is appropriate to the complexity of personal history in Gauguin's situation.

What else might have led Williams to overlook or discount the possibility of this kind of ambivalence? He suggests at one point that we need to identify a possible mode of expression for negative sentiments if their ascription to the agent is to be plausible (p. 32). The idea seems to be that this requirement cannot be met in a case in which agents are also unable to experience all-in regret about what they have done. But what exactly is the problem supposed to be? One possible mode of expression of guilt in these cases, after all, is to affirm conversationally the normative judgment that provides the content of the attitude, admitting that one ought not to have acted as one did. The form of expression suited to cases of ambivalence would then include conversational acknowledgment of the two different judgments that guide agents' retrospective emotions about their own history.

One thing that would block this line of response would be skepticism about the judgments that allegedly provide the content of the conflicting retrospective emotions. Thus, suppose we deny the credentials of normative or evaluative discourse, as a domain of genuine judgments about what is or is not the case. What look on the surface to be judgments are really vehicles for the expression of desiderative attitudes, of the kind that are capable of motivating to action the person who is subject to them. On this kind of expressivist view, to affirm conversationally that one ought, all things considered, not to have gone to Tahiti is to express an on-balance preference that one should not have acted in that way. But a preference of that kind is unavailable to Gauguin, given the other features of the standpoint from which he looks back in reflection on his earlier decision. If success determines that he cannot regret that decision in the all-in way, then it thereby rules out the attitude that would find expression in his thinking that the decision was nevertheless one that he ought not to have made. Williams writes that the feature of this case that crucially makes possible retrospective justification is the way Gauguin's later "stand-point of assessment" will be colored by the success or failure of the project that he decided to pursue as a younger man (p. 35). If the locus of justification in this case is normative thought about what he ought or ought not to have done, and if this kind of thought is understood in turn in the expressivist terms just sketched, then we can perhaps begin to see why Williams might have concluded that Gauguin's choice can be justified by his later success.

Williams is somewhat cagey about his basic metaethical views, and he certainly eschewed a simple-minded emotivism about moral and other forms of evaluative thought.[28] But there are places in his work where an unacknowledged expressivism seems to lie just

---

28. See, for example, his "Morality and the Emotions," as reprinted in Williams, *Problems of the Self: Philosophical Papers, 1956–1972* (Cambridge, U.K.: Cambridge University Press, 1976), pp. 207–29.

beneath the surface of his argument, and "Moral Luck" may be one of those locations.[29] If this helps us to understand what Williams may have been thinking, however, it does not in my view render his conclusion plausible or convincing. Indeed, the inability to make room for emotional ambivalence in cases of this kind is one among many reasons for rejecting the sort of expressivism that would lend support to his account of Gauguin's susceptibility to moral luck. Guilt and anguish can be significant human emotions even in situations that do not allow for all-in regret, and it is important that a theory of normative thought should accommodate our susceptibility to such emotions in these situations. This is especially clear in cases in which the retrospective normative judgments that undergird the agent's anguish have a significant moral basis that implicates their relations with other people.[30]

Thus, Gauguin's family members have claims against him that he has not lived up to and a corresponding objection to his decision that nothing in his subsequent biography has silenced. His continuing guilt and torment about his decision reflect an awareness that these objections retain their force, even in the face of his subsequent life history. A fitting expression of the negative emotions will therefore include acknowledging to his children (for instance) that he has wronged them, and that they have a legitimate grievance against him, together with an apology and a sincere effort to make amends (to the extremely limited extent that it may still be possible for him to do so).

29. There are other themes in Williams's work, however, that seem in tension with this kind of expressivism, including his internal reasons theory; according to that theory, whether Gauguin ought to have gone to Tahiti is determined not by Gauguin's present preferences but by the preferences he had at the time. See Bernard Williams, "Internal and External Reasons," as reprinted in Williams, *Moral Luck*, pp. 101–13.

30. Note that Williams himself is elsewhere alert to the possibilities of emotional ambivalence; it is one of the themes of "Ethical Consistency," for instance, that agents who live through a tragic conflict of values will inevitably, and also appropriately, be subject to retrospective regrets whatever they end up doing. See Bernard Williams, "Ethical Consistency," as reprinted in his *Problems of the Self*, pp. 166–86.

That he is unable to feel all-in regret about his decision, looking back on it, no more precludes these expressions of residual sorrow in Gauguin's case than it does in the different but epistemically simpler case of the young girl's child.

To summarize: it can make sense for someone in Gauguin's position to continue to be concerned about the justification of his earlier decision; furthermore, the emotional counterpart of that concern is something that Gauguin might both experience and express, even if he is not susceptible to all-in regret about the decision that is its object. But there is a different and more troubling basis for ambivalence in Gauguin's situation that we now need to confront. To this point I have granted, and attempted to elucidate, two important assumptions that Williams makes about the standpoint of assessment of the later Gauguin: first, that Gauguin's artistic success in Tahiti gives him powerful reasons to affirm the earlier decision that was the necessary condition of that success; and second, that the successful Gauguin will not, as a result, be subject to all-in regret about the earlier decision. The idea is that Gauguin unconditionally affirms his actual life on the basis of the artistic projects that have given it meaning and value; this in turn commits him to affirming unconditionally those projects themselves, as well as their necessary conditions.

Even if Williams is right about these assumptions, however, it doesn't strictly follow that an affirmative attitude toward his fateful earlier decision is one that is warranted on balance. That is, we might agree that Gauguin's affirmative attitude toward his actual life gives him good reason to affirm the earlier decision but think that there are also powerful reasons to regret the decision as well. Indeed, candidate countervailing reasons of this kind are not hard to find. One might think that they are provided by the very moral considerations that told against his decision at the time when he made it, and that I have argued provide him with a continuing basis for guilt and sorrow about the decision even on the hypothesis that he affirms it on balance. The fact is that he wronged the members of his family, neglecting their claims in order to pursue his artistic projects. This fact continues to have normative weight in the retrospective point of view, giving Gauguin a reason of some kind to prefer that he should not have acted as he did. Of course, the successful Gauguin also has reasons to affirm his earlier action, which are provided by his attachment to his life and by the values that undergird that attachment. It may be that the nature of Gauguin's unconditional attachment to his life is such that he cannot realistically help but affirm the earlier decision that has given that life such meaning and value as it has. This is a point about psychological necessity, however, not about normative warrant. It is possible that Gauguin's affirmative attitude toward his earlier decision might not stand up to reflective scrutiny on account of the kinds of objections that can still be brought against it. Until this possibility is ruled out, we cannot conclude that Gauguin is really entitled to the affirmative attitude that his success might determine him to adopt.

To be clear about the possibility that is under consideration, it should be emphasized that Gauguin's affirmative attitude toward the earlier decision is not a matter of brute psychological compulsion. As I noted above, he has reasons for preferring on balance that he should have acted as he did back in the day. These reasons are provided by his attachment to the life he has actually led and by the values that undergird that affirmative attitude toward his life. The nature and structure of these commitments are questions that I shall come back to in the next chapter, but for the present the point is that they provide Gauguin with a serious normative basis for his affirmative attitude toward the decision that has so dramatically shaped his artistic career. To be warranted on balance, however, Gauguin's retrospective preference regarding the earlier choice needs to satisfy a further condition. Not only must he have strong reasons for preferring that he should have made the decision that he did; it must also be the case that there are no comparably strong reasons on the other side, for preferring that he should not have made that decision. The question to be considered is whether the moral objections to the decision, which tell against it in the deliberative perspective that Gauguin occupied when he originally made the choice to abandon his family, have this kind of continuing significance for his retrospective attitudes, giving Gauguin powerful reasons for regret. If so, we should conclude that Gauguin's inability to experience all-in regret about the decision is not really warranted, even if it is an attitude that he cannot help adopting. The only stance that Gauguin is really entitled to, we might say, is deep ambivalence, involving a set of conflicting preferences about whether the decision he looks back on is one that he should have made.

If this is the right way to think about the situation of the successful Gauguin, however, then we might suppose that it would also be the right way to think about the situation of both the mother and the daughter in the case of the young girl's child. There, too, we have powerful reasons for affirming the young girl's decision to conceive, but also strong objections to that decision, which continue to register for retrospective thought as possible grounds for guilt and resentment. Perhaps we should conceptualize those objections as retrospective reasons for preferring that the young girl had not decided to conceive after all, which are comparable in their strength and significance to the reasons that both mother and daughter have for affirming the same decision. If this is a plausible interpretation of the case, then there would similarly be in it a basis for deep ambivalence about the event that is contemplated in retrospective reflection. The mother and her daughter might as a matter of fact find that they affirm the mother's decision to conceive when they look back on it from the perspective of the attachments it has shaped and brought into existence. But that would not be an entirely warranted attitude for them to adopt, on account of the powerful reasons that also obtain for preferring that the young girl should not have decided to have a child when she did.

I do not believe, however, that this is the right way to understand the situation of the mother and her daughter in this case. One of its distinctive features is that the deliberative objections to the earlier decision are grounded in the claims of the very people whose attachments give them reason to affirm that decision. The main objections are of a moral nature, and I have suggested that they can be traced to the daughter's claim to an adequate level of attention and care from the mother who brought her into existence. But the bearer of that claim, the daughter, is also someone who is now deeply attached to the life she has led, and who by hypothesis strongly prefers that life to the alternative scenario that she should not have lived at all. This deprives the deliberative objection of continuing force as a basis either for her or for her mother to prefer, retrospectively, that the decision to conceive should not have been made by the mother. Similar remarks apply to the prudential objections to the decision that could be brought on the mother's own behalf. It is unwise to enter into motherhood when you are still in your early teenage years, in part because of the effects such a decision is likely to have on your own life prospects and opportunities. But the person whose interests ground this objection is also someone who, as a mother, now has powerful reasons to affirm the earlier decision she made, on account of its relation to the existence of the child she has come to love. Her ongoing attachment to her daughter leaves her with a strong on-balance preference that she should have conceived when she did, as she looks back on that decision from the later point of view. And this feature of her situation renders the prudential considerations unsuited to serve as reasons for preferring retrospectively that that decision should not have been made after all.

The general principle at work in this example, it appears, is that the normative force of claims as grounds for retrospective preference is undermined if the bearers of those claims themselves now actually prefer, on balance, that their claims should not have been acknowledged. Their de facto present preferences regarding the past action, based in their own ongoing attachments, trump their moral claims as potential normative bases for regret, at least so long as those preferences are based on a truthful understanding of their objects. We might put this in terms of the authority agents generally have to waive objections that might be brought on their own behalf. This authority is hardly absolute, but it is undeniably significant, and in a wide range of situations it can make a difference to questions about the justification of attitudes and responses. In the present context, in which our attitudes toward past actions are at issue, it makes a difference whether the bearer of the claims that undergird potential objections to the actions themselves prefer that their claims should have been honored. If not, then it is hard to think of those claims as grounding important reasons for preferring, against their bearer's wishes, that the claims should have been honored after all. The de facto preferences of the mother and her daughter seem dispositive in this context, provided that they are well-informed (as they are in the case at issue). Those preferences do not completely deprive the claims of all normative significance; as we have seen, they continue to constitute grounds for resentment and guilt, which express emotionally the fact that the young girl acted in ways that wronged the daughter whom she brought into existence.[31] But when the preferences involved in regret and affirmation are at issue, the bearers of the claims ought to have the last word.

---

31. Compare Derek Parfit, *Reasons and Persons* (Oxford: Clarendon, 1984), p. 364. Parfit suggests that the child's affirmative attitude toward her own life amounts to a form of consent to her mother's treatment of her, which effectively undermines any moral objection to that treatment that might be grounded in her rights. I disagree, thinking that consent serves to undermine rights-based objections only when it is given in advance of the behavior to which the consenting agent might object. But I think that the child's affirmative attitude toward her life might have a different kind of significance for her mother's retrospective point of view, depriving the moral objection to the mother's earlier action of its continuing force as a reason for wishing that she had not performed it.

But Gauguin's later perspective seems different in precisely this respect. As he looks back on his decision to abandon his family, the objections to it that he acknowledges are grounded in the claims of his family members to his attention and support. Unlike the case of young girl's child, however, the bearers of those claims do not affirm in retrospect the fact that they were disregarded. It is Gauguin's attachments, not those of his family, that ground an affirmative attitude toward his earlier choice to pursue his art in Tahiti. But he has no authority to waive potential objections on behalf of the partner and children whom he wronged. Whether their claims continue to ground strong bases for preference concerning the earlier action is ultimately dependent on their own retrospective attitudes. Assuming, with Williams, that the fate Gauguin left them to was truly grim, we may safely surmise that they still take an attitude of all-in regret about the fact that Gauguin decided to follow his artistic muse rather than honor his obligations to them. The force of their neglected claims, as a normative basis for retrospective preferences about Gauguin's action, thus remains fully intact. It is not for Gauguin to decide whether those claims are to count in this distinctive context, and his retrospective affirmation of his decision therefore has no tendency to drain them of normative significance for attitudes of this kind.[32]

To this it will perhaps be objected that it is ultimately up to Gauguin to decide for himself whether to affirm or to regret his

---

32. The historical Gauguin fathered two children during later stays in the South Pacific. Though there is little evidence that he was deeply attached to these offspring, one might think that they gave him a different and more powerful reason to affirm the earlier decision to leave behind his bourgeois life in Paris, a reason that silences the objections of his older children to the same decision in his retrospective point of view. But I do not myself share this intuition. The crucial difference between the cases of Gauguin and the young girl's child is not the difference between reasons for affirmation that do and do not stem from one's attachment to individual human beings, but the fact that the moral objections to Gauguin's decision are based in the complaints of individuals who continue to prefer that he should have acted otherwise. As I go on to write in the text, it follows that those objections are "available" to retrospective reflection, as powerful reasons for regret, in a way they are not in the case of young girl's child.

earlier decision. He cannot determine the retrospective attitude that others will or should adopt toward that decision, but his own attitude toward it is something that it falls to him to determine. The standpoint from which he exercises his authority in this matter is one that is conditioned fundamentally by his own attachments, which as we have seen give him reasons for affirming the earlier decision in reflection on it. That the members of his family are unable to affirm it for themselves, from the different point of view that they now occupy, is of no relevance to the question of the attitudes that Gauguin will and should adopt.

The grain of truth in this objection is that Gauguin's retrospective attitudes are his alone, which means that it is finally for him to determine what these attitudes will be.[33] We have conceded that he has good reasons for affirming his earlier decision, and also that the basis of these reasons is his attachment to his own life, a basis that makes it virtually inevitable that he will in fact adopt an affirmative stance, on balance, when he looks back on what he has done. The question, however, is whether this affirmative attitude is fully warranted, or whether instead a more ambivalent stance would better reflect the normative complexities that confront him in the retrospective point of view. In particular, we are asking whether the deliberative objections to Gauguin's earlier decision might also be strong reasons for him to prefer retrospectively that he should not have made it, reasons that counterbalance his grounds for affirmation, leaving him in a normative situation in which ambivalence and mixed feelings would be the only justifiable stance to adopt.

This is the question to which the retrospective attitudes of Gauguin's family members seem relevant. If they, looking back on it, found that

---

33. I do not mean to suggest that it is fully under Gauguin's volitional control whether he adopts an affirmative attitude toward the earlier conditions and decisions that he looks back on. He may not be able to help adopting such an attitude toward his own life and the normative conditions of his affirmative attitude toward it. Still, the attitudes in question are his alone.

they wholeheartedly affirmed Gauguin's decision to leave them, despite the fact that it neglected their claims to his attention and support, this would have a bearing on the justifiability of Gauguin's own retrospective endorsement. In particular, the fact that they on balance prefer that he should have made his decision would undermine the standing of the moral objections to it as reasons for Gauguin to regret it himself. This is essentially the situation of the mother in the case of the young girl's child. But it is of course not the situation of the successful Gauguin in Williams's example. As I have explained, the wife and children he left behind do not affirm the decision that wronged them but are subject to all-in regret about it on account of its dire effects on their lives (about which they may be assumed to be very well-informed indeed). The moral objections to the decision thus continue to have standing, for them, as bases for regretting that it was made, and they are therefore available in general for retrospective reflections about the decision. But if they are available, in general, then they are available specifically for Gauguin, as considerations that count strongly in favor of preferring now that he should not have made the decision after all. Gauguin might not be able to help adopting an affirmative attitude toward the decision, but the continuing objections to it raise a serious question about the rational warrant of that affirmative stance.

The last step in this argument might well be questioned, however. Let us grant that the moral objections to Gauguin's decision are in general available as potential bases for retrospective preference, in a way they would not have been if Gauguin's partner and children themselves took an affirmative attitude toward the decision. From the fact that they are available in general, however, it might not follow that they are available specifically for Gauguin. Williams himself, for instance, would undoubtedly question this inference. Whether a given consideration counts for Gauguin as a reason for regret, Williams would presumably say, is a question of his retrospective standpoint in particular, and it cannot simply be assumed that considerations that in general potentially speak in favor of regretting an event are reasons specifically for Gauguin to regret the event.[34]

There are two arguments that might be marshaled in support of this objection. First, one might take it for granted that reasons are relativized across the board to the subjective motivational sets of the agents whose reasons they are. This is the kind of position that Williams himself subscribes to regarding reasons for action,[35] and it could be extended to apply to reasons of other kinds as well, including reasons for such attitudes as regret and affirmation. If we accept a view of this kind, then whether the moral objections to his earlier action are reasons for Gauguin to wish that he had done otherwise will depend on the subjective attitudes that shape his outlook at the point in time when he looks back on it in reflection. And it might well be doubted that Gauguin's later subjective motivational set is such as to imbue these considerations with the force of reasons for him to regret his earlier decision. After all, we have granted that he will in fact take an affirmative attitude toward the earlier decision, preferring on balance to have made it on account of its role as a condition for the things that have come to give meaning and content to his life. But someone who adopts this stance arguably lacks the kind of subjective outlook that would confer on objections to the decision the status of comparably weighty reasons to wish he had not made it after all.

The question, however, is whether we are entitled simply to assume a subjectivist view of reasons for regret in the context of an interpretation of Gauguin's normative situation. A view of this kind would, to be sure, deliver the result that the moral objections to his decision do not count for the successful Gauguin as powerful bases for regretting that he made it. Furthermore, Williams himself was attracted to this general

---

34. The question, again, is whether his "his decision can be justified, *for him*, by success," "Moral Luck," p. 36 (italics mine).

35. See Williams, "Internal and External Reasons," and Williams, "Internal Reasons and the Obscurity of Blame."

approach to reasons, defending it influentially in other work. But I do not accept this approach myself, nor have I taken it for granted in the argument of this book. The perspectival aspect of retrospective assessment that has been my theme is not merely a special case of the more generally perspectival character of normative reasons, but derives more specifically from the distinctive role of attachments in the retrospective standpoint from which we look back on our lives with affirmation or regret. I would therefore not wish to appeal to a general subjectivism about reasons in thinking about the availability of moral objections as reasons for Gauguin to regret his earlier choice. Those who accept Williams's subjectivism on this score will perhaps arrive at a different interpretation of Gauguin's reasons for regret, but it is an interpretation that rests on premises many philosophers would reject.

There is, however, a different basis for questioning the availability of moral objections as reasons for Gauguin to regret his decision. This derives from the fact that he actually affirms the life he has led unconditionally, and is therefore committed psychologically to affirming the decision as well, insofar as it is a condition for the meanings that ground his affirmative stance. But if Gauguin is psychologically committed in this way to affirming the decision, the question whether there are powerful reasons against doing so might seem moot. There is, for him, no real question of regretting the decision, once he is clear about its relation to the things in his life that give him a basis for affirming it in the unconditional way that he does. Reasons for adopting this stance would therefore seem to have no place in his retrospective standpoint.

This line of thought has the comparative advantage that it does not simply presuppose a controversially subjectivist view of reasons for regret. But it should be rejected all the same. There can be reasons for and against attitudes, even if it isn't ultimately up to us whether or not we have the attitudes in question. With emotions in particular, it seems that there is wide scope for the application of questions about justification and warrant, even in cases in which the emotions that are subject to assessment are not under our direct control. Think of the familiar cases of people who are irrationally afraid of spiders, or who cannot summon the gratitude they know they ought to feel about a kindness that has been done to them. We raise questions all the time about the justification of emotions and other attitudes that it may not be a real option for us to acquire or to modify, and the question that is now at issue about Gauguin's attitudes can and should be thought of in these terms. He may not be able to regret his decision fundamentally when he reflects on it from the perspective of his later success. It doesn't follow from this psychological fact about him, however, that he does not have good reason to regret the decision, in virtue of the compelling moral objections to it that continue to provide his family members with reasons to regret what he has done to them.

For most of this chapter I have accepted Williams's contention that the successful Gauguin is justified in affirming his decision on balance when he looks back on it in thought. I have argued that even if this is true about Gauguin's perspective of retrospective assessment, nothing would follow about the justification of the decision that Gauguin thus affirms. It remains the case that it was not all right for Gauguin to have left his family behind in Paris, and he can both acknowledge this point emotionally and give appropriate expression to the emotions he feels, compatibly with his inability to experience all-in regret about the fact that he acted as he did. We have now seen, however, that Gauguin's later normative situation may be more multifaceted than it initially seemed to be. In particular, the deliberative objections to his earlier decision are still available from the retrospective standpoint as potential reasons for regret about what he did to his wife and children. We therefore cannot rule out the possibility that his affirmative attitude toward the decision, however firmly anchored it might be in the structure of his retrospective attitudes, cannot stand up to critical scrutiny, and that an attitude of deep ambivalence would better correspond to the complexity of the history that he looks back on.

Chapter 5

The Bourgeois Predicament

In the preceding chapter we saw that our attachments can lead us to affirm actions of ours that might not really be worthy of affirmation on the whole. Unconditional affirmation can in this way outrun its normative basis, committing us to prefer on balance to have acted in certain ways, even in the continuing presence of powerful reasons to regret those actions. But the affirmation dynamic that leads to this result can extend not just to our own earlier actions, but also to impersonal circumstances in the world that condition the things to which we are directly attached. In this chapter I explore an important example of this phenomenon.

We reasonably aspire to live lives that are worthy of retrospective affirmation. Not complete affirmation, of course; any realistic survey that agents might conduct of their lives, however admirable they may have been on balance, will uncover countless occasions for regret and remorse. But it is compatible with this that one might nevertheless think that it was worth it on the whole: there were things in one's life that gave it meaning and purpose from one's own point of view, and these are sufficient to redeem the many setbacks and failures it inevitably will contain.

In this chapter I want to consider a potential obstacle to the satisfaction of this normative condition. For virtually everyone who is likely to encounter the ideas in this book, the projects that provide the evaluative content of their life have a distinctive economic and social basis. They involve activities that are possible only for those who enjoy a comparatively privileged position in the global distribution of material resources, and who have access to an array of institutional and social advantages that are denied to most people in the world. For want of a better word, we might describe them as characteristically bourgeois projects and activities. The difficulty, then, is this: Our ground projects are the basis of our affirmative attitude toward the lives that we lead. But their bourgeois character means that those projects implicate us in social and economic disparities that we cannot possibly endorse (not at any rate if we are reasonable and thoughtful). The result is to undermine the rational basis of the affirmative attitude we take toward our lives, and to frustrate our concern to live in ways that are worthy of that kind of attitude. This is the bourgeois predicament of my title.

My main aim in this chapter is to explain the bourgeois predicament, and to show that it is a genuine challenge to our aspiration to lead lives that we can wholeheartedly affirm. The chapter begins (section 5.1) with a more detailed discussion of some issues that were already touched on in chapters 3 and 4, concerning the role of projects in providing a basis for the unconditional affirmation by agents of their own lives. In section 5.2 I address some potential normative obstacles to the achievement of this kind of affirmation, focusing in particular on conditions that might make an agent's projects unworthy of unconditional affirmation from the retrospective point of view. Section 5.3 applies the lessons of this discussion to the relation between our projects and impersonal injustices and misfortunes that our projects implicate us in, laying out the bourgeois predicament. The final section considers three possible responses to the predicament, and argues that they are futile.

5.1. MEANING AND ITS CONDITIONS

Let me start by conceding the obvious, which is that for the vast majority of us, there is no practical question of whether we do or will continue to adopt an affirmative attitude toward life as we are living it. We love life, we are attached to it, we cling to it, as it were, for dear life. Moreover, these are attitudes of attachment not to life in the abstract—to the mere fact that there are beings in the world who are alive—but to *our own* lives, the fact that we in particular are among the living. That we are attached in this manner to the lives that we lead is presumably the expression of an elementary biological imperative of some kind; it is prior to reasons and justifications, and hence impervious in some degree to normative challenge or support.

Even if our ongoing attachment to life does not require justification, however, the question can be raised as to whether it is a reasonable attitude to adopt. We are reflective creatures, after all, and with the capacity for reflection comes the ability to ask critical questions about tendencies that are given to us with our biological nature. We can ask, in particular, whether the lives we are living are worthy of the kind of ferocious attachment that we are unreflectively inclined to go in for. The ongoing attachment to life I have been discussing is in the first instance an attachment to our lives as they are unfolding. We value being alive, in a way that involves the kind of emotional vulnerability discussed in chapter 2, and among the primitive expressions of this emotional attachment is a strong preference to continue living. Indeed, this preference is strong enough that it generally makes it unnecessary to ask the question as to whether we should carry on in life.

When we do put to ourselves this unnecessary but existential question, however, where might we look for materials to answer it? Not, I think, *simply* to the future. There are cases in which people cite future circumstances to explain why they are interested in hanging in there for a few more weeks or months: they want to see their book through to completion, or meet the grandchild who was recently born abroad. But these future considerations are anchored in things that are already part of the person's life, such as their family attachments or their ongoing literary pursuits. It is, most basically, our attachments to individuals and activities in the life we are already living that potentially provide a normative basis for our attachment to life.

As we noted in chapter 3 above, Bernard Williams referred to these bases of affirmation as our "ground projects."[1] He also characterized them as "categorical" desires, observing that they "do not depend on the assumption of the person's existence, since they serve to prevent that assumption's being questioned, or to answer the question if it is raised."[2] The idea is presumably not that the causal efficacy of ground projects is independent of the person's existence; projects operate through the agency of those to whom they are ascribed, and in that respect they always depend on the continued existence of their subjects. Williams's idea, I believe, is rather that the normative significance of ground projects is independent of the assumption that the person who bears them will continue to exist. The test for whether a given concern meets this condition is whether the concern would give a person reason to continue with their life, if the question were to arise for them. Consider, in this connection, two different fans of the local baseball team. Fan A cares about the team, enjoys watching them play, and reads press accounts of them when he can; but A isn't terribly invested in his fandom, and it wouldn't occur to A to think that the continued opportunity to follow the team is a positive reason for going forward with his life. Fan B, by comparison, is profoundly invested in the role of a fan, with all of the social and psychological consequences that entails. B's involvement with the team is among the things she lives for, as we might say, and for B the commitment to fandom would plausibly

---

1. Bernard Williams, "Persons, Character and Morality," as reprinted in his *Moral Luck: Philosophical Papers, 1973–1980* (Cambridge, U.K.: Cambridge University Press, 1982), pp. 1–19

2. Williams, "Persons, Character and Morality," p. 11. Categorical desires also figure importantly in the argument of Williams's paper "The Makropulos Case: Reflections on the Tedium of Immortality," in his *Problems of the Self: Philosophical Papers, 1956–1972* (Cambridge, U.K.: Cambridge University Press, 1972), pp. 82–100.

count as a reason for carrying on with her life if the question were seriously to be entertained by her.

Ground projects, then, may be thought of as attachments to activities or individuals that provide a potential normative basis for our ongoing attachment to life itself. They help to constitute the perspective from which we conduct our lives, and are among the conditions that give us a distinctive character and point of view as individuals—a "practical identity," in the expression of Christine Korsgaard.[3] But does every attachment that in this way shapes our identity also give us a compelling reason to live? I am doubtful that this is the case. Character comes in many different varieties, and people whose fundamental attachments are to ends that are empty or evil do not thereby acquire a genuine reason to carry on with their lives. Their will to live may find psychological expression in a drive to realize the goals to which they are committed, and those goals might in turn be the sort of thing that it would occur to them to mention, in the perhaps unlikely event that they were reflective enough to think seriously about the existential question. But that question is a normative rather than psychological one, and there are objective constraints on what counts as a satisfactory answer to it. To provide the materials for a convincing response to the existential question, an agent's attachments must be attachments to things that it is genuinely worthwhile for humans to engage with, such that engagement of the relevant kind can be acknowledged interpersonally to be something to live for. People can be propelled forward in life by malicious or trivial ambitions—a compulsion to dominate and defeat others, or to accumulate meaningless material trophies—without it being the case that they thereby have good reason for carrying on.

3. See Christine M. Korsgaard, *The Sources of Normativity* (Cambridge, U.K.: Cambridge University Press, 1996), lecture 3.

In a different kind of case, agents are sustained by ambitions that have real normative significance but that are nevertheless too thin to contribute much on their own to the meaning of the agents' lives. Consider the person who sees little to live for but who carries on out of a sense of moral duty or because there is someone else who needs them. These considerations, it seems to me, might genuinely ground a preference to remain alive. But they are not the sort of thing that can really fill out a human life, or make it one that is worthy of wholehearted affirmation from the agent's retrospective point of view. Agents in this situation might prefer to carry on with their lives while they are living them, an outlook that we can think of as involving a conditional preference to continue living, given that they already exist (and that moral obligation, or the needs of someone else, requires this of someone in the agent's position). But if this is all that propels them forward, the agents might at the same time fail to affirm unconditionally the lives that they have led. Looking backward, and taking everything into account, they might regret on balance that they ever came into existence in the first place, and wish devoutly that things had been otherwise in this crucial respect. I will stipulate that persons in this situation do not take a fully affirmative attitude toward their own life. There are attachments that are barely sufficient to ground their forward-looking preference for continuing in existence. But these attachments lack the texture and complexity that ordinarily impart meaning to one's activities, and that therefore provide a basis for being glad that one has lived.

This is a kind of limiting case, however. Ordinarily, the projects that ground a person's forward-looking preference for continued existence are also things that support an affirmative attitude toward one's life of the kind discussed in section 4.2 above: a retrospective preference to have lived life one's actual life, as against the alternative that one should not have lived at all. The attachments that carry us forward through life are the very things that we hope will provide a basis for being happy in this way that we have lived when we look back from the perspective of the identity and character those projects have helped to constitute. We might say that an aspiration to live a life that is worthy of unconditional affirmation is thus immanent in the structures of personality that undergird our existential attachment to our lives while we are living them.

There is an interesting question that can be raised, however, about the scope of this aspiration. Why should we focus on the issue of whether our lives as a whole are worthy of unconditional affirmation? Why take the unit of one's life, as one has actually lived it, as the focus of retrospective assessment or evaluation? There are, after all, several alternative issues that might be broached when we look back in thought on the lives we have led. Rather than asking whether those lives as a whole are or are not worthy of affirmation, we might contract our focus, asking only about particular actions or activities of ours, and whether they are worthy of affirmation or regret when considered individually. Did we respond well to the circumstances and challenges we were confronted with on some occasion, or do we regret rather that we then acted as we did? Alternatively, we might expand our focus, assessing not merely our own lives and activities but those of some more extensive group or community with which we connected (our families, say, or professional associations, or the nation states to which we belong).

We can and do put to ourselves, of course, these more or less expansive questions of retrospective assessment. But we also can and do put to ourselves retrospective questions about the lives we have led as a whole, and these are natural and even important questions to ask. Their significance derives in large part from their connection with our identity. As we saw in chapter 4, our lives acquire whatever unity and coherence they may have through their connection with us; they consist in that set of experiences and actions that may be ascribed to us as either subject or agent. But a life in this sense is what we leave behind as a result of having lived. The difference that we have made, as individuals, is the difference that has been made in the world by the inclusion in it of those experiences and actions that may be attributed to us.

It is the difference that has been made in the world by the cumulative effects of the life that we cling to in medias res, as we are living.

There are affinities between the retrospective concern we have for the lives we have led and Aristotle's question in the *Nicomachean Ethics* about what it is to live well as a human being. Two points in particular stand out in this connection. First, Aristotle's question is about the human life as a unit of assessment, the lives that individuals lead as a whole, and not merely the actions or activities that persons may have been engaged in during a part of their life. This is connected to Aristotle's suggestion that we can only determine finally whether people have lived well at the end of their lives, from the standpoint of what I have called retrospective assessment.[4] Second, Aristotle's question about human lives is not simply the question as to whether their subjects have managed to cope as well as could be expected with the conditions that they encountered as they lived. People who are unusually unfortunate in their formative circumstances or in the challenges they confront as adults, for instance, may not succeed in living well on Aristotle's account, even if they cope admirably with the obstacles and hindrances that life places in their way. Living well, in the Aristotelian sense, is in this way hostage to fortune, as is the question of whether our lives are worthy of unconditional affirmation. The affirmation of individual actions is, as we saw in chapter 2, often merely conditional, involving a preference that the actions should have been performed under the conditions that the agents were faced with, which are taken as given and screened off from

---

4. See Aristotle, *Nicomachean Ethics* 1.10. The claim that the goodness of one's life can finally be assessed only from the retrospective standpoint is not to be equated with the different claim that (e.g.) the deathbed is the best epistemic context for reaching conclusions about whether one has lived well. The process of dying, after all, might well have peculiar features that distort one's judgment rather than facilitating clear thinking about the character of the life one has led. These might range from a disposition to existential pessimism on the negative side to a tendency to wishful thinking that would make one overlook the bases for regret as one surveys the life one has lived.

assessment themselves. But the affirmation of a life is different in this respect; it requires an on-balance preference to have lived the life that is up for assessment, including a preference that the conditions should have obtained that made that life possible in the first place.

Aristotle was of course not particularly interested in the phenomenon of affirmation in this sense. Unconditional affirmation is connected to attachment; it results from the activity of retrospective reflection that is engaged in either by agents themselves, who are attached to the lives they have led, or by others who are attached to those agents by bonds of friendship or love of one kind or another. But Aristotle's investigation of the good life concerns a subject that is continuous with the one I have been exploring, concerning the conditions that make a life worthy of this kind of affirmation. His own theory famously holds that these conditions centrally involve the activities expressive of the conventional ethical virtues, engaged in through a complete human life. I shall bracket the question of whether he is right about this in what follows. My own view is that it is an important challenge for moral theory to show that compliance with moral requirements typically contributes to making our lives worthy of affirmation in retrospective thought, even if it is not the only thing that does so.[5] But I shall not take it for granted that this Aristotelian challenge can successfully be met.

---

5. See my "The Rightness of Acts and the Goodness of Lives," in R. Jay Wallace, Philip Pettit, Samuel Scheffler, and Michael Smith, eds., *Reason and Value: Themes from the Moral Philosophy of Joseph Raz* (Oxford: Clarendon, 2004), pp. 385–411. We might distinguish two ways in which compliance with moral requirements might contribute to making one's life worthy of affirmation: it might have the kind of importance to the agent that could make it sufficient on its own to render the life one has led worthy of affirmation; or its importance to the agent could be such that it is a necessary but not sufficient condition for one's life to be worthy of affirmation, so that one wouldn't achieve this normative goal if one didn't live in a way that basically complied with moral requirements. The discussion above of the person who only continues living out of a sense of moral obligation suggests that the second way of thinking about morality's contribution in this connection might be more plausible than the first.

The framework suggested above for thinking about these issues sees ground projects in Williams's sense as the primary normative basis for the affirmation of the lives that they contain. These are the things that we live for as we make our way through life, and the hope is that they will provide a basis for unconditional affirmation when we look back on the lives we have led. This is an extremely ambitious aspiration, however. As we saw in earlier chapters, unconditional affirmation involves a distinctive dynamic, committing us to affirming the necessary historical and causal conditions of its immediate object (in this case, our lives), as well as the normative conditions of our affirmative attitude. When we affirm our lives in this way, we do not merely prefer them on balance to the alternative scenario that we should not have lived at all, taking the necessary conditions of our lives as given. We affirm those conditions themselves, preferring also that they should have obtained, and taking into account everything that it is reasonable to believe about their causal and historical and social prerequisites; this much results from the realism condition on retrospective attitudes that was introduced in section 2.4 above. This affirmation dynamic, however, already renders our aspiration to live lives that are worthy of such an attitude hostage to fortune, in much the way Aristotle's conception of living well seems to be. We ultimately have no direct control over many of the conditions and consequences of our lives, and whether these are ultimately such as to make the attitude of affirmation a reasonable one to adopt toward them is therefore a matter of luck relative to our powers as the agents of our lives. My larger aim in the present chapter will be to trace one particular way in which the aspiration to live a life that might justify unconditional affirmation is thus affected by conditions that we are ourselves unable to shape.

The projects that most readily contribute on the positive side to satisfying this aspiration are ones that involve a combination of objective value and subjective engagement.[6] They center around relationships and activities that are intrinsically worthwhile, and hence capable of being acknowledged interpersonally as meriting our interest and attention. But if they are to contribute to our capacity to affirm our lives, these projects must also be such as actually to engage us, so that we are invested in them emotionally. Within the pluralist framework that I shall presuppose for purposes of this discussion, we may take it as given that there are a variety of differently valuable activities and kinds of relationship that persons could build a life around.[7] We constitute ourselves as individuals in part by choosing to engage with some values rather than others, through activities that have the result of making those values our own. If all goes well, these activities will involve a cumulative deepening of our emotional commitment to the corresponding values, so that we come to care about them and to be identified with them, to some extent. To take an example that lies ready to hand (and that I shall return to later), think of a complex intellectual pursuit such as philosophy and the way that someone who is initially drawn to this pursuit might eventually become deeply invested in it through continual engagement with its problems and activities. Projects that satisfy these subjective and objective conditions lend meaning to our lives, and provide a normative basis for retrospective affirmation. They are the things that ground an unconditional preference to have lived, taking into account retrospectively everything that has in fact happened in our lives.

Obviously, meaning in this sense is a matter of degree. It is possible to live a life that is better or worse along this dimension of assessment, and there is no exact answer to the question as to how much meaning a given life has to contain to be worthy of retrospective

---

6. See Susan Wolf, *Meaning in Life and Why It Matters* (Princeton, N.J.: Princeton University Press, 2010).

7. For an important presentation of this kind of pluralism, see Joseph Raz, *The Morality of Freedom* (Oxford: Oxford University Press, 1988), chap. 14.

affirmation from the agent's point of view. It is equally obvious that meaning in this sense can coexist with the presence in a life of much that is worthy of serious regret and remorse, including missed opportunities, serious lapses of imagination or will, poor decisions, and a lot of low-level moral and nonmoral failure. (As Philip Larkin writes: "There is regret. Always, there is regret."[8]) Insofar as agents fundamentally regret these aspects of their life, they will wish on balance that things had been otherwise in the relevant respects. But this attitude is compatible with unconditional affirmation of one's life as one has actually lived it, even taking realistically into account its lamentable elements. To affirm one's life in this unconditional way is not to affirm absolutely everything that it contains, but merely to think (to a first approximation) that the good outweighs the bad. It is to think that the meanings that the life has achieved are substantial enough to make it worthy of affirmation on the whole, despite the presence of its many regrettable aspects. The aspiration to live a life that is worthy of affirmation is, I believe, an aspiration to live in a way that satisfies this condition. We hope to achieve meanings that are sufficient to warrant an on-balance retrospective preference for the life we have actually lived, as against the hypothetical scenario that we should not have lived at all. But even if we realize this aspiration, there may be many things in our life that we also wish on balance that it had not included.

5.2. OBSTACLES TO AFFIRMATION

In some cases, of course, the balance will tip in the other direction, so that the lamentable elements dominate the potential bases of affirmation from the standpoint of retrospective assessment. Looking back, the agent might feel that the projects that sustained the ongoing preference

8. Philip Larkin, "Love, We Must Part Now."

for continued life did not have enough texture or value to warrant an unconditional preference to have lived. In a still different scenario, agents may find that their life is filled with meaning, but also that it is filled with occasions that call for serious remorse and regret. Consider, for instance, people who have rich personal relationships and attachments in the private sphere, but whose professional life is dominated by ruthless and destructive ambition. Such persons might find it hard to conclude honestly that an on-balance attitude of affirmation is called for in regard to the lives they have led, taking into account not only their personal attachments but also the devastating effects on others of the way in which they have conducted their professional affairs. The only realistic attitude to adopt toward the lives they have lived would then be one of profound ambivalence.

A couple of brief comments about this scenario are called for. In saying that ambivalence might be the only realistic attitude to adopt toward the life the agents have led, I don't mean merely to be suggesting that the agents might have lived in a way that calls for retrospective regrets. As we saw in the previous chapters, some degree of ambivalence is compatible with an attitude of on-balance affirmation as one looks back on the life one has led. In the cases now under consideration, however, this affirmative attitude might not be warranted from the ex post facto point of view; a more fundamental form of ambivalence seems to be called for, along the lines of the deep ambivalence that was discussed in connection with the case of Gauguin in section 4.4. above. Second, even if deep ambivalence of this kind is the only justified attitude of the agents we are considering, it would not follow that those agents will in fact necessarily be ambivalent when they look back on their life. The same tenacious attachment that propels us forward also typically leads us to be glad that we have lived, even in a situation in which there are powerful reasons for regret and remorse. We are attached to our lives not only while we are living them but also in the retrospective point of view, and this often

means that it isn't really open to us to revise the on-balance preference to have lived. If I am right, however, we want to live lives that are
worthy of this kind of unconditional affirmation, and the point is that
this normative condition might not be satisfied in the case of those
who have systematic reasons for deep regret about the way they have
conducted their professional affairs. Agents who satisfy this description will fail to have lived in a way that makes their on-balance preference to have lived a reasonable one to adopt.

Note, in addition, the potential relevance of moral considerations
in this scenario to the question of whether agents have lived in a way
that warrants retrospective affirmation. I suggested earlier that obligation by itself might not have enough texture and interest to make
for a really meaningful life; people who hang in there out of a sense of
duty will be acting on important reasons they have to carry on, without their doing so necessarily providing a positive basis for retrospective affirmation. It is compatible with this point, however, that
morality might have relevance of a different kind for questions of retrospective affirmation. In particular, systematic moral failure, of the
sort that profoundly disrupts one's relationships to the other people
one has interacted with in life, can leave the agent with a correspondingly profound basis for regret, one that is sufficiently powerful to
undermine the possibility of reasonable on-balance affirmation.

A further noteworthy feature of these cases is the following. We
have been supposing that there are bases in the lives we have been
considering for both affirmation and profound regret. But these bases
of conflicting attitudes are located in separate spheres of activity: the
grounds of affirmation are provided by the rich personal attachments
that the agents have achieved, while the grounds for regret can be
traced to the largely disparate professional activities in which the
agents have also been engaged. This separation between the normative sources of affirmation and regret in the agents' lives opens space
for a consoling retrospective thought about them. It is open to the

agents who have lived them to think that while their reprehensible activities provide them with strong reasons for regretting the lives they have actually led, those reasons do not infect the separate bases of affirmation in the retrospective point of view. The things in their lives that are worthy of being affirmed are not compromised by the distinct grounds for regret, insofar as the two are independent of each other. There is thus conceptual and psychological space for the agents in these cases to wish on balance that they had not done the reprehensible things that now give them powerful reasons to regret their lives, even while they cling to the meanings that their personal activities have conferred on those lives. They have lived in a way that would have provided a sufficient basis for on-balance affirmation, if only they had conducted their professional affairs on a different basis; furthermore, nothing in their attitude toward the meanings that their personal activities have realized commits them to affirming that they should have acted as they did in the professional sphere. There is in these lives, as we might put it, an uncontaminated basis for on-balance affirmation, and the recognition that this is the case is a potential source of consolation.

The feature of these cases that leaves room for this consoling thought is the postulated independence of the bases for retrospective affirmation and regret, which are located in distinct activities or phases or aspects of the agent's lives. A different possibility, which will bring us closer to my eventual topic, is that the bases for affirmation and regret in the agents' lives are more tightly connected to each other. I am not thinking here of those cases mentioned above in which the putative sources of meaning are projects that are intrinsically evil or empty. In those scenarios, the projects in question will not turn out to provide any genuine ground of affirmation at all, however powerfully committed to them the agents may have been while living. But we can imagine other cases, in which agents pursue inherently valuable ends, but in ways that are fundamentally conditioned by immorality or other factors that provide a basis for regret.

Consider, for instance, a group of distinguished scientists who are actively engaged in systematic and illuminating research into basic questions of genuine importance and interest, but who interact with their subordinates in their laboratories in ways that are morally objectionable. To be more specific, we may suppose that they are exploitative (willing to take advantage of their power over their students and postdocs to extract from them a level of contribution in the lab that it would otherwise be unreasonable to demand); inconsiderate and even cruel (oblivious to the interests and vulnerabilities of their co-workers, and prone to mock and humiliate them publicly if they make mistakes or show signs of being slow-witted); and egomaniacal (relentlessly focused on advancing their own professional standing and power). Basic scientific research into fundamental questions, I take it, is a deeply worthwhile activity, valuable in itself, and not just for the benefits to human health or well-being that it might eventually produce. When research of this kind is successful and engages the interests of its agent, it will be precisely the sort of thing that could be expected to contribute positively to the meaning of the agent's life, and to provide a powerful basis for retrospective affirmation. In the case at hand, however, the scientists also have powerful reasons for regret. Furthermore, these reasons are not provided by activities that are independent from the agents' scientific projects, but are rather grounded in those projects themselves. That is, the way the agents have carried out their scientific research involves a pattern of activity that could only occasion remorse if the agents were to face up to it truthfully.

In thinking about the situation of these imagined scientists, we may stipulate that their regrettable comportment does not compromise the scientific value of the activities in their laboratories. The research that is conducted there is imaginative, illuminating, and important, and it represents a real advance in our understanding of the phenomena that it investigates. But at the same time the scientists have conducted their research investigations in a manner that exploits and undermines the other people who are involved in them. There are some who might question the assumption that activities can be valuable along any dimension if they are conducted in such a morally reprehensible way. One thinks in this connection of Kant's suggestion in the *Groundwork* that morality is a condition of all other values, something in whose absence acts and activities cannot be said to be good at all.[9] But the suggestion does not seem very plausible in application to examples such as the one under consideration. There are clear internal criteria for successful scientific research, and it is easy enough to imagine that those conditions might be satisfied, with the result that the laboratory activities have genuine scientific value, even if they were brought about in a way that was morally and humanly questionable.

Indeed, the relation between the scientific value and the immorality of the laboratory activities in the example could conceivably be even more perverse than I have so far imagined. In particular, we might plausibly suppose that the character traits that lead to the scientists' questionable comportment are instrumental to the outstanding scientific results that are attained in their labs. The valuable work that is done there would not have been quite so voluminous and cutting-edge, we may suppose, if the scientists had been less ruthless and exploitative in the ways they have comported themselves. Their ambition and egocentric drive, which disposed them to disregard moral niceties in their dealings with their subordinates, might well have been the very personality traits that also enabled them to persist and to succeed with their research program during the long period of

9. See Immanuel Kant, *Groundwork of the Metaphysics of Morals*, sec. 1.

its gestation and development. And their willingness to mock their less clever and confident subordinates—their incapacity to "suffer fools gladly"—might have created an atmosphere of intimidation that ultimately made for a more innovative and productive workplace. It would be nice to believe that there is a holism of value, such that valuable achievements in domains such as science are possible only if the activities that bring them about also satisfy the conditions of moral value. But this doesn't strike me as a realistic outlook.[10] The plurality of kinds of value allows for situations in which outstanding accomplishments in the scientific domain might not only be compatible with constitutive immorality but may even be made possible and sustained by that immorality.[11]

It might be objected that this way of thinking rests on a failure to distinguish the research produced by the scientists' academic activities from those activities themselves. In this spirit, one might maintain that, though the results obtained by the scientists in their laboratories are valuable as contributions to research in their field, the activities that gave rise to them are not valuable along any dimension, precisely insofar as they involve forms of systematic exploitation and oppression. But the distinction between activities and their results doesn't undermine the point I am making. The scientists' activities might well be morally objectionable without it being the case that they are on that account *scientifically* deficient. Indeed, insofar as

10. In saying this, I don't mean to deny the plausibility of a more limited version of holism. It might reasonably be maintained, for instance, that scientific activities involve a built-in sensitivity to at least some moral values (those of truthfulness and integrity, for instance), so that they cannot really be scientifically excellent if they offend against those moral values. For this suggestion, see. T. M. Scanlon, *What We Owe to Each Other* (Cambridge, Mass.: Harvard University Press, 1998), pp. 166–67. Even if this is true, however, it would not follow that a project can achieve scientific excellence only if it is appropriately responsive to all moral values and requirements.

11. See Raz, *The Morality of Freedom*, chap. 14, and Bernard Williams, "Conflicts of Values," as reprinted in his *Moral Luck*, pp. 71–82.

they are so organized that they regularly produce outstanding research results, it is plausible to suppose that they are themselves exemplary instances of scientific practice. Of course, the moral objection to those activities is itself a very powerful one; my own view, and my working assumption in this discussion, is that it clearly outweighs whatever scientific advantages might be made possible by the scientists' careerist immorality in the perspective of deliberation. They had decisive reason to comply with moral requirements in conducting their research, and the fact that flouting those requirements might facilitate the research is not really a good reason for people in their position to act in that way. Still, the value of the research activities, once they have been conducted, is considerable, and it provides a basis for retrospective affirmation on the part of the autocratic scientists who were primarily responsible for it.[12] This is what I mean in saying that both the scientists' activities and the results they attained through them had scholarly value, despite the immorality that was their condition.

In fact, we encountered an example with a similar structure in the preceding chapter in our discussion of Williams's Gauguin. His affirmative attitude toward the life he looks back on is grounded in the artistic achievements that he realized through his sojourn in the South Sea Islands. But those valuable achievements were in turn made possible by his decision to leave his family behind in Paris, a decision that by hypothesis was morally indefensible, wronging the wife and children who were directly and adversely affected by it. Here, too, it does not seem plausible to maintain that the things that

12. Indeed, on the buck-passing view to which I am attracted, the fact that the activities provide retrospective reasons for affirmation is precisely what their being valuable consists in. The peculiar feature of this case is that the scientific excellence of the research activities can provide such retrospective reasons, even though it isn't prospectively the case that the scientists have good reason to engage in those activities in the perspective of deliberation on account of their intrinsic immorality. (They have good reason to pursue their scientific research, of course, but not in the way they actually did.)

Gauguin achieved in his paintings were not really valuable in the dimension of the artwork just on account of the fact that they were conditioned by immoral behavior. The criteria of artistic value seem sufficiently autonomous that they can be satisfied even through activities that are gravely deficient along other dimensions of assessment, such as the moral. The main difference between the cases of Gauguin and of the scientists is in the relation between the postulated immorality and the activities that generate value in the two scenarios. With Gauguin, we imagine that there is a single, discrete break with his family, which has momentous consequences both for them and for him, but which is not extensively interwoven into his later patterns of artistic activity (the practices that generated the valuable works of art whose meaning gives Gauguin reason to affirm his actual life as he looks back on it). With the scientists, by contrast, we are supposing that the immoral behavior is partly constitutive of the laboratory activities that give rise to the outstanding results that their professional lives are organized around.

What the cases have in common, however, is more important for our immediate purposes. Above all, there is present in both of them a necessary connection between the bases for retrospective affirmation and the things that the agents have reason to regret. The agents' reasons for affirming the lives they have led lie in their significant life projects, as those have actually played out: in Gauguin's case, the project is one of singular artistic accomplishment, while with the researchers it is a sustained and brilliant course of scholarly research that addresses important scientific questions. But the things the agents have powerful reasons for regretting are necessary conditions for these bases of affirmation. Looking back, the agents cannot really wish on balance that they hadn't wronged others in the ways they did without thereby undermining the potential basis for affirmation that their scientific and artistic achievements represent. They cannot, in other words, be glad on balance for the lives they have led, on account of the role of their valuable projects in those lives, while wishing on balance that they hadn't conducted themselves in flagrant violation of moral requirements. This combination of attitudes is pragmatically ruled out, because a world in which they acted more justifiably toward their coworkers and family would not contain the very scientific projects that are the basis for an affirmative attitude toward the lives they have actually led.

This suggestion requires a bit of unpacking. Let's start with the bases of affirmation in these lives. We have been assuming that their valuable projects provide both Gauguin and the scientists with grounds for preferring the lives they have actually lived to the alternative scenario that they should not have lived at all. Their projects are in this way necessary normative bases for the affirmative attitudes they adopt when they look back on their lives. As we saw in earlier chapters, however, a situation with this structure generates a commitment on the part of the agents to affirm the projects that provide their grounds for affirming their lives. The affirmation dynamic, as I have called it, extends not just to the necessary causal conditions of the things that we unconditionally affirm but to the necessary normative conditions of that affirmative attitude as well.[13] In the case at issue, those normative conditions include the scientific and artistic projects that constitute the meanings of the lives our agents have lived, and that provide them with grounds for affirming those lives as they look back on them in reflection. So if they unconditionally affirm their lives, they must affirm in the same way the projects that constitute the meaning of those lives—assuming, that is, that they are aware of the role of the projects in providing a basis for the affirmative attitude that that they have adopted.

Of course, our agents might not be aware of the role that their actual projects play as normative conditions of their ability to affirm

13. See especially sec. 3.4 above.

the lives they have led. They might affirm their lives unconditionally, without reflecting at all on the conditions that ground this attitude; under these circumstances, there would be psychological space for them to continue to affirm their lives, even while they regret on balance their artistic and scientific projects and activities. But this would not be a very stable set of attitudes, since it would be subject to being undermined as soon as the agents became aware of the normative significance of their scientific and artistic projects for their affirmative attitude toward the lives they have actually led. Their unconditional affirmation of their lives thus commits them to affirming the things in their lives that make them worthy of being affirmed, which in the cases at issue are the valuable projects the agents have pursued. So these projects, too, become objects of unconditional affirmation. The agents in question could escape this dynamic only if they were willing to give up the attitude of unconditional affirmation that they take toward their own lives. But this is by hypothesis not a real option for them.

As we saw in the preceding chapter, an argument of this sort rests on assumptions about the values that are realized in the agents' projects. Their situation is one in which the values that in fact contributed to the meaning of their lives are conditioned by forms of immorality that they also have good reason to regret. That is to say, those values would not have been achievable in the absence of the immoral behavior that stains the lives our agents have led. It is of course compatible with this point that, had the agents not comported themselves in such objectionable ways, there would have been some other source of meaning that was achievable in their lives, something that could provide a normative basis for affirming the lives they would then have led. Thus Gauguin might still have become an important painter, and the scientists could have produced brilliant research, under this counterfactual condition. But the values they might have realized under those conditions are different from the values that confer meaning on the lives they have in fact led; they are therefore not available within retrospective reflection, to provide a basis for the agents' affirmative attitude toward their actual lives.

This point was discussed extensively in section 4.2 above. As I argued there, Gauguin's decision to decamp for Tahiti had momentous consequences for the trajectory of his career, so that it becomes very plausible to assume that the values achievable through his artistic activities would have had a very different character if he had not made that decision. With the scientists, by contrast, things might seem different in this respect. A resolution on their part to conduct themselves with decency and consideration in their laboratories would not, after all, have precluded them from pursuing their scientific investigations. We have been supposing that their ruthlessness and egocentric drive, which render them oblivious to the moral requirements that properly regulate their interactions with their subordinates, are also character traits that facilitate their academic work, enabling them to make scholarly advances that they would otherwise have been unable to achieve. Even if this is granted, however, it doesn't follow that the scientific values realizable under the alternative scenario are significantly different from the valuable work they actually have succeeded in doing. Perhaps there would have been fewer published papers in that scenario, with results that are a little less brilliant and imaginative. But it seems implausible to assume that they couldn't have made many of the same contributions to important research in their fields if they had treated their subordinates with greater consideration and respect. In this way, their situation seems to contrast with that of the successful Gauguin.

On the other hand, there is a further difference between the cases that is also relevant in this connection, and that seems to cut the other way. As I noted above, the regrettable comportment that provides a basis for the scientists' regret is much more extensively interwoven through their professional activities than is the case with Gauguin.

His project was decisively shaped by a single act that was morally objectionable, but the feature that makes it objectionable does not characterize his activities as an artist once he has left his family behind in Paris.[14] With our scientists, by contrast, morally questionable behavior is a continuing characteristic of their scholarly activities. It is in the nature of those activities, as they have actually played out, that they involved forms of interaction in the laboratory that were exploitative and demeaning for those who were working there. Our scientists' actual research projects just are the unfolding activities of people who are talented and driven and ambitious, but also egomaniacal and autocratic and exploitative. Their immorality, in other words, is not just a causal but also a constitutive condition of the ongoing projects that give meaning to their lives. To the extent this is the case, we cannot truthfully say that the values that provide them with a basis for affirmation would have been available in a world in which they had comported themselves more respectfully. They might have achieved many of the same scientific results under that counterfactual scenario. But what is valuable in their actual lives is not merely the results they have obtained but the activities through which those results were realized, and those activities constitutively involve the immorality that gives the scientists a retrospective basis for regret about their lives.

With both the scientists and Gauguin, then, there is a necessary connection between the bases for regret and for affirmation in the retrospective point of view. This is a different and more troubling source of ambivalence than in the case we encountered earlier, in which agents deeply regret their activities in one sphere of their life while finding much that is worthy of affirmation in a different and unrelated sphere. In that situation, agents can entertain a consoling

14. This is, once again, a simplifying assumption about the example that probably doesn't apply to the historical Gauguin, who showed a continuing pattern of sexual exploitation and indifference to family claims in his life as a painter in the South Pacific. See, for example, David Sweetman, *Paul Gauguin: A Life* (New York: Simon & Shuster, 1996).

thought, wishing that their lives had been different in the lamentable respects, without that undermining their basis for affirming the life that they have actually led. It is just that the actual bases of affirmation are counterbalanced by the actual grounds for regret, so that a kind of ambivalence becomes the only reasonable retrospective outlook for the agents to take. In the cases of Gauguin and the scientists, by contrast, the bases of affirmation and regret are not in the same way independent from each other. Instead, the thing that the agents have powerful reasons to regret conditions (in the case of Gauguin) and helps to constitute (in the scientists' case) the very thing in the agents' life that warrants affirmation. For people in this kind of scenario, the bases of affirmation are themselves infected by the grounds for regret, with the result that there is no realistic scenario accessible to retrospective reflection in which the sources of meaning are preserved while the deeply regrettable aspects of their life are avoided. I shall stipulate that situations of this sort involve noncontingent grounds for ambivalence, insofar as the actual bases for affirmation and regret are thus bound up with each other.

5.3. THE BOURGEOIS PREDICAMENT

The cases of noncontingent ambivalence considered above involved valuable activities that are conditioned and constituted by regrettable behavior on the agent's part. But a similar structure can emerge in situations where the basis for regret is an impersonal condition that shapes the agent's life, rather than something the agent has done. This brings me to the bourgeois predicament.

It is noteworthy that many of the most significant sources of affirmation in our lives are attachments that of their nature presuppose a certain degree of material well-being. Meaningful work, for instance, is something that is generally available to people only under conditions of comparative affluence, under which they are freed from the banal rigors of bare subsistence. Meaningful work involves active and continuous engagement with problems that are important and challenging, under conditions that involve some measure of variety as well as some opportunities for initiative and self-determination. Those of us fortunate enough to work in good universities typically have jobs that satisfy these conditions in high measure, but of course there are lots of other possibilities as well, in contexts ranging from industry and public service to economic development and the arts. Many other sources of meaning in peoples' lives similarly presuppose freedom from material necessity; consider in this connection the passionate interests in literature, film, or opera that sustain many people. Even personal relationships exhibit this feature to some degree. Many of the most valuable forms of interpersonal attachment are built up out of the activities of an essentially leisured class, including shared participation in artistic or athletic pursuits, or simply the kind of conversation and banter that is possible only when one is not constantly struggling to figure out where one's next meal is going to come from.

I am not, to be clear, maintaining that a meaningful life is possible only under conditions of material well-being. A lot of the paradigm examples that come to mind when we think about valuable attachments in human life involve bourgeois activities such as the ones I have just mentioned, but it is surely possible for people who are struggling with life's basic necessities to form significant attachments of various kinds. Having said that, however, it is striking that for those of us who enjoy the material advantages of upper-middle-class life in a developed economy, the attachments that are in fact our most significant sources of meaning have a distinctly bourgeois character. Our rewarding professional and personal projects are those of people who have the kind of educational and cultural opportunities available only under conditions of general affluence. Even if we are not ourselves *especially* wealthy (measured by the income distribution in our society), we profit directly from the amenities that advanced economic activity makes available, if only through the accessible schools and universities and museums that affluent societies support and the other generous public goods they are able to provide. Our relationships and personal attachments, too, are structured around activities that presuppose significant material advantage. Even our family lives are deeply colored by the conditions of relative prosperity under which we live. Our ability to plan and manage our families—to decide for ourselves when to have children and how large our families should be—is conditioned significantly by material well-being and educational attainment. And of course the activities that organize our family relationships and give them their value are themselves largely the activities of a comparatively prosperous class. Think of the vacations, the outings to museums and historical sites, the opportunities for structured play, the music lessons and soccer games and educational challenges, the collective meals and conversations, that modern family life is largely organized around in the strata that most of us actually occupy.

We might summarize these truistic points by saying that the significant sources of affirmation for most of us are distinctively bourgeois attachments.[15] They are projects and relationships that could exist only under conditions of comparative material advantage, and that presuppose both the opportunities and the freedom from material necessity that such advantage makes possible. The next observation I want to make is that the material circumstances that in this way condition our bourgeois attachments are constitutive parts of larger social and historical patterns that are impersonally lamentable. The

---

15. To be clear, I am using the adjective "bourgeois" here and throughout in a general way, to refer to individuals who occupy a comparatively privileged position in the global distribution of resources, and to activities that can be engaged in only by those who are so situated. I do not wish to import into the discussion some of the other connotations sometimes attached to this expression (such as the idea that the bourgeoisie form a discrete social class whose interests are diametrically opposed to those of the proletariat, or the assumption that they are essentially philistine in their cultural outlook).

affluence that supports our educational and social opportunities, and that underwrites our whole way of life, coexists with circumstances of extreme deprivation in many parts of the contemporary world. In some epochs, and to varying degrees in virtually all developed economies, there are striking inequalities of wealth and power within the state, so that the advantages of affluence are not fully available to all of its members. This is, on most plausible conceptions, a serious injustice. Furthermore, even those developed societies that are comparatively egalitarian in their distribution of social advantage make resources available to their citizens that are unheard of in other parts of the contemporary world. According to data from the World Bank, there were around 2.5 billion people living in extreme poverty in 2004 (39.7 percent of the world's population),[16] and even the developing countries that have made progress in reducing the level of absolute poverty are far behind the standard of economic attainment that prevails in the more developed parts of the world. Whether these global disparities of material advantage should be considered matters of injustice, strictly speaking, is not a question I wish to enter into here.[17] But they are, it seems to me, indisputably regrettable. Things would be better, the world would be a better place, if material resources could be redeployed in a way that would eliminate absolute poverty and dramatically improve the life prospects of those in the contemporary world who are currently least advantaged.[18]

16. See Thomas Pogge, *World Poverty and Human Rights: Cosmopolitan Responsibilities and Reforms*, 2nd ed. (Cambridge, U.K.: Polity, 2008), p. 2.

17. This question is under dispute in the debate between more and less cosmopolitan conceptions of liberalism as it applies to questions of international justice. Some important contributions to this debate include John Rawls, *The Law of Peoples* (Cambridge, Mass.: Harvard University Press, 1999); Charles Beitz, *Political Theory and International Relations*, rev. ed. (Princeton, N.J.: Princeton University Press, 1999); and Thomas Pogge, *Realizing Rawls* (Ithaca, N.Y.: Cornell University Press, 1989).

18. This is true, it seems to me, regardless of whether one assumes that distributive equality is intrinsically valuable or holds instead (for instance) that people should have a level of resources sufficient to meet their needs and to enable them to participate in social relations on a basis of equality.

There is a historical dimension to this point as well. Not only are the material conditions that sustain our valuable ways of life connected to contemporary patterns of distribution that are objectively problematic. They essentially involve institutions and practices that are connected through their histories with massive inequities and injustices in the past. It is very hard to believe that those of us who live in affluent Western societies, for instance, do not derive meaning and significance from activities that would not have been possible in their contemporary form without lamentable historical developments of various kinds, including the emergence of corrupt hierarchies of power and wealth, colonial exploitation, and the oppression of the weak and the vulnerable. The institutions and practices that sustain us today have a particular history, one that connects them through relations of causal dependence to social conditions that were objectionable in the recent and more distant past.

If this is correct, however, it has significant implications for our attitudes toward our own lives. For most of those who make up the audience of this book, the things that provide a basis for affirming our lives are in the nature of bourgeois attachments. They are projects and relationships that are possible only under conditions of significant material advantage. Yet the broader distribution of resources that makes these material advantages possible is impersonally regrettable, as are the historical events and circumstances that conditioned the emergence of the contemporary bourgeois world. We have good reason to wish that things were otherwise with respect to the distribution of material resources and opportunities—both within developed societies and across the world as a whole; both at the present historical moment and in the past. But the satisfaction of these preferences would undermine the basis we have for affirming our lives as we have actually lived them. The result is a situation similar to the one that was diagnosed in the preceding section, in which we have noncontingent grounds for ambivalence about our lives.[19]

To make this more concrete, let's consider realistically the professional activities that many (if not most) readers of this book are actively engaged in, and that provide a significant source of meaning in the lives that we actually lead. These activities revolve around teaching and research in philosophy, conducted in expensive institutions that are selective in the students they admit and that invest significant resources to support scholarship at a reasonably high level. I shall assume that these are worthwhile activities to be involved in, and that a life of active engagement with philosophical questions in this kind of context is one that is on that account worthy of affirmation from the agent's point of view. At the same time, it is striking that the activities at issue are extremely resource-intensive; they are characteristically bourgeois activities, and this makes our involvement in them vulnerable to the line of argument I have been sketching in abstract terms.

There are three connected aspects of the problem. The first of these is that the institutions that sustain contemporary philosophical research have a distinctive history. They are institutions that emerged in earlier centuries under social conditions that involved dramatic forms of oppression and deprivation, and their development and growth were decisively influenced by these objectionable conditions. Universities were, in the earlier phases of their history, flagrantly

---

19. One is reminded in this connection of the famous aphorism of Theodor Adorno "Es gibt kein richtiges Leben im falschen" ("Wrong life cannot be lived rightly", from his *Minima Moralia: Reflexionen aus dem beschädigten Leben* (Frankfurt am Main: Suhrkamp Verlag, 2008), p. 58 (sec. 18); English translation by E. F. N. Jephcott, *Minima Moralia: Reflections from Damaged Life* (London: Verso, 1974), p. 39. In this connection, a life lived rightly would be one that warrants unconditional affirmation in the sense characterized in this book. And the wrong life would involve conditions that are both impersonally objectionable, such as nobody has reason to affirm, and also implicated in the attachments that give our lives meaning. (The German original, unlike Jephcott's translation, carries the suggestion that it is impossible to live rightly in the context of wrong life, a suggestion that is appropriate to the bourgeois predicament as I am developing it.)

elitist institutions that were closed to most members of the broader societies in which they were located, and that profited from their functional role in perpetuating prevailing social hierarchies. Consider in this connection the munificent endowments and bequests that many private and even public universities have received over the decades and centuries, and that have contributed crucially to their ability to sustain outstanding research in the arts and sciences today. Presumably it would have been possible for scholarly and educational associations of some kind to develop under conditions that were less unjust and oppressive, and even under the conditions that actually obtained in the societies in which they emerged, they might have assumed forms that were less extensively interwoven into the existing patterns of injustice that prevailed. But for better or worse, the research universities that actually sustain philosophical activity today have a history that is questionable at best, and they would not be able to support valuable scholarship in the ways they do if they had not been connected to practices of social hierarchy and exclusion in the past.[20] Our affirmation of the activities that give our own lives meaning thus commits us, via the institutions that support those activities, to affirming historical conditions that we have powerful reasons to wish had been otherwise.

There is a second, contemporary dimension to the problem, which has to do with the continued connections that link the institutions in which we work to the injustice and deprivation that prevails in the world today. The universities that support philosophical research are made possible by educational policies that invest far more in the training of the most advantaged members of our societies than is invested in the education of those who are less well off. This is arguably the opposite of the pattern that would prevail under a more

20. For a detailed study of one small aspect of this history in the United States, see Jerome Karabel, *The Chosen: The Hidden History of Admission and Exclusion at Harvard, Yale, and Princeton* (Boston: Houghton Mifflin, 2005).

just set of educational policies.[21] The practices that enable high-level research and teaching in the liberal arts appear all the more questionable when we consider the scale of absolute and relative poverty in the modern world. Surely better use could be made of the resources that sustain our philosophical activities and that gave us the kind of background and training that prepared us to participate in them. Seen in the context of the massive suffering and want afflicting so many people across the globe, university research programs in a subject like philosophy are a luxury that it is very difficult to justify; indeed, their existence appears to be a kind of absurdity. In light of these considerations, it seems very plausible to think that we have strong reason to regret the contemporary conditions that make possible one of the activities that most significantly contribute to the meaning of our lives as we actually live them.

But are modern institutions of higher education really so extensively dependent on the objectionable social conditions that I have been calling attention to in this section? Most of the abject misery to which the destitute in the world are currently subject could arguably be alleviated with comparatively modest contributions to development and medical relief on the part of people in the more developed countries.[22] Presumably contributions at this level are compatible with the continued existence and even flourishing of the research universities that sustain contemporary philosophical activity. But what is seriously objectionable about the social conditions that prevail in the contemporary world is not merely the amount of sheer misery that people are subjected to; it extends to things that would

21. See John Rawls, *A Theory of Justice* (Cambridge, Mass.: Belknap Press of Harvard University Press, 1971), p. 101.
22. See Pogge, *World Poverty and Human Rights*, pp. 2–3, where it is pointed out that a shift of a mere seventieth of current consumption expenditures in the affluent economies would provide the $300 billion in additional annual consumption that the global poor require to escape from severe poverty.

persist even if severe poverty could be eradicated across the globe. These include lack of access (on a vast scale) to such basic goods as health; an education, suited to one's abilities, that enables one to participate in the cultural life of one's community; meaningful work; opportunities for leisure and play; and the conditions for a dignified old age. The persistence of these problems in a world that makes unimaginable luxuries available to a small segment of its population would be something that we would have strong reason to lament, even if we could eliminate the most acute poverty, malnutrition, and disease that the destitute suffer from today. And it is doubtful that contemporary research universities as we know them would survive if we made a serious effort to address these issues on a global scale.

In saying this, I don't mean to deny that cultural goods, including philosophical and other kinds of scholarship, might find a place in a just global society.[23] Nor do I wish to imply that the institutions that support academic teaching and research are the most egregious contributors to the social ills that afflict much of the world's population in the contemporary world. We can, perhaps, barely imagine a transformation of social conditions that would ameliorate those ills while preserving the institutions and practices that sustain philosophical research in something close to their current form. But while a transformation of this kind is conceivable, it is not, I believe, socially or historically realistic. The institutions that currently sustain scholarship at the highest levels are too extensively embedded in the massive contemporary inequalities to make it plausible to suppose that they could continue to exist in anything like their current incarnation under a more just set of social arrangements. Modern universities serve as gateways to power and influence for the students who pass through their classrooms and lecture halls, and they function in the

---

23. A helpful discussion of this question is Véronique Munoz-Dardé, "In the Face of Austerity: The Puzzle of Museums and Universities," *Journal of Political Philosophy*, forthcoming.

ways they do in part because they continue to play this role in perpetuating political and economic hierarchies. To take the most obvious point, the level of funding that they receive—through student tuition, government provision, philanthropic support, etc.—is crucially connected to their role in sustaining objectionable social inequalities. Given this fact, I think it fair to say that we have no realistic idea what forms academic research might assume under the vastly different social conditions that I have been imagining.[24]

There are, to be sure, significant differences between institutions of higher education in the contemporary world. The United States, to take just one example, has a vastly diverse and pluralistic system of tertiary education. Its public institutions include accessible establishments that focus on professional skill acquisition, as well as research universities that are among the most selective and prestigious in the world, and many institutions that are somewhere between these extremes. There may be even more variety in the private sphere, where we find for-profit colleges that hardly offer an education worthy of the name, as well as the elite institutions of the Ivy League, which control vast fortunes, and which offer correspondingly lavish educational opportunities to the handful of students they are willing and able to cater to. The points I have been making about the dependence of philosophical research on objectionable social conditions will apply with different levels of force to the different institutions of higher education within this diverse and multifaceted system. My third and final observation, however, is that this dependence becomes virtually incontrovertible as we move up the hierarchy of academic

---

24. Our situation is in this respect similar to Gauguin's. Just as the artistic values he might have realized had he remained in Europe would almost certainly have been very different from the actual artistic values he achieved in the South Pacific, so too with us: the academic institutions that would realistically be possible in a more just and equitable social world are so different from our actual institutions that we can only assume that the philosophical activities we would have engaged in under those institutional arrangements would have been massively different as well.

prestige. The elite institutions of higher education in the most developed economies are connected through extremely tight bonds to the plutocratic forces that control the levers of wealth and power in the world today and that would simply not exist under a more just and equitable system of social arrangements. Those of us who are fortunate enough to work in such universities should acknowledge that our research and teaching activities are dependent, in fairly manifest ways, on social structures that we have good reason to regret.

Of course, elite universities produce huge quantities of research that has direct benefits for the larger human population, research that drives progress, for instance, in medicine and technology, and that contributes in countless ways to our cultural life. Many of the people who work in these institutions are sincerely concerned to address the egregious social and developmental problems that face people in the contemporary world and to maintain and enhance the access to their educational programs enjoyed by students from less privileged backgrounds. But the most prestigious institutions control tremendous resources, in ways that tie them inextricably to the unjust economic relations in which they are embedded. The result is that such institutions arguably serve to perpetuate injustice in the modern world as much as they contribute to improving the human condition. They are able to offer fantastic salaries and working conditions to their own tenured professors, something that is of course good for the direct beneficiaries of this largesse but that also contributes directly to objectionable inequalities within the larger ecosystem of higher education. (Witness the increasingly stratified academic hierarchy in the United States, featuring professorial stars on one extreme and poorly paid foot soldiers on the other, who do a lot of the grunt work of teaching undergraduate students in jobs that provide low pay and little job security.) They also function, in effect, as central cogs in the larger system whereby economic gains are siphoned off with relentless efficiency by a small sliver of the population within the developed countries. The shocking percentage of graduating seniors who have gone directly from Harvard, Princeton, and Yale to the socially toxic finance industry in the past decade or so speaks for itself.[25]

To this it will perhaps be objected that there are a lot of worse things we could be doing with our lives than writing and teaching in philosophy, even if we pursue these activities within the elite institutions I have just been referring to. These are hardly the most resource-intensive of the many professional occupations available to people in developed economies, and they seem comparatively harmless in their broader effects. We could have gone to work for arms manufacturers, for instance, or joined our former students in developing innovative arbitrage strategies for some predatory bank or hedge fund. These observations are true, but beside the point. Presumably many of the lives that are led under conditions of great affluence are not really worthy of affirmation at all, in the sense I have been discussing in this chapter, because the activities that they revolve around are fundamentally corrupt or otherwise without merit. My working assumption has been that there is a plurality of personal and professional values that can be realized in human lives, and that these values exhibit a degree of autonomy from each other. It doesn't follow from this assumption, however, that all projects that people are attracted to in the modern world are genuine sources of meaning. Indeed, there is probably a dynamic in modern economies that tempts us to devote more time than we should to undertakings that are intrinsically empty and morally questionable.[26] We are encouraged to participate

25. See Catherine Rampell, "Out of Harvard, and into Finance," *Economix* (blog), *New York Times*, December 21, 2011: http://economix.blogs.nytimes.com/2011/12/21/out-of-harvard-and-into-finance/.
26. I insisted in the preceding section that activities can be intrinsically valuable even if they are conducted in a way that is subject to important moral objections; the examples were cases of artistic and scientific activity. It is compatible with this point that there might be other cases in which an activity is without any intrinsic value at all on account of the immoral character of its most fundamental constitutive aims. The contemporary finance industry seems a fertile source of examples that might fit this description.

in the rat race, to engage in pointless and environmentally catastrophic levels of consumption, to acquire bigger and flashier gadgets and baubles as a way of distracting ourselves from the inherent boredom of our lives. That is perhaps a kind of bourgeois predicament, but it is not the predicament that is my subject in this chapter.

My view is that concentrated affluence, in addition to its many deleterious effects, also makes possible an array of activities that are of undoubted intrinsic value. It is the material substructure that supports the cultural undertakings that we hold in especially high esteem, including institutions that enable outstanding achievements in science, scholarship, and the arts. It also makes available to many people opportunities to support themselves through work that is interesting and honorable, in lives that are also rich in the personal relationships and other activities they involve. These are the kinds of attachments that provide many of us with the most convincing basis for an affirmative attitude toward the lives that we actually lead. The predicament that is my concern derives from the fact that the material and historical circumstances that condition and make possible these genuine bases of affirmation are themselves circumstances that we have good reason to regret impersonally. Furthermore, the fact that our bourgeois sources of affirmation are in this way conditioned by lamentable circumstances does not deprive them of their intrinsic value. We have good reason to be glad that the world contains such things as opera and philosophy and museums of art, even if those things have historical and material presuppositions that are objectively regrettable. When our participation in such activities gives meaning to the lives that we ourselves have led, our attachment to life will involve our affirmation of those projects. And this in turn, via the affirmation dynamic, will commit us to affirming unconditionally the objectionable conditions that make the projects possible in the first place. This is the bourgeois predicament.

I said above that in a situation of this kind, agents have noncontingent grounds for ambivalence about how they have lived their lives. The bourgeois predicament in this respect resembles the situations of Gauguin and of the driven scientists who were discussed in the preceding section. The main difference from those earlier cases consists in the fact that the bases of regret are here provided by the impersonal circumstances of our existence (in both the present and the past), rather than by the comportment of the agents who look back on their own lives in reflection.[27] The idea is that there are lamentable impersonal conditions that are essential causal conditions of the activities in which our valuable projects consist. We would not have been able to launch ourselves on our valuable projects and relationships in the first place, nor would be able to sustain our commitment to them over time, in the absence of those conditions. The attachments that confer meaning on our lives would thus not be possible in a world in which resources were distributed more equitably—either today or in the past—and this constitutes a noncontingent link between the sources of meaning in our lives and the impersonal material conditions that we all have good reason to regret. In virtue of this link, we become *implicated* in the objectionable impersonal structures that we inhabit, insofar as the sources of meaning in our lives are activities that would not be possible in the absence of those structures.

One response to this line of thought would be that it is a misnomer to refer to it as a specifically "bourgeois" predicament. There are lots of ways in which people might similarly be implicated in objectionable impersonal conditions without their having bourgeois projects and

---

27. Because of this difference, the affirmative attitude that we are committed to in this case differs interestingly from the corresponding attitude at issue in the case of Gauguin. As I noted in sec. 2.3 above, preferences about the past have a less straightforwardly agential character when they take as their object impersonal conditions rather than actual or potential actions on the part of the person who is the subject of those preferences.

relationships, in the narrowest sense of the term. An analogous predicament might have faced certain artists and aristocrats in the ancient world, for instance, before the emergence of the forms of economic organization that the adjective "bourgeois" strictly presupposes.[28] And as I shall come back to in the following chapter, there are still other ways in which our attachments can commit us to affirming objectionable social and historical conditions. But I think it nevertheless makes sense to single out the particular links that in fact connect many of us to objectionable impersonal conditions by speaking of the bourgeois predicament. One thing that is distinctive about these links is that they operate in the modern world via our involvement in activities that have a recognizably bourgeois character; there is a set of values that are capable lending meaning to an agent's life, but that also presuppose that the agent occupies a position of comparative material privilege, and my intention is to highlight this conspicuous feature of them by referring to the position they put us in as the bourgeois predicament. A further reason for singling out their bourgeois aspect is that its salience has epistemic significance, giving us excellent reasons for believing that we are committed through our attachments to affirming conditions that are impersonally objectionable. Precisely because the activities that provide a basis for affirming our lives have a conspicuously bourgeois character, we can grasp how our affirmation of them commits us to affirming impersonal conditions that there is good reason for everyone to lament. As we will see in chapter 6, this epistemic dimension is missing in many of the other situations in which we are similarly committed via our attachments to affirming the impersonally objectionable.

A second response to my argument might question how widespread the specifically bourgeois predicament really is. I have taken as

---

28. These agents would face a situation that is identical in all but name with the bourgeois predicament that is my concern.

my focal example a case that involves fairly expensive professional activities. But, it might be argued, this example is not representative of the attachments that give meaning to our lives. There are plenty of valuable projects in bourgeois societies that are not intrinsically resource-intensive at all—think of the person who paints or sings or participates in a soccer league as a hobby, and who is passionately devoted to these pursuits. Furthermore, the personal and family relationships that for many of us are the most important sources of meaning might appear to escape the predicament altogether. Friendship, for instance, does not by its nature require an elaborate institutional infrastructure; it might therefore seem that our participation in this practice does not implicate us in the lamentable patterns of unequal distribution that are directly presupposed by such activities as scientific scholarship and opera. The same might be said for the relationships between close family members.

It is not my intention to maintain that all of the activities that sustain us in life have an essentially bourgeois character. For my purposes it is enough if many of the familiar attachments that provide a basis for meaning and affirmation in our lives rest on and require the affluent material conditions I have been discussing. That will suffice to get us caught up in the bourgeois predicament. Having said that, however, I would add that the problem seems to me to extend to a much wider range of activities than the objection just canvassed acknowledges. Amateur practices such as painting and music and organized sports, for instance, presuppose the kind of leisure that is typically available only under conditions of general prosperity, where people are not consumed by the mundane task of satisfying their basic material needs. Moreover, they derive at least some of their significance for us from being embedded in social structures that also support much more resource-intensive forms of professional practice. It is important to the amateur singer or painter or football player, for instance, to be engaged in the same activities that are conducted at a high level by the leading practitioners of these disciplines; this is part of what lends the amateur activities their value and significance. As for relationships, as I noted earlier, it is a striking fact that friendships and family attachments in developed societies are largely organized around activities that are possible only for the members of a comparatively affluent middle class. These are the activities that help to constitute the relationships, to a considerable degree, and to that extent the relationships themselves take on a bourgeois character.[29] They are essentially the relationships of people who live under conditions of material privilege, and they therefore presuppose those conditions.[30]

The thesis at issue, it should be stressed, is not that the affluent burgers who are my subject would not have lived meaningful lives if

29. There are two points to make in this connection. One is that relationships have an essentially historical dimension. They are constituted in part by interactions between two individuals at particular times and places, involving shared activities of one kind or another. If this is right, however, then there is a sense in which my actual friendship with you would not have existed in a world in which the conditions were absent that made our joint activities as friends possible. I could have entered into a friendship with you under those conditions, but it would by hypothesis have been a different personal relationship. Second, what is valuable about the relationship, as something that contributes a basis for affirming my life, is in part a function of the value of the activities that constitute the relationship in the first place. So if those activities would not have been possible in a world that lacks the lamentable inequalities we have been discussing, then the actual basis my relationships provide for affirming the life I have led would be lacking in that world. It is consistent with these points to acknowledge, however, that once a valuable personal relationship is in place, it may evolve going forward in ways that change its nature, so that its constitutive activities come to take on a different character. This is a point that I shall return to in sec. 5.4 below.

30. One might respond that the value that is at issue in the case of relationships is the value of the persons who are involved in the relationship, and that this value is neither causally nor otherwise contingent on the material conditions that happen to obtain in the larger world. The grain of truth in this reply is that each person possesses a kind of value that could aptly be described as unconditional; this is the value that makes the person a bearer of moral claims, someone who is worthy of being treated with respect and consideration. These essentially moral values, however, are not the values that ground the personal significance of attachments. Friendship provides a basis for affirming my life, and contributes to its meaning, insofar as it is a valuable *relationship* between two individuals, not insofar as it is a relationship between morally valuable *individuals*. The question, then, is whether and to what extent the things that make the relationship valuable would be able to persist under radically different material conditions from the ones that the bourgeois actually inhabit.

they hadn't been borne to the conditions of comparative material advantage that they in fact inhabit. There are in fact two counterfactual scenarios in which the basis for regret about my actual life might not have been present. I might have lived in a world in which material advantages and life opportunities were much more equitably distributed across the entire global population, so that everyone has access to the basic amenities of life. Or I might have lived in a world that is distributionally much like the actual world, but occupied a position in that world of deprivation rather than privilege. Under both scenarios, it seems plausible to assume that I might have lived a life that is worthy of retrospective affirmation. If I had grown up in moderate poverty, for instance, I could still have had friendships and family bonds with the kind of richness and texture that provide a basis for affirmation. The same of course goes for a fundamentally egalitarian world, which might even have presented opportunities for me to engage in valuable intellectual pursuits of some kind or other— philosophical reflection, after all, is not an activity that strictly requires an institutional context of the sort that elite modern research universities provide.

But these are not the attachments that provide a basis for affirming my life as I am actually leading it now. The philosophical activities I might have engaged in under the counterfactual circumstances just described are not at all the same as the professionalized teaching and research that my life is currently devoted to, undertakings that can take place only within an elaborate and costly institutional framework. For reasons already canvassed, they are therefore not so much as available to provide a basis for retrospective affirmation as I look back in reflection on the life I have actually lived. The bourgeois predicament stems from the role of objectionable historical and material conditions in making possible the attachments that, as a matter of fact, fill out our lives and render them worthy of retrospective affirmation. The very things that give us reason to be glad that we have lived are conditioned by circumstances that we can only wish had been otherwise. That there might have been different bases for affirmation in our lives if those material circumstances had been different is not to the point.

A third and still different response to the argument would maintain that I have misdiagnosed the source of ambivalence in the cases I have been concerned to analyze. My suggestion is that the predicament stems from the fact that the bourgeois projects that give many of us reason to affirm the lives we lead also implicate us in impersonal economic and historical structures that we have powerful reasons to regret. But perhaps the basis for regretting the bourgeois life lies not in the impersonal conditions of inequality we are borne into but in the personal choices we have made about how to conduct ourselves under those conditions. Specifically, it might be argued that it lies in our failure to fulfill our moral obligation to contribute what we can to alleviating the suffering and misery of people who live under much less privileged conditions than we do. The bourgeois life, on this view, is also a life that is morally objectionable, and the moral objection to the way that life is led is what really provides the agent with a basis for retrospective regret about it.[31]

The moralistic interpretation of the bourgeois predicament should be rejected, however. In saying this, I do not of course mean to deny that we have moral obligations of mutual aid to assist people who are in dire straits when we are in a position to do so at little cost to ourselves. These are important moral responsibilities, and people who fail to live up to them thereby acquire a significant basis for regret about the way they have conducted their lives. But it is not essential to the bourgeois predicament, as I understand it, that those

---

31. This interpretation would bring the cases involving bourgeois activities into alignment with the cases discussed earlier involving personal immorality that is a causal or constitutive condition of the things that make an agent's life worthy of affirmation.

who are subject to it should have displayed this kind of moral failure. The predicament derives its force from the nature of the bourgeois attachments that make our lives worthy of affirmation, not from the assumption that we are necessarily immoral in they way we have pursued those attachments.

This assertion requires some qualification. It is a famously vexed question what exactly the moral duty of mutual aid requires of those who are in a comparatively privileged position in the global distribution of world resources. A plausible assumption, I believe, is that any reasonable account of this obligation should have the consequence that agents who comply with it are still able to have meaningful lives, including the kinds of bourgeois attachments that for many of us are in fact our primary sources of affirmation.[32] If this assumption is correct, then it will be possible to pursue bourgeois projects in ways that are not necessarily morally objectionable, even if many of us in fact fail to do all that we should to alleviate the plight of those much less fortunate than ourselves. My point is that there would still be grounds for retrospective ambivalence under these conditions, in virtue of the fact that the bourgeois projects that make our lives worthy of affirmation are premised on historical and material conditions that there is strong impersonal reason to regret. There presumably are moral failures of benevolence and mutual aid that most of us are guilty of, to one degree or another, and that give us some reason for regret about our lives when we look back on them. But these failures are only contingently connected to the real sources of meaning in our lives, whereas the bourgeois predicament that is my concern involves a basis for regret that is noncontingently linked to the things we actually live for.

32. See, e.g., Garrett Cullity, *The Moral Demands of Affluence* (Oxford: Clarendon, 2004); also Liam B. Murphy, *Moral Demands in Nonideal Theory* (Oxford: Oxford University Press, 2000).

Some philosophers will presumably find this assumption about the obligation of mutual assistance too complacent. It could be argued, for instance, that there is in fact a moral complaint that could be lodged against any project or activity that involves bourgeois patterns of consumption, so long as there exist acute human needs somewhere in the world that those resources could have been used to address.[33] A position of this kind would have the consequence that there is after all a moral objection to a life that is organized around basically bourgeois attachments, as I assume the lives of most of us to be. For the record, I do not find this interpretation of the duty of mutual aid to be especially plausible (and I shall come back to it in the following section, offering a partial diagnosis of its appeal). Even if I am wrong about this, however, the result would not be to undermine the argument of this chapter. It would turn out, on this interpretation of our responsibilities, that those of us with bourgeois projects will necessarily have comported ourselves in ways that give us moral grounds for remorse. But it would remain the case that we *also* have reason to regret the impersonal historical and material conditions that make those projects possible in the first place. The presence of impersonal grounds for regret of this kind just is the bourgeois predicament, as I have described it; the predicament would therefore persist, even on the most rigorous interpretation of the moral requirement of mutual assistance.

Of course, if an interpretation of that kind is correct, it would have been possible for those of us who are subject to the predicament to have avoided it, by conducting our lives from the start in strict compliance with moral demands. But that in turn would have precluded the projects that give meaning to our lives as we have actually

---

33. A locus classicus for this position is Peter Singer, "Famine, Affluence, and Morality," *Philosophy & Public Affairs* 1 (1972), pp. 229–43. See also Shelly Kagan, *The Limits of Morality* (Oxford: Clarendon, 1989), and Peter Unger, *Living High and Letting Die: Our Illusion of Innocence* (New York: Oxford University Press, 1996).

led them, and that provide us with concrete grounds for affirming those lives. Under these assumptions, we would have personal grounds for remorse about the sources of meaning in our lives, as well as impersonal reasons for regretting their historical and contemporary conditions. This complicates somewhat the bourgeois predicament, but it does not fundamentally alter its basic structure.

5.4. REDEMPTION, WITHDRAWAL, DENIAL

The argument of this chapter rests on a fairly simple truth about the nature of value. The world is complex and interconnected, and many of the things that we have reason to value are linked to other things that we have reason to deplore or to condemn. A much-discussed example of the general phenomenon is the so-called problem of dirty hands, involving cases of political action whose outcomes we can only welcome and celebrate, even though they were made possible by means that are undeniably lamentable (the ruthlessness of politicians working for a good cause, say, or their willingness to trample on the legitimate claims of individuals in order to get the job done). Much of the debate about these cases approaches them from the point of view of agency, asking whether it can ever be permissible or required for people acting in a political capacity to violate some of the most fundamental moral requirements, such as those that prohibit torture or the targeted killing of the innocent.[34] However we answer these questions, there is a different set of issues that comes into focus when we reflect on them from the perspective of a third party. In particular, we then encounter structures of retrospective attitude that parallel those

---

34. See, for example, Michael Walzer, "Political Action: The Problem of Dirty Hands," *Philosophy & Public Affairs* 2 (1973), pp. 160–80, and Bernard Williams, "Politics and Moral Character," as reprinted in his *Moral Luck*, pp. 54–70.

that have been my concern in the present chapter, such as an inability to experience fundamental regret about moral atrocities when they were necessary to achieve supremely valuable ends (such as the prevention of oppression on a massive scale). A still different set of examples involves large-scale historical processes of various kinds. Bernard Williams was wont to remark on the ironic fact that the achievement of liberal values involved and probably required social processes that had a decidedly nonliberal character, involving terror, oppression, and severe injustice.[35] Someone who celebrates those values will therefore find it challenging to regret unconditionally the lamentable conditions that enabled them. Or we might think of artistic and cultural triumphs that were made possible by the existence of various forms of slavery in ancient Greece.[36]

The deep ambivalence that seems natural when contemplating these kinds of developments and practices is also deeply reasonable; indeed, it is the only realistic response that is available to us once we acknowledge the profound interpenetration of value and disvalue in the world as we find it. The bourgeois predicament that I have been at pains to lay out can be thought of as a special case of this more

35. See, for example, Bernard Williams, "Reply to Korsgaard," in Korsgaard, *The Sources of Normativity*, pp. 210–18, at p. 217, and Bernard Williams, "Moral Luck: A Postscript," as reprinted in Bernard Williams, *Making Sense of Humanity and Other Philosophical Papers, 1982–1993* (Cambridge, U.K.: Cambridge University Press, 1995), pp. 241–47, at p. 245; see also Bernard Williams, "Human Rights and Relativism," in his *In the Beginning Was the Deed: Realism and Moralism in Political Argument*, ed. Geoffrey Hawthorn (Princeton, N.J.: Princeton University Press, 2005), pp. 62–74.

36. Compare Friedrich Engels, *Anti-Dühring*, as excerpted in Bruce B. Lawrence and Aisha Karim, eds., *On Violence: A Reader* (Durham: Duke University Press, 2007), pp. 39–61, at p. 58:
    It was slavery that first made possible the division of labour between agriculture and industry on a larger scale, and thereby also Hellenism, the flowering of the ancient world. Without slavery, no Greek state, no Greek art and science; without slavery, no Roman Empire. But without the basis laid by Hellenism and the Roman Empire, also no modern Europe. We should never forget that our whole economic, political and intellectual development presupposes a state of things in which slavery was as necessary as it was universally recognised. In this sense we are entitled to say: without the slavery of antiquity no modern socialism.

general phenomenon. But there is something distinctively disturbing about the predicament I have described, which can be traced to the role of attachments in defining it. The predicament arises for agents when they contemplate the way they have lived, reflecting on the projects and relationships that give their lives meaning and the conditions for the realization of those projects. The immediate object of affirmation in this case is the agent's own existence, and this is not something that the agent can take a complacent or resigned attitude toward. As I mentioned above, we cling to our lives, assuming toward them a default stance of unconditional affirmation, an attitude that extends to the things in our lives that make them worthy of affirmation and to their conditions in turn. This stance of unconditional affirmation precludes the kind of deep ambivalence that is open to us to adopt when reflecting on other valuable features of our world.[37] That our attachments might implicate us in objectionable impersonal structures in ways that undermine the normative basis of unconditional affirmation is for this reason a peculiarly unnerving prospect to contemplate. At issue is the question of our relation to ourselves

---

37. Commenting on Nietzsche's question of whether one can will the eternal recurrence of the same, Bernard Williams writes: "[O]ne has to recall that in facing the question one is supposed to have a real and live consciousness of everything that has led to this moment, in particular to what we value. We would have to think in vivid detail, if we could, of every dreadful happening that has been necessary to create Venice, or Newton's science, or whatever one thinks best of in our morality"; see Bernard Williams, "Introduction to *The Gay Science*," as reprinted in his *The Sense of the Past: Essays in the History of Philosophy*, ed. Myles Burnyeat (Princeton, N.J.: Princeton University Press, 2006), pp. 311–24, at p. 319. It is not clear, however, that valuing achievements of this kind commits us in any way to affirming or willing the necessary conditions for their existence; there is psychological space, in other words, for deep ambivalence when we reflect on the relationships to which Williams is calling attention here. The special problem of this chapter arises only when attachments enter the picture, in particular when the object one values is the basis for one's affirmative attitude toward one's own life, for unconditional affirmation, unlike mere valuing, commits one to affirming the necessary conditions of the immediate object of affirmation. (It is of course consistent with this remark that for some people, engagement with the glories of Venice might be among the life projects that give their lives such meaning as they have.) I return to Nietzsche's idea of eternal recurrence in chapter 6.

and the lives we have led, and the possibility that our best efforts will leave us only with grounds for retrospective ambivalence and estrangement.

The bourgeois predicament is thus a matter of existential significance for the agents affected by it. It mobilizes anxieties about our deepest aspirations for our lives, forcing us to face up to the distressing fact that those aspirations might not be achievable in the world as it is. It is tempting to suppose that there must be some way of escaping from the predicament as I have laid it out. I shall consider three possible avenues of escape, arguing that none of them can possibly succeed; this should serve to give us a deeper appreciation for the severity of the problem that we confront.

Redemption. The bourgeois predicament stems from our implication, through the activities that give meaning to our lives, in social structures that are impersonally objectionable or unjust. If this is the problem, however, the solution might seem to lie in selecting the right activities to engage in. Suppose we devote ourselves with single-minded focus to the project of alleviating or ameliorating the impersonal conditions of inequality and deprivation that prevail in the contemporary world. We might thereby reasonably hope to achieve some measure of redemption, escaping our implication in lamentable social structures by the concentrated effort to redress them.

In the previous section I touched on the vexed question of the interpretation of our moral duties of assistance or mutual aid toward those who are much worse off than we are. There are strong pressures within moral thought that move us toward the conclusion that these duties are much more demanding than many of us ordinarily take them to be. Claims that are grounded in circumstances of severe deprivation and suffering are extremely compelling, and it is hard to see what might be set against them within moral thought to justify the conclusion that it is permissible for us to allow those claims to go unmet when it is in our power to address them. Of course we each have lives of our own to lead, lives that are given texture and content by the projects and relationships that fill them out. But if we take seriously the idea that everyone's interests count equally in moral reflection, it can seem self-indulgent or worse to suppose that our projects and relationships protect us against claims of others that are grounded in basic human necessities.

This is a difficult issue for moral theory, one that I do not propose to go into here. What I want to do, instead, is to call attention to a distinct consideration that can motivate the conclusion that we should devote ourselves personally to projects of emergency assistance and social justice. This consideration has its source in the bourgeois predicament I have been discussing in the present chapter. Thus, suppose for the sake of argument that it is morally permissible, once we have made some substantial personal contribution to assisting the impoverished and the suffering, to go about our own lives, engaging in activities that advance our individual projects and relationships. Insofar as those projects provide our basis for affirming our lives, we are likely to find that we remain entangled in the bourgeois predicament under these circumstances. Our reasons for regretting the impersonal conditions that enable our projects are pragmatically at odds with the grounds we have for affirming the lives that we have actually led. Under these circumstances, the aspiration to live a life that is worthy of unconditional affirmation can generate pressure to redefine the projects that give meaning to our lives. In particular, we can feel that it is imperative that we dedicate ourselves personally to alleviating the impersonally regrettable conditions that characterize the world in which we live. This imperative, however, does not have its source in a sense of moral inadequacy but in our personal hopes about our own lives. Its origin is a conception not of what we owe specifically to others but of our relation to ourselves, involving our aspiration to find a way of living that is worthy of unconditional affirmation.

G. A. Cohen confronted political philosophy (and political philosophers) with the excellent question "If you're an egalitarian, how come you're so rich?"[38] His argument is that anyone who is seriously committed to equality as a political and moral value cannot ultimately justify a life of comparative affluence and privilege. He meant, I believe, that there is no moral or political justification for the effective betrayal of one's ideals through the personal conduct of one's own life. But his argument derives at least some of its force from its implicit reliance on the existential dialectic I have been sketching. There is a sense of anxiety, which Cohen effectively taps into, that one's own life is inevitably compromised or undermined somehow if it is conducted in ways that presuppose the conditions of impersonal inequality that one officially deplores. In this situation, the only way out seems to be to turn one's political ideals into personal aspirations, dedicating oneself to the project of improving the conditions of those much worse off than oneself. This is the strategy of redemption, and as Cohen himself acknowledges, it has more in common with certain religious patterns of thought than with the requirements of conventional morality.

But the strategy is hopeless. In saying this, I do not of course mean to imply that the personal efforts we might make as individuals are necessarily pointless or ineffective. We cannot on our own solve the problems of injustice, poverty, and deprivation on a global scale. But we can make some small contribution toward addressing them, a contribution that makes a real difference to the lives of those affected by our efforts. Furthermore, dedicating ourselves to projects of this kind is unquestionably a valuable thing to do, and it can be one way of giving meaning to our own lives. Considered as a response to the bourgeois predicament, however, the strategy necessarily fails. Those

---

38. G. A. Cohen, *If You're an Egalitarian, How Come You're So Rich?* (Cambridge, Mass.: Harvard University Press, 2000).

who seek to escape from their implication in impersonally lamentable conditions by dedicating themselves to improving those conditions rely on the very thing that they are trying to escape. It is only those who stand in a privileged position in the distribution of resources who have the luxury of giving meaning to their lives through the project of helping to address the plight of the least advantaged members of our social world. The attempt to achieve personal redemption thus reenacts the very dialectic it is trying to overcome.

To this it may be replied that the strategy of redemption is not best understood as an attempt to escape from the bourgeois predicament altogether. It is, rather, an effort to compensate for its effects, placing something at the center of one's own life that can be set over against one's inevitable implication in larger social structures that are impersonally regrettable. But this reply concedes the only point I am trying to make in my discussion, which is that the predicament cannot be evaded through the strategy of reshaping one's personal projects in the light of it. Furthermore, it may be wondered whether the reply succeeds even on its own terms. If redemption is achieved by having something in one's life that can be set over against one's implication in the impersonally objectionable, why should this require of us that we dedicate ourselves specifically to alleviating the objectionable conditions themselves? It has been an assumption throughout my discussion that the ordinary agents who are caught up in the predicament *already* have something in their lives that can be set over against the impersonally lamentable structures that affect them. They have, in particular, attachments to individuals and to projects that are worthy of pursuit, where these things provide them with a basis for affirming the lives they have led. The idea that we achieve some special redemption by reshaping our projects in the image of the predicament rests on the assumption that doing so represents an avenue of escape. But that assumption is, for reasons I have advanced, simply implausible.

A different way to understand the strategy of redemption is in terms of the idea of implication. The challenge, it will be recalled, is presented by the fact that the projects that give our lives meaning are conditioned by social structures that we have on-balance reason to regret. This links us essentially to those structures, in a way that undermines the goal of a life that is worthy of unconditional affirmation. Those who dedicate themselves to combating the objectionable conditions to which they are in this way linked, however, might hope thereby to lessen their implication in the objectionable conditions that they inhabit. It isn't that they are trying to find something to set over against their implication in deplorable social conditions. Rather, they are setting *themselves* against those conditions, showing in the most dramatic way available that they do not approve of them. Nor is this oppositional stance of merely expressive significance. As I noted above, we should concede that those who fight global inequality and deprivation often bring about some genuine progress through their efforts, insofar as those efforts result in improvements in the material conditions of at least some of the individuals who are worst off in the world. The aspiration is to put some distance between oneself and the lamentable social conditions, so that the sources of meaning in one's life are not any longer bound up with them.

I concede that the strategy of redemption has something to be said for it on this way of understanding it. Implication is a multifaceted phenomenon, and one of its dimensions involves a person's attitudes. Complacency or even approval of a social condition puts one in a different relation to it from active opposition, and those who adopt the latter stance may succeed in distancing themselves from the conditions they are fighting to change, at least in one respect. But if implication in the objectionable is in this way ameliorated through the strategy of redemption, there is another respect in which it is actually exacerbated. Dedicating one's life to the project of combating inequality and deprivation has the perverse effect that one comes to define oneself primarily in terms of the lamentable conditions that one sets oneself against. It is not just that those conditions are causally necessary for the realization of the projects that give meaning to one's life, as in the generalized version of the bourgeois predicament. More specifically, the content of one's projects makes direct and essential reference to the regrettable conditions that are at issue.

This difference might be given expression in modal terms. With an ordinary valuable project, such as philosophical research and teaching, I have taken it to be the case that lamentable inequalities are causally necessary for the activities in which the projects consist. We would not, as a matter of social and historical fact, be able to engage in those activities in a world in which severe global inequalities were eliminated. But these inequalities are not conceptually necessary for the projects in question. We can imagine a world in which we and others give ourselves over to the kind of philosophical teaching and research we are actually engaged in, but in which the relevant global inequalities do not exist; it might for example be an (admittedly utopian) world in which everyone who is alive has access to the level of resources and opportunities that our philosophical projects actually require. By contrast, people whose defining project is that of combating global inequality and deprivation could not retain that source of meaning in a counterfactual situation in which those conditions had been altogether eliminated. The conditions are, for such people, not merely causally necessary for the realization of the things that make their lives worthy of affirmation but constitutively or conceptually necessary. This is what I meant in suggesting that devoting oneself to projects of this kind has the perverse effect of deepening one's implication in the lamentable structures that one opposes.

This observation, to be clear, is not meant in the spirit of criticism, moral or otherwise, of those who respond to injustice and poverty and suffering by dedicating themselves to the project of trying to alleviate such conditions. Those activities are immensely valuable, and we should admire people who are willing to give themselves self-lessly to such ends. Nor am I suggesting that this kind of heightened implication in the lamentable is in general a reason not to pursue activities that have this particular effect, in the perspective of agency. Someone with the appropriate talents and interests might be very well advised to pursue a career in international famine relief or as a social worker or a researcher combating AIDS. The fact that such professional activities presuppose the regrettable conditions that they aim to eliminate or improve does not in general tell against pursuing them.[39]

My point is restricted to activities of this kind when they are conceived in the spirit of the strategy of redemption. Considered as responses to the bourgeois predicament, there is a tragic dimension to the choice of such oppositional pursuits: the very attempt to achieve distance from deplorable social structures, along one dimension of connection, ends up deepening one's implication in them in a different dimension. One is reminded of those soldiers who display extraordinary heroism and cunning on the battlefield in the cause of a fundamentally just war and who later define themselves primarily in terms of their military achievements.[40] The value that their lives come to be organized around is one that couldn't exist in the absence of the very injustices they were fighting against, insofar as that value consists precisely in effective and heroic opposition to the injustices. People in this position have a genuine basis for retrospective affirmation of the lives they have actually led. But that basis connects them,

39. Remember that increased implication in the lamentable in this dimension goes together with diminished implication in the dimension of the agent's oppositional stance. Taking everything together, then, those who make it their life goal to fight injustice and oppression are no worse off with respect to the bourgeois predicament than are people with ordinary expensive projects.

40. Consider also the firefighters of sec. 2.4 above, on the assumption that the ameliorative values realized in their heroic rescue activities become the primary basis for their affirmative attitude toward their own lives.

not just causally but also constitutively, to conditions that are worthy of rejection and regret (indeed, to the very conditions that they so heroically opposed in their military youth). Insofar as implication in the lamentable is a threat or a problem, it would be better to move on with one's life, and find other sources of meaning in it that are not in the same way conceptually linked to the injustices one fought so hard to defeat.

Withdrawal. There is a different way that we might attempt to reshape our projects in response to the bourgeois predicament. Rather than dedicating ourselves to the goal of alleviating the regrettable conditions we are implicated in, we might attempt to escape the predicament through a strategy of withdrawal and retreat. We could, for instance, opt out of participating in contemporary consumer society, taking up a life of modest Thoreauvian self-sufficiency. The goal of these efforts would be to organize our lives around simple projects that do not rest on the structures of social inequality that generate the bourgeois predicament in the first place.

But this strategy, too, seems hopeless. For one thing, it is unrealistic to think that completely opting out is a genuine option for those of us who occupy positions of comparative privilege in the contemporary world.[41] We are social creatures, and our activities are essentially conditioned by the complex webs of convention, law, and practice that constitute the social realm. We might purchase a small plot of land somewhere, erect a modest wooden house on it, and proceed to scratch out an existence of contemplative subsistence in that setting. A life with these characteristics would perhaps involve a

---

41. Adorno makes this point in sec. 18 of his *Minima Moralia* (which ends with the well-known aphorism about the impossibility of living rightly under wrong conditions, cited in note 19 above). He suggests that the best contemporary life might be the private life of suspended commitment to the larger social world, but then observes (in effect) that this is an impossible ideal for us, illustrating his point with reflections on the complexity of our relations to the system of private property.

lower level of consumption than we would otherwise be engaged in. But it would be a fantasy to suppose that it would be a life that is completely decoupled from the objectionable patterns that prevail in the larger social world. I am reminded in this connection of the city in which I live, Berkeley, California, which is constantly and quixotically attempting to extricate itself from the many aspects of contemporary American political and economic life that its citizens find objectionable. Our city council will declare its opposition to unpalatable aspects of US foreign policy, for instance, or erect signs at the city borders stating that Berkeley is a "nuclear-free zone."[42] There is an expressive function that gestures of this kind can play, and in some circumstances this function is politically important. But considered as an effort to extricate the city from involvement in the policies and practices it deplores, the strategy is manifestly futile. The myth of liberation through retreat is a recurrent one in our culture, associated today with the assorted hippies and survivalists who occupy depopulated corners of the American countryside, but it doesn't provide a realistic template for avoiding the predicament I have been describing.

Against this, it could be pointed out that withdrawal is a matter of degree. Perhaps it is a mere fantasy to suppose that we might completely decouple ourselves from the broader social structures to which we object. But we can still make some progress along the path of withdrawal. We could give away (to a worthy cause) most of our possessions, and devote ourselves going forward to cultivating our garden, literally and figuratively, at a considerably reduced level of consumption and expense. There are real questions that many of us would confront about how exactly we would sustain ourselves if we were to opt out in this partial way. Assuming those questions could be

---

42. These local policies might also be interpreted as oppositional gestures, in the spirit of the strategy of redemption (though they are equally futile when understood in that way).

answered, however, the result might be to put us at some distance from the lamentable structures that originally generated the bourgeois predicament. Furthermore, there would still be room, within such a reduced life, for continued engagement in some of the activities that earlier gave our lives their meaning—for the activities of friendship, for instance, and for philosophical reflection and conversation. Once attachments of this kind have a foothold in one's life, it is possible to make adjustments that preserve their value while rendering them less dependent on objectionable social conditions than they may have been at first.

At this point, however, two different problems arise. First, the strategy of partial withdrawal shares with the strategy of redemption the feature that it reenacts the dialectic that it was meant to escape. It is a kind of luxury to have the option of giving oneself over to the simple life, something that itself presupposes that one occupies a position of comparative advantage in the global distribution of resources. By choosing this option, one therefore exemplifies the bourgeois predicament rather than escaping from it. The basic point here is that projects of modest consumption have a different character, depending on whether they are undertaken by someone who lacks expensive alternatives or instead by an agent who is attempting to scale back from a position of comparative affluence. As a response to the bourgeois predicament, the strategy of withdrawal is one that is engaged in by the privileged; it is a way of giving meaning to one's life that thus presupposes the regrettable conditions it is designed to retreat from.

The second and more basic problem stems from the partial character of the withdrawal that is at issue. So long as it is not a realistic option for the bourgeois to decouple themselves completely from the larger patterns of objectionable consumption and distribution, the strategy of withdrawal will not really represent an avenue of escape from the predicament they face. We can dedicate ourselves to the goal of reducing our level of expensive activity, with the result that our lives over time are increasingly filled with comparatively modest projects and pursuits. But even those activities will presuppose a position of comparative privilege in the global distributional order, so long as they are undertaken within the political and social context of a developed economy. Withdrawal is an intelligible response to the bourgeois predicament psychologically, but it is not a genuine solution.

Denial. A final set of responses to the problem I have described involves denial. By this I do not mean philosophical denial—the attempt, through argument, to refute the claims I have made about the nature and sources of the bourgeois predicament. I mean, rather, the refusal to face up to the predicament and the problems it involves. A response of this kind would not even purport to be a solution to it. But it is a common response, perhaps even the most prevalent amongst those who are affected by the predicament, and it deserves at least brief comment.

One form that denial can take is rationalization. The bourgeois predicament takes as its starting point the assumption that the attachments that give many of us the most important reasons to affirm our lives themselves presuppose conditions that are impersonally regrettable. In rationalization, we reject this important assumption, without being able to advance convincing reasons for doing so. We might, for instance, deny that our expensive projects really do presuppose a distribution of resources that leaves most of the world's population with greatly reduced capabilities and prospects. Everyone could have the same opportunities that we enjoy, the argument might go, if only they would apply themselves; so it isn't really true that our ability to affirm our lives rests on the availability to us of resources that aren't available to many others. A different and perhaps less manifestly implausible line of rationalization would concede that vast inequality is indeed a condition of our bourgeois projects but deny that this is a matter that is really worthy of regret. There is a virtual cottage industry of ideology production devoted to defending the conclusion that the epic inequalities that prevail within and between many contemporary societies do not involve any form of systematic injustice or preventable oppression. This conclusion, if correct, would go some way toward exonerating us from the charge that the actual sources of meaning in our lives depend on impersonal conditions that are genuinely lamentable.[43] My hypothesis is that the fact that it plays this functional role helps to explain the appeal of a position that is hard to take very seriously on the merits.

In *What We Owe to Each Other*, T. M. Scanlon cites the reactions of Americans to the profound transformations of their society in the 1960s and 1970s in support of his claim that it matters to us greatly whether we are able to justify ourselves to others. Americans experienced a sense of shock at the suggestion that their institutions were not uniquely fair and principled, and this led many of them to react by "vehemently denying that the charges of injustice at home and criminality abroad had any foundation."[44] This reaction, I would add, has only hardened in the decades to follow, becoming in recent years a virtually reflexive tendency on the part of some Americans to dismiss any suggestion that our institutions and practices might be in need of serious reform. I agree with Scanlon that this tendency to rationalization is a perverse reflection of the importance we attach to being able to justify ourselves to others. But its visceral character indicates that our relations to ourselves are also in play. Our sense of meaning and self-worth are threatened by the suggestion that the social institutions in which our activities are structured might be fundamentally unjust or objectionable; we react by rejecting such

---

43. The conclusion would go only some way toward this goal, because there would arguably still be impersonal social conditions that we have reason to lament, even if those conditions are not forms of injustice that, e.g., resulted from lapses of agency on anyone's part.

44. Scanlon, *What We Owe to Each Other*, p. 163.

suggestions, even when they are extremely plausible, with a fervor that would otherwise be difficult to make sense of.[45]

A different and perhaps even more common strategy of denial is simply to refuse to face the existential question that gives rise to the bourgeois predicament in the first place. This method of avoidance, as I called it in section 2.3, is one that is all too easy to put into practice. The predicament arises within a distinctive kind of retrospective reflection that it is possible for us to engage in. We step back and ask whether we are happy that we have lived, taking into account everything that has happened in our lives; we also ask whether there are impersonal conditions of our meaningful activities that we have compelling reason to regret on balance. These are strikingly abstract questions, however, which do not correspond to any genuine deliberative issue that we might be called on to resolve as we go through life. It is not as if we will at some point be confronted with a choice as to whether to have lived the lives we have actually led. At the time when we pose to ourselves the retrospective question, both our lives and the conditions of their meaning confront us as a matter of facticity, which it is no longer within our power to affect one way or another. Nor is anybody likely to call us to account for the conduct of our life as a whole, the way we are often called on to answer for specific things we have done within the lives we have led. The questions that generate the bourgeois predicament are thus decoupled from the specific contexts of deliberation and accountability that we confront as we

---

45. There are also more subtle possibilities of rationalization, which are opened up by the inherent difficulty of assessing counterfactual claims about the relation between global inequalities and the individuals' valuable projects and activities. People might maintain, for instance, that their *individual* pursuit of such projects as philosophy or opera or artistic production does not presuppose global inequalities, even if the larger communities to which they belong in virtue of these pursuits (and the institutions that sustain them) are made possible by the objectionable social conditions. But rationalizations of this kind often betray a lack of realism or imagination—an unwillingness, for instance, to face up to the fact that one wouldn't have been able to practice philosophy in the way one does if those communities and institutions hadn't existed.

move forward through life, and this practically invites us to deploy the method of avoidance. We simply refuse to engage in the distinctive form of reflection that would lead us to the uncomfortable conclusion that the sources of meaning in our lives have conditions that are impersonally regrettable.[46]

There are, of course, many people who do not have the luxury of grappling with existential questions about the meaning of the lives they have led, because they are too busy struggling to get on with things while they are alive. This brings out a further respect in which the predicament sketched in this chapter has a bourgeois aspect: it is a predicament that can be faced up to only by those who have the leisure of engaging in abstract reflection about the character of their lives. But this does not lessen the significance of the predicament; there are many important questions of value that can be addressed by people only if they are comparatively well-off, so that they do not have to devote all their energies to figuring out where their next meal is going to come from. Indeed, the ability to engage in reflection about such abstract questions is famously among the things that can contribute to the meaning of an affluent existence.

Even if we are in a position to face up to the retrospective question, however, there are more subtle possibilities for avoidance. I have assumed throughout this chapter that we entertain a specific aspiration for our lives, the aspiration to live in ways that warrant affirmation. But some might simply deny this, disavowing the concern about whether they have lived in a way that is worthy of being retrospectively affirmed. They might look back on their lives from time to

46. See Williams, "Introduction to *The Gay Science*," p. 319, on "forgetting" as a reaction to the problem posed by Nietzsche in *The Gay Science* (which as I discuss in the following chapter is continuous with the problem at issue here). Williams quotes the narrator's description of Tom and Daisy in F. Scott Fitzgerald's *The Great Gatsby* as an illustration of the attitude of forgetting, and the quotation has particular relevance to the specifically bourgeois predicament: they "retreated back into their money and their vast carelessness, or whatever it was that [kept] them together."

time and form attitudes of various kinds about episodes within those lives, or even their lives as a whole, but affect a lack of interest in the question of whether the attitudes they form are really warranted on balance. But a failure to take an interest in the question of retrospective justification does not deprive that question of its significance. There is a real difference between attitudes that are warranted by the normative considerations to which they respond and attitudes that are not so warranted; the latter ultimately don't make sense to us, even if we find that we cannot help adopting them. The bourgeois predicament brings out one particular way in which our attitudes toward our own lives fail to make sense, and it is an important aspect of our situation in the world that it saddles us with absurd attitudes of this kind. We can avert our eyes from the absurdity of our attitudes, but in doing so we will be failing to honor the deeper value of truthfulness, a value that calls on us to acknowledge uncomfortable facts about our lives, even when doing so is disconcerting.[47]

Humans are adept at avoiding such unpleasant truths. We compartmentalize, we erect elaborate mental barriers, and we find ways to distract ourselves from confronting things about ourselves that are difficult to come to terms with. These tendencies probably have some survival value for members of our species; certainly they make it easier than it would otherwise be to deal with the practical issues that need to be resolved as we move forward in life. But the method of avoidance does not provide a solution to the bourgeois predicament. The bases of meaning in our lives implicate us in impersonal conditions that we have powerful reasons to regret, with the result that even the best life we might lead will not be worthy of unconditional affirmation. This is a genuine predicament for those who live under conditions of affluence and comparative advantage, even if most of us manage to find ways to avoid facing up to it as we go about our lives.

---

47. Compare the realism condition from sec. 2.4 above.

Chapter 6

A Somewhat Pessimistic Conclusion

The thesis I have defended in chapter 5 is a pessimistic one. We aspire to live lives that are worthy of unconditional affirmation, but this aspiration cannot be satisfied under the conditions that most of us inhabit. In particular, the bourgeois attachments that give most of powerful reasons for affirming the lives we have lived also implicate us in impersonal structures of inequality and suffering that are worthy of unconditional rejection. We may cling to our lives and be glad to have lived them as a matter of psychological fact. But this isn't an attitude that can stand up to rational scrutiny. At the level of reasoned assessment, we are left at the end of the day with grounds for deep ambivalence when we look back on how we have lived.

Though this is a pessimistic conclusion, it is not the most pessimistic conclusion that might be reached about the questions I have been addressing. There are philosophers, for instance, who believe that the world is essentially inimical to the realization of our existential aspirations. These thinkers hold that the elemental conditions of human life are such as to preclude the possibility of a life that is worthy of affirmation, on account of abstract but universal features of the human situation, such as the nature of desire and its relation to suffering.[1] That is

---

1. One might interpret certain elements in Schopenhauer's philosophy in this spirit; see, e.g., Arthur Schopenhauer, *The World as Will and Representation*, Vol. 1, ed. and trans. Judith Norman, Alistair Welchman, and Christopher Janaway (Cambridge, U.K.: Cambridge University

not the position I have defended. The bourgeois predicament, as its name indicates, arises only under certain historical and cultural conditions, and then only for those who occupy a certain role within the contingent social structures that those conditions make available. Since the relevant conditions are ones that apply to virtually everyone who participates in contemporary philosophical discourse, the predicament is apt to be of interest to all of us; but it is not strictly universal, nor is it grounded in features that are endemic to human agency. As a result, it is possible to hold out coherent hope for the eventual achievement of political and economic conditions in which the predicament would not arise. These would be conditions under which people could lead lives that are worthy of unconditional affirmation, such that the sources of meaning in them do not presuppose impersonal structures that warrant rejection. The day is of course still very far off when we can expect these conditions to be realized. But their conceivability suggests that the particular predicament I have tried to analyze may not be a built-in feature of human social relations.

We should not take too much comfort in this conclusion, however. Even if we can imagine (and work toward) a world without the social inequalities that generate the bourgeois predicament, there is some ground for thinking that a generalized version of the predicament would persist. The predicament arises from the fact that our valuable life projects presuppose social conditions that are impersonally objectionable, in ways that are readily accessible to reflection. This gives those of us who pursue bourgeois projects understandable reasons for regretting the conditions that make them possible, reasons that are epistemically salient to us. But for all we know, our valuable projects and relationships may always implicate us in historical conditions that are objectionable in this way—not in virtue of abstract features of the human condition,

---

Press, 2010). A critical account of Schopenhauer's a priori pessimism can be found in Julian Young, *Schopenhauer* (Abingdon, U.K.: Routledge, 2005), chap. 8.

but in virtue of our contingent causal connections to events and circumstances that there is good reason for anyone to deplore.

A single hypothetical example may serve to illustrate a point that could be made in any number of ways. Consider, then, the historical contingencies that may have been causally necessary for the existence of the individuals whom we love. We may not know very much about those contingencies. But we do know that those individuals would not even have existed if our actual parents hadn't met, and if their parents in turn hadn't met, and so on through the generations of our lineage; the reasons are similar to those that supported the conclusion, in chapter 3, that the young girl's decision to conceive was a necessary condition for the existence of the child she is now attached to. We can also readily imagine that somewhere along the line, the actual ancestors of those we love would not even have encountered each other if not for historical events that were momentously disastrous: a catastrophic and pointless war, for instance, that forced a distant progenitor into the refugee camp where she met her future husband, or a natural calamity of some kind that had a similar effect. Under these conditions, our unconditional affirmation of the person we love will commit us to affirming the objectionable historical conditions that were necessary for that individual person's existence.

Scenarios of this kind are apt to be salient in the thinking of those whose loved ones were born within one or two generations of some historical catastrophe, especially when the ancestors were actually caught up in the catastrophe in ways that make their descendants aware of their causal implication in it. People in this epistemic situation will have a hard time avoiding the uncomfortable fact that their attachments commit them to affirming circumstances that are objectively deplorable. But it is easy to see that their predicament probably applies to the rest of us as well, even if we are in the dark about the precise nature of the causal chains that link us to objectionable events and circumstances of various kinds. We may lack good reasons for believing that we are committed to affirming any particular historical catastrophe in the distant past. But there are very good reasons for supposing that any number of such catastrophes were necessary conditions for the existence of the individuals whom we love and whose lives we unconditionally affirm. Other regrettable events and circumstances are likely to be historically necessary conditions for our pursuit of the valuable projects and activities that actually give meaning to the lives that we have led (if only in virtue of representing conditions for our own existence as individual persons). It is thus very plausible to suppose that we are all committed by our attachments, in ways we are not able to spell out very exactly, to affirming historical conditions that are objectively lamentable, and that we would remain so committed even in a world in which the specifically bourgeois predicament was dissolved.

This situation represents an even more general threat to our aspiration to live lives that are worthy of unconditional affirmation. The main difference between the generalized threat and the bourgeois predicament lies in our ignorance of the precise ways in which our attachments might generally implicate us in regrettable historical circumstances. This epistemic difference perhaps provides some emotional comfort, shielding us from having to confront directly the ways in which the affirmation dynamic might commit us to affirming lamentable historical circumstances.[2] At the same time, however, it also raises the bar for the attitude of unconditional affirmation. Since we don't know exactly how we might or might not be causally implicated in disastrous historical events of various kinds, we have to be prepared, in principle, to affirm any of them if we are really going to affirm our own lives unconditionally. Indeed, at the limit, we might have to affirm the entirety of world history, since it cannot be ruled out that a change in any aspect of the past might have ramified in ways

---

2. In particular, it makes it far easier to apply the "method of avoidance" discussed in sec. 5.4 above.

that would have undermined the objects to which we are attached and the bases for meaning in the lives that we have led.

This is, in my view, the grain of truth in Nietzsche's doctrine of the eternal recurrence of the same. His basic idea seems to be that we can honestly affirm our lives only if we are prepared to affirm the recurrence of world history for all eternity, an attitude that we might think of as involving a wholehearted preference that that history should have played out precisely as it did, rather than differing from the actual course of events in any respect. But why might we be drawn to such an extreme doctrine? Some have taken it to be connected to a philosophical view about the metaphysics of the self, to the effect that we are just the totality of our connections to other things, so that alterations in those things would in turn eliminate the subject whose actual life is a candidate for affirmation in the first place.[3] But a more plausible suggestion is that the idea of eternal recurrence is tied to our epistemic situation. This situation is one in which we have excellent reason to believe that our unconditional affirmation of our own lives commits us to affirming all manner of regrettable events and circumstances in the past, but without our knowing of any particular event or circumstance that we are implicated in it in particular. Under these conditions, the idea of the eternal recurrence might be understood to function as a regulative ideal: only if we are prepared to will the totality of world history can we honestly adopt an attitude of unconditional affirmation toward our lives and the other things to which we are attached. Because for all we know, that attitude already commits us to affirming as well the most catastrophic and egregious aspects of the larger histories in which our lives are caught up.[4]

---

3. See, for example, Alexander Nehamas, *Nietzsche: Life as Literature* (Cambridge, Mass.: Harvard University Press, 1985), chap. 5.

4. A natural question to ask about the Nietzschean idea, on this interpretation of it, is why we should be enjoined to will the recurrence of history eternally; wouldn't it suffice to consider whether one is prepared to will the recurrence of the actual history of the world even one

Nietzsche himself seemed to think that this condition could be satisfied only if we are prepared to undertake a "revaluation of values," questioning or undermining received assumptions about the good that might prevent us from affirming the eternal recurrence in all its gory detail.[5] If the difficulty is that the regulative ideal requires us to affirm things that do not seem worthy of affirmation, then perhaps the solution is to revise the evaluative judgments that underlie such conclusions. But this does not strike me as a viable response to the difficulty. I have taken it for granted, throughout my discussion, that our actions and attitudes are subject to normative assessment, and that the terms of such assessment are fixed by principles that are independent of us. Confronted with the disturbing fact that our attitudes commit us to affirming things that do not seem worthy of affirmation, we cannot resolve our discomfort by revising the normative judgments that give rise to it (any more than we can resolve it by revising the factual assumptions at issue, about our causal connections to the apparently lamentable circumstances). The problem is created by a clash between our attitudes toward our lives and normative commitments that are independently plausible; it is simply not open to us to evade it by making an ad hoc decision to withdraw those normative commitments.

---

time? See, e.g., Bernard Williams, "Introduction to *The Gay Science*," as reprinted in his *The Sense of the Past: Essays in the History of Philosophy*, ed. Myles Burnyeat (Princeton, N.J.: Princeton University Press, 2006), pp. 311–24, at p. 319. A speculative answer to this question might be that the willingness to will the *eternal* recurrence of the same functions as a criterion of the wholeheartedness of one's preferences about the past. The ideal is meant to test for whether one is prepared to affirm the possible conditions of meaning in one's life unconditionally, and this requires that one will always come down on the same side of the question of whether things should have played out as they in fact did. (Someone prepared to will the recurrence of things once, but only on the condition that they could leave it open what will happen should there be further opportunities to decide the issue, might reasonably be thought not to have achieved an attitude of wholehearted affirmation of the things they are contemplating.)

5. This aspect of Nietzsche's position is emphasized by Bernard Reginster in *The Affirmation of Life: Nietzsche on Overcoming Nihilism* (Cambridge, Mass.: Harvard University Press, 2006), chap. 5.

But what about the attitude of unconditional affirmation itself? Couldn't we revise this attitude, adopting toward our lives a more ambivalent stance once we are clear about our potential implication in historical catastrophes of various kinds? This is a theoretical possibility—there are people, after all, who give up on life while they are in the midst of it, and they would not appear to affirm their lives unconditionally. But this is not how things are for most of us. The same vital forces that lead us to cling to life as we are living also give rise to an unconditional preference to have lived—a preference, looking backward, to have lived our actual lives, as against the alternative that we should not have lived at all. They also involve, I have argued, an unconditional preference that our lives should have included the attachments that provide a positive basis for this attitude toward our lives. If we are honest with ourselves, we cannot really take seriously the suggestion that we might give up or modify these preferences in light of our connection to historical conditions that are worthy of condemnation and regret. Philosophers sometimes suppose that there are brute forces of desire or conatus to which human beings are subject, which precede all evaluative and normative thought and eventually determine its contours. This is not a position that I find convincing. When it comes to our most basic attitudes toward life, however, it seems to me that we should acknowledge the role that is played by a kind of affirmation that is prior to reasons, and ultimately not subject to revision in response to normative criticism. Our plight as humans might be that we are condemned, in virtue of our attachment to life, to affirming conditions in the world that we cannot possibly regard as worthy of this attitude. There is something absurd about this situation, involving as it does the persistence of attitudes that don't fundamentally make sense to their bearers. But the absurdity may be one that is endemic to the human condition.

This is a somewhat pessimistic conclusion, which might accurately be said to incorporate an element of nihilism. There are, of course, many forms that a nihilistic outlook might assume. A general framework for understanding the range of such outlooks might distinguish between two elements: (a) the general orientation that people take toward life and the world, whether this is one of affirmation or constructive striving, on the one hand, or rather a tendency to despair or resignation or active destruction and violence on the other; and (b) the potential bases or grounds for general orientations of these different kinds. The most theatrical forms of nihilism will involve distinctive positions along both of these two dimensions. Thus someone might adopt an orientation of resignation or despair or even active violence in response to the conviction that there is nothing in the world as we find it that might justify a more affirmative orientation toward life.[6] But for the reasons mentioned in the preceding paragraph, I do not believe this theatrical position to be a very common or stable one in practice. For better or worse, we generally cling to life as we are living, and this goes together with an affirmative attitude toward the lives we have led as we look back on them in reflection.

The more interesting forms of nihilism, as it seems to me, do not involve the adoption of a negative or regretful orientation toward the world, but the recognition that the affirmative attitude we assume by default is not one that ultimately makes sense. The root idea is that there is a discrepancy between our actual outlook on life and the grounds for such an outlook, a discrepancy whose recognition might naturally occasion anxiety more than active despair. It is anxiety about meaning, rather than resignation or other more theatrical forms of adjustment in orientation, that is the real hallmark of nihilism in the contemporary world. But here too distinctions are possible. Some

---

6. Why violence or destruction should be a better response to this recognition than, e.g., resignation or withdrawal is an excellent question. In fact, some of the nineteenth-century political movements that went under the heading of nihilism and that advocated violence or negative political action were not really animated by a concern for the unattainability of meaning in human life.

philosophical positions postulate a dramatic discrepancy between our affirmation of our lives and the possible grounds of this affirmative orientation. One might hold, for instance, that there are no genuine distinctions of value, so that none of the projects or relationships that might be realized in our lives is capable of providing warrant for an affirmative attitude toward them. Or one might maintain that such values as we are capable of achieving are relativized by the fact of our mortality, in ways that undermine their capacity to justify the affirmation of our lives. We could describe these positions as immoderate forms of nihilism, since they maintain that there is nothing on the positive side that could possibly contribute to justifying the affirmative orientation we adopt toward life by default. A more modest position, by contrast, might allow that there are genuine values that can be realized in our lives, and that these provide a real basis for affirmation, but insist that these grounds for affirmation are historically and socially connected to comparably weighty grounds for regret.

This modest nihilism, as I shall call it, is the kind of position I have been sketching in the present chapter. It identifies a distinctive basis for anxiety about meaning, which lies in the implication of our lives and our attachments in historical and social conditions that we have powerful reasons to regret. Anxiety about meaning, on this interpretation of it, derives from our recognition that the deep aspiration to live lives that are worthy of unconditional affirmation may not be realizable at the end of the day. As I suggested above, however, anxiety is not the same as resignation or despair. Agency matters, and from the fact that we cannot extricate ourselves from the larger world of lamentable processes, it does not follow that it makes no difference how we conduct ourselves while we are living. On the contrary, as I suggested in section 2.3 above, the on-balance preferences involved in our attitudes about the past have a distinctive character when they focus on things we have ourselves done, rather than on impersonal conditions that did not involve our own actions. When we look back on our lives, we take a special kind of interest in the expressions and effects of our own agency, forming intention-like preferences about those things that closely resemble, and often in fact involve, ordinary conditional intentions for the future. But if these attitudes focus on expressions of our agency, it follows that we have some control over whether we will eventually be subject to them through the way we comport ourselves while we are making our way through life.

More specifically, I would suggest that there are three particular ambitions that are capable of being realized through our agency, despite our implication in the impersonally objectionable, and that are of great significance for our retrospective attitudes. One of these is that there should be something in our lives that can be set over against the objectionable conditions that we inhabit, something that gives us a positive basis for affirming our lives when we look back on them. This is perhaps the most important component in the ideal of a life that is worthy of unconditional affirmation, since it is the part of that ideal that is under our own control (at least to some degree).[7] We can't really do much about our causal implication in a larger world of regrettable occurrences, but our efforts make some difference when it comes to the value of the projects that are realized in our own lives. Immoderate nihilists take even this aspiration to be incapable of realization, holding that nothing we might do is of genuine value, so that we could never have any grounds at all for affirming our lives. But the more modest form of nihilism that I have defended rejects this assumption. It holds that there are real differences of value between the different attachments that people organize their lives around; some

---

7. The qualification here acknowledges the fact that there is a significant element of grace or luck in the satisfaction of this ambition. We need suitable opportunities to take advantage of whatever natural talents we might have been endowed with, and it is a matter of good fortune whether the right people enter our lives (people with whom it is possible for us to form significant relationships).

of these attachments are empty and pointless and banal, while others are complex and interesting, with a character that enriches the lives of those who are devoted to them. The predicaments I have been discussing mean that the aspiration to live a life that is worthy of unconditional affirmation cannot be realized. But there is still something that it is reasonable and important for us to strive for, which is to engage in activities that are of genuine value. To live a life that is worthy of being looked back on with ambivalence is itself a kind of achievement, and the failure to realize this ambition is something that will properly attract distinctively personal forms of disappointment and remorse.

A second important ambition for our lives concerns their moral quality. Not only do we hope that our lives will contain genuine bases for retrospective affirmation, we also hope that they will not provide others with a basis for reproach and moral complaint. It matters to us that we should interact with people on terms that are acceptable to them, and this too is something that we have control over as we make our way through life. That this is distinct from the first ambition is illustrated by some of the examples considered in the earlier parts of this book. Both the young girl and Williams's Gauguin, for instance, have attachments that provide a basis for affirming their lives, but they have also conducted themselves in ways that justify the opprobrium of others and that leave the agents themselves with significant grounds for guilt.[8] Nobody is completely blameless, of course, and it is not realistic to suppose that one might achieve a life that is entirely free from moral blemish. What we can expect of ourselves and each

---

8. As I argued in sec. 3.3, a susceptibility to guilt can coexist with an inability to will that things should have been otherwise in the respects that occasion guilt. The difference between the young girl and Gauguin, however, is that the moral failings of the former do not provide her with a retrospective reason for wishing that she had acted otherwise, whereas the moral failings of the latter are available as reasons of this kind in Gauguin's retrospective point of view. This difference between the cases is discussed in sec. 4.4 above.

other, however, is conduct that does not flagrantly wrong the people it affects and that is basically justifiable to them.[9]

The value of this ideal is sometimes called into question; it is challenged, for instance, by those moral skeptics who deny the normative significance of moral requirements (without necessarily questioning the value of all human accomplishments—moral skeptics need not be immoderate nihilists). But most of us take the value of relating to other people on moral terms to be extremely important, and major lapses from this standard are occasions for some of our most profound retrospective regrets. It is up to us whether we live in a way that satisfies the most basic demands of morality, and it is therefore a distinctively personal failing when we offend against those demands. We might not be able to avoid entanglement in objective conditions that are worthy of rejection, and that therefore frustrate our aspiration to live in a way that warrants unconditional affirmation. But we can pursue our significant projects and relationships in a way that deprives others of a serious basis for reproach, and it rightly matters to us when we look back on our lives whether this ambition has been achieved.

Finally, there is a still more specific value that we can reasonably aspire to achieve in our lives, mentioned at the end of the preceding chapter, which is the value of truthfulness. Fidelity to this value is not always easy to pin down,[10] but it involves, at a minimum, a willingness to face up to unlovely aspects of our lives and our relation to the social world, rather than retreating from the facts into fantasy or denial.

9. Thus, in a distinctively moral sense of "rightness," it seems to me that there is the possibility of "living rightly" even under conditions that are objectively wrong or false; compare the famous aphorism from Theodor Adorno, *Minima Moralia: Reflexionen aus dem beschädigten Leben* (Frankfurt am Main: Suhrkamp Verlag, 2008), p. 58 (sec. 18): "Es gibt kein richtiges Leben im falschen."

10. A thoughtful exploration of this question is Bernard Williams, *Truth and Truthfulness: An Essay in Genealogy* (Princeton, N.J.: Princeton University Press, 2002). See also his "Introduction to *The Gay Science*," pp. 319–24, on the significance of the ideal of truthfulness to questions about the affirmation of life.

Those who are truthful take their attitudes to be answerable to what I have called the realism condition, acknowledging a responsibility to understand the facts about both the causes and the consequences of those attitudes. In the scenario currently under consideration, we may not know precisely how our attachments commit us to affirming objectionable historical and social conditions. But we have good reason to believe that we are implicated in such conditions, one way or another, just in virtue of our unconditional attachment to life and to the people and projects that ground this orientation. The Nietzschean thought experiment of the eternal recurrence can be understood as a way of forcing ourselves to acknowledge this feature of our existential situation and to deal with the anxiety that is induced by the recognition that one of our aspirations for our own lives might not be capable of being realized in the world as we find it. There is independent value in this way of living, and this is shown by the fact we admire people who can unflinchingly confront the absurdity of their own ambitions, despite the distress this insight is apt to occasion.

INDEX

accountability. *See* responsibility

action, voluntary. *See* agency, voluntary exercises of

Adorno, Theodor, 215n, 241n, 260n

affirmation, 3, 5–6, 10–16, 53, 65–77, 84–86, 97n, 99, 105, 112–113, 115, 117n, 118–119, 126, 196, 199, 201, 204–205, 211–212, 223n, 227, 253n, 254, 259 (*see also* attachment, and unconditional affirmation; preference, and affirmation; realism condition on affirmation and regret (the); reasons, for affirmation)

    of an action or decision, 4–5, 65–66, 68, 74–76, 79, 97n, 98, 105–107, 109–111, 113, 116, 118, 126–127, 136, 142–145, 150–152, 156–157, 160–161, 164, 166–167, 169, 175–186, 193, 200

    and (in)compatibility with all-in regret, 69–74, 78–79, 88, 96–97, 121–123, 125, 134–140, 157, 166, 175, 177, 184, 205–207, 233

    conditional, 11, 74–75, 105, 142, 193–194

    dynamic, 5, 7, 77, 97–98, 105, 118, 120, 123, 143, 150, 186, 195, 206, 222, 252

    is not an emotional state, 65–68

    extends to the necessary conditions of what one affirms, 7–8, 13–14, 16, 73, 75–77, 95, 97–98, 105–106, 109, 118–121, 123–126, 128, 134, 138–139, 142–146, 150, 186, 195, 205–206, 216, 222, 224, 233n, 251–252, 261

    of one's own life, 10, 12–13, 65–66, 68–69, 71n, 75n, 76, 104–105, 108–109, 118–130, 133–134, 138–157, 167, 175–176, 179n, 181, 184, 186–187, 191–201, 204–210, 214–215, 221, 224–225, 226nn, 227–231, 233, 235, 237–240, 244, 247–250, 252–253, 255–260

    of a person or state of affairs, 7–8, 12, 14, 65–66, 68–73, 76, 79, 89, 91, 95, 97n, 98, 105, 108, 110, 117–118, 124, 126, 130–131, 134, 137, 139, 143, 150n, 186–189, 191, 224, 251–253, 255–256

    of a project or practical identity, 119–125, 148, 151–152, 156–157, 167, 175, 206–207, 210, 216, 222

    unconditional, 5, 9–10, 11, 13, 16, 75–78, 88, 96–98, 105–109, 114n, 118, 116–125, 130, 134–153, 156–158, 160, 167, 175–178, 181, 184–187, 191–201, 204–209, 215n, 222, 226n, 233, 235, 238, 248–261

    voluntary aspect of, 66–67

agency, 12, 16–18, 39n, 51n, 54–59, 61n, 66–68, 92, 114–116, 125n, 189, 192, 223n, 240, 250, 257–261 (*see also* intention; preference(s); reasons; regret, agent-; regret, personal; willing)

INDEX